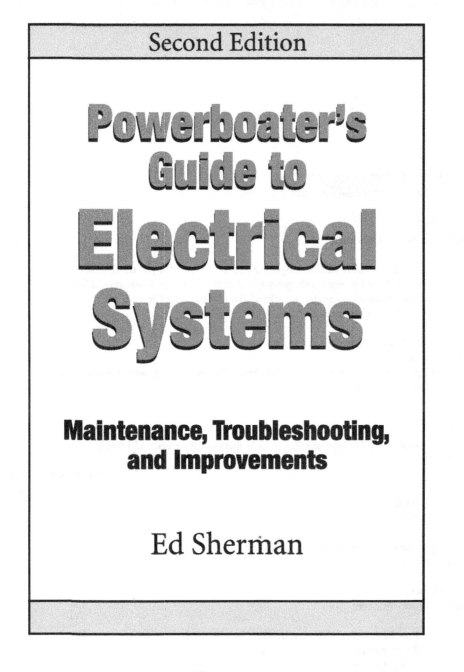

## Second Edition

# Powerboater's Guide to Electrical Systems

## Maintenance, Troubleshooting, and Improvements

### Ed Sherman

Camden, Maine • New York • Chicago • San Francisco • Lisbon
London • Madrid • Mexico City • Milan • New Delhi
San Juan • Seoul • Singapore • Sydney • Toronto

## The *McGraw·Hill* Companies

7  8  9  10  QVS QVS  15

*Library of Congress Cataloging-in-Publication Data*
Sherman, Edwin R.
  Powerboater's guide to electrical systems : maintenance, troubleshooting, and improvements / Edwin R. Sherman. — 2nd ed.
     p.    cm.
  Includes index.
  ISBN 978-0-07-148550-0 (hc : alk. paper)
  1.  Boats and boating—Electric equipment. 2.  Motorboats—Maintenance and repair.
  VM325.S54 2007
  623.8'503—dc22                                                                    2007006587

ISBN 978-0-07-148550-0
MHID 0-07-148550-3

Questions regarding the content of this book should be addressed to
International Marine
P.O. Box 220
Camden, ME  04843
www.internationalmarine.com

Questions regarding the ordering of this book should be addressed to
The McGraw-Hill Companies
Customer Service Department
P.O. Box 547
Blacklick, OH  43004
Retail customers: 1-800-262-4729
Bookstores: 1-800-722-4726

Photographs courtesy Susan Thorpe Waterman and the author.
Illustrations by Geoffrey Skog unless otherwise indicated.
Electrical icon by Chris Van Dusen.

*Dedication*
To my wife, Nancy, and son, Mason, who have to put up with
me when I'm involved in projects like this!

# Contents

CONTENTS

## Chapter 10. Engine Instrumentation Problems and Solutions .147

## Chapter 11. Alternating Current and AC Equipment .........156

## Chapter 12. Installing Marine Electronic Equipment ........180

# Foreword to the Second Edition

It can arguably be said that harnessing the electron has been one of humankind's crowning achievements. For thousands of years, people—including those who have sailed the seas—have been fascinated by lightning, static electricity, and harnessing light. Early humans must have wondered how to put that kind of power to practical use. But it wasn't until the close of the 18th century that the path to everyday use of electrical power would begin to have a profound and lasting impact the world over, including at sea.

We all know about Benjamin Franklin, who in 1752 proved that lightning was electrical when he flew a kite during a thunderstorm. He tied a metal key onto the string and, as he suspected it would, electricity from the storm clouds flowed down the string, which was wet, and he received an electrical shock. Maybe not the smartest of ideas, but it sure brought the point home fast!

Throughout the next hundred years, many inventors and scientists tried to find a way to use electrical power to make light. In 1879, Thomas Edison was finally able to produce a reliable, long-lasting electric light bulb in his laboratory. From that point forward, the world would witness profound technological advances.

By the end of the 1880s, small electrical stations based on Edison's designs were springing up in a number of U.S. cities. But each station was able to power only a few city blocks. Elementary electrical systems were beginning to find their way onto ships, and onto pleasure craft reserved for the affluent few. During those early days, electrical safety standards were virtually nonexistent, both on land and at sea.

Although the majority of people living in larger towns and cities had electricity by 1930, only 10 percent of Americans who lived on farms and in rural areas had electric power. But that was about to change rapidly through the 1940s and 1950s as America was thrust onto the world stage fighting a second world war, the Korean conflict, and the Cold War.

Today, the standard of living across the globe has risen as more and more people experience the convenience of electric power at home, school, work, and at sea. If there is any doubt in your mind, try to exist for one day without any influence of the power of the electron. You'll quickly discover that you will literally be back in the Dark Ages.

In harnessing the power of the electron, it was recognized early on that standards were needed for reasons of both practicality and safety. For recreational boats and yachts, the American Boat & Yacht Council (ABYC)—a nonprofit industry membership organization—has been developing, writing, and updating the safety standards for boatbuilding and repair in the United States for over 50 years. This includes electrical safety standards.

Over the past half century, the ABYC has come to be known as the recognized global leader in marine safety standards research, development, international harmonization, and co-recognition. ABYC standards are endorsed and used by the United States Coast Guard, Transport Canada, the National Marine Manufacturers Association (NMMA) Boat and Yacht Certification program, the international community, and by virtually every industry segment. Over 400 of our member volunteers donate time, expertise, and research while serving on technical committees that develop and revise the ABYC standards and technical information reports.

The positive, lifesaving impact of the ABYC standards cannot be overstated, but perhaps none more so than in the area of wiring and electrical systems installation, maintenance, and repair of boats and yachts. Proper electrical system design, wiring type and size, overcurrent protection, wire termination, power source management, proper installation and integration of electronic sensing and control components, and the networking of all critical systems have and will significantly reduce injury and fatalities caused by electrical fires and shock and damage to watercraft components, accessories, and systems. Simply put, ABYC standards, and in particular, ABYC electrical standards, save lives and property!

In addition to developing and disseminating industry standards, the ABYC has taken the lead in advocating, providing, and promoting technical workforce professional development, continuing education, and technical workforce certifications. Three courses that make extensive use of Ed's book are the ABYC Basic Electricity course, the ABYC Electrical Certification course, and the ABYC Marine Systems Certification courses. Additionally, his book is a resource for all boaters and want-to-be boaters who want to take ABYC "boater" courses, seminars, and workshops. Visit www.abyc.com to learn more about the ABYC, its mission, and its educational offerings. And when buying a boat, ensure that it is NMMA certified using ABYC standards!

Over the years I have come to know Ed as both a professional and as a friend. As a professional, he has designed both the ABYC Basic Electricity course and the ABYC Electrical Certification course. He also has recently completed the National Marine curriculum guidelines for secondary schools that offer ABYC-endorsed technical marine programs, and he has codeveloped a post-secondary Marine Systems Curriculum that is scheduled to be implemented in a number of schools across the country. Ed's teaching and writing skills and his rapport with students are legendary and beyond reproach. He is regarded as an industry expert in the area of electricity and marine electrical systems, and as such, is an active member of the ABYC's Electrical Committee. And yes, Ed holds an ABYC Electrical Certification!

The first edition of *Powerboater's Guide to Electrical Systems* has been read and used as a reference document by tens of thousands of marine professionals, technicians, students, and boating enthusiasts. It is considered a "must-have" reference guide because it is able to convey concepts and practical knowledge of complex material in a user-friendly manner. It speaks to both the technically minded as well as to the novice boatowner. It also stresses the importance of adhering to industry standards in order to "do the job right the first time."

The second edition has new information, takes a fresh look at industry technological advances, and captures the essence of what you need to know regarding electricity and electrical systems used on boats, yachts, and marine craft. It discusses the basics as well as advanced techniques concerning maintenance, troubleshooting, and repair of marine electrical systems. More importantly, it does all this in the context of the latest ABYC standards, which have significantly evolved and changed since the publication of the first edition.

In closing, as a friend and work associate, Ed Sherman can be counted upon to give you candid and sage advice and expert counsel. I look to him to help shape and guide the future of the ABYC and our education, training, and certification programs. He's a team player who is looking out for the industry and the boaters we serve, and as such, has his eye on the end goal—safer boats for safe, fun, and memorable boating experiences for all. I encourage you to read, digest, understand, and use the material in the second edition of *Powerboater's Guide to Electrical Systems*—you'll be glad you did!

Skip Burdon
President and CEO,
American Boat & Yacht Council

# Preface to the Second Edition

Since the first edition of the *Powerboater's Guide to Electrical Systems* was published in 2000, there have been many evolutionary and some revolutionary changes to marine electrical systems, and significant updates to the standards that dictate how designers and field personnel should carry out their work. The basics of marine electrical system troubleshooting haven't changed much, but certainly some of the equipment we install and use has. This second edition of the *Powerboater's Guide* reflects these changes and provides an update to where we are in 2007. Examples of some of the new material found within this second edition include complete reference updates to all the applicable ABYC electrical standards. Since the first edition notable changes have been made to both the ABYC AC and DC standards in that what were once Standards E-8 and E-9 are now combined into Standard E-11. The ABYC battery standard has some significant changes within it and they are discussed here. We've also seen a major change in ABYC Standard A-28, Galvanic Isolators, which now requires a status-monitoring system to be integral with the isolator; that information has been added to this edition.

Additionally, and not standards based, we've seen some major improvements in both battery technology and battery combiner systems. Components that used to rely on either fully mechanical or electromechanical control have gone completely solid-state, and have added intelligence built in to provide much more accurate control of multiple battery systems. New information is provided here about this new era of battery control.

In the area of engine-specific electrical systems, we've moved from traditional distributor ignition systems on gas engines to computer-controlled DIS (distributorless ignition systems). Flat serpentine drive belts used to run engine-driven alternators are now the norm rather than an anomaly, so some additional information has been provided relative to the maintenance of these very important drive belts.

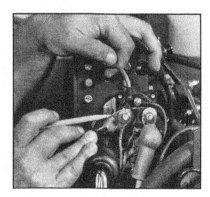

Next, we are now seeing the broad use of networked engine control systems from such companies as Mercury Marine with its SmartCraft system, and Teleflex with a similar system. The use of these systems will ultimately simplify things, but for now it looks daunting to the untrained eye. Now we're distributing data from one point to another in addition to basic electrical distribution. We'll discuss these changes in chapter 10.

Additionally, we're just beginning to see entire electrical systems that are reduced to many fewer wires from such companies as Paneltronics, with its PowerSign System, and Capi2's three-wire system. These systems go beyond the scope of this book, but my book *Advanced Marine Electrics and Electronics Troubleshooting* covers them in more detail.

Finally, we've seen the increased use of alternative energy systems, specifically solar panels, on cruising powerboats. The need-to-know information relative to these systems is provided in this second edition.

# Introduction

This book has been evolving in my head for years. Of all the different areas I work in, diesel and outboard engine mechanics and onboard systems, electricity is one of the most interesting as well as one of the most perplexing to many people. Even boating professionals who have worked in and around watercraft all their lives sometimes find the fundamental principles of electricity difficult to understand. Electricity is often seen as a mysterious force that, except when it shows itself in a spark or in the fluctuation of the needle or dancing digits of a multimeter, is invisible in a controlled state. The effects of electricity, however, can be quite profound, as anyone who has inadvertently bridged the terminals of a freshly charged battery or latched onto the wrong wires in a hot AC circuit can attest.

I was fortunate in that I recognized the arcane and slightly magical qualities of electricity early in my career, and this gave me a distinct advantage over my colleagues. As a teacher and practitioner of the electrical arts as well as a mechanic, I was forced into a deeper comprehension of the underlying principles of electricity. In order to teach others the fundamentals of electricity, I had to translate the technical mumbo-jumbo, that obscure language that's so popular with the technophiles and engineers who write most of our electrical manuals, into plain English—first so I could understand it myself, and then so I could help others to understand it. The very act of translating electrical technobabble into English and rewriting it into plain, simple explanations got me on my way as a technical writer.

I first became involved with electricity as an automobile mechanic about 30 years ago. The automotive electrical systems of those days were fairly simple, and I spent most of my time troubleshooting faulty components and repairing factory-engineered wiring harnesses. The wiring diagrams we had back then showed in minute detail the complete electrical system for each make and model of automobile, and these diagrams were readily available and easy to understand.

When I became involved with boats, however, things changed dramatically. Before the formation of the American Boat & Yacht Council, Inc. (the ABYC, which I talk about much more later on), electrical anarchy reigned unchecked in the marine field. There were no uniform standards, no universal system of color coding, and no governing body to bring order to the prevailing chaos. Boatbuilders developed their own, largely proprietary wiring systems, and technicians and owners alike made changes and additions without restraint of reason or common standards. Boats were often one-of-a-kind or limited production, and customers frequently ordered extra or specialized equipment added after the boat had been built and the electrical wiring installed. Many entire electrical systems were created by self-trained technicians who had even less experience in designing reliable and safe marine systems than I myself had at the time. Problems with these do-it-yourself electrical systems were many, and frequently I found myself reengineering work that had been improperly, poorly, and sometimes dangerously installed. Wiring diagrams, when they were available at all (which wasn't often), were rudimentary and often inaccurate to the point of being useless. Uniform color-coding of wiring was nonexistent.

I spent quite a few years muddling about with these perplexing and difficult-to-understand electrical systems, and I was lucky enough not to burn up anyone's boat or to make too many other disastrous mistakes. Then I discovered the ABYC and became

> ► **ABYC**
>
> To find out more about the ABYC, contact them at 613 Third Street, Suite 10; Annapolis, Maryland 21403; Phone: 410-990-4460; Fax: 410-990-4466; www.abyc.com.

familiar with its comprehensive *Standards and Technical Information Reports for Small Craft*. Suddenly, my work as a marine electrician became much easier. I now had uniform electrical standards to work with and to learn from. Information on wire types, insulation materials, color codes, and wire sizing was clearly laid out and understandable even to those of us with limited training and experience. The hearsay, guesswork, and old wives' tales that had dominated the old school were no longer a part of my work. I had found, at last, a guiding light to lead my electrical efforts through the dark jungle of naïveté and ignorance.

The good news for boaters is that today more and more boatbuilders are building their craft to the ABYC standards, and a genuine effort is being made industry-wide to improve owners' manuals and wiring diagrams so that they can be more easily understood by engineers and laypersons alike. This trend toward universal standards of marine electrical work has also had a profound effect on the expertise of all professional marine technicians, from the person who designs the boat right down to the one who changes your oil and checks the gap in your spark plugs. This includes you, the boatowner. Once you finish this book and develop a few of the analytical skills we will cover in the following pages, your comfort level when working with things electrical will be increased dramatically.

The *Powerboater's Guide to Electrical Systems* is not intended to turn you into an expert electrician. It should, however, help you wade through the technical mumbo-jumbo and electro-speak that you're bound to encounter in your other reading on marine electricity. Once you understand the basics, much of the rest will follow in a clear, concise, and easy-to-understand manner. All instructions and recommendations found in this guide are in accordance with the very latest of the ABYC's electrical standards, and the procedures described herein have all been tried and tested many times over by me personally and by my students. Many of the tests and procedures that I have detailed here are identical to those used in my curriculum for the ABYC's electrical technician certification program.

By following the recommendations in this guide you will be taking a long step toward keeping your boat's electrical system in top working order. Then, in those rare instances when a failure does occur, the procedures outlined here will get you to the source of the problem quickly and easily so that you can effect repairs and be back underway without the stress and frustration normally associated with electrical problems.

There are several points in this book where I clearly state that a professional marine electrician should be called in or consulted for certain complicated, difficult, or dangerous operations. Some of these procedures require either specialized equipment or expertise (and often both) that goes far beyond the scope of this book. Please do not take these warnings lightly or fail to heed them. Expensive and delicate electronic equipment can be damaged and even destroyed by improper installation and repair techniques, and the high-voltage AC system on your boat can be extremely dangerous if proper procedures are not understood and followed to the letter. Household AC current when misapplied to a human body is unpleasant in the best of circumstances, and in the worst it is lethal. Extreme care must be taken any time your boat is plugged in to shore power, has a generator running, or has an operational inverter on board. If, after reading through chapter 11 of this book, you still don't feel confident in your abilities to sensibly and safely perform the tests and procedures I have outlined, you should stay away from the AC service on your boat.

I hope you enjoy the *Powerboater's Guide to Electrical Systems* and find it a useful addition to your arsenal of onboard tools.

As always, good luck, and happy boating!

# Chapter 1

# Electrical Basics You Need to Know

## What Is Electricity?

One of the first things to confront a new student of electricity is the concept of just what the stuff is. We all know that electricity travels through wires, but when we inspect a cut cross section of one of these wires we see nothing more than copper, and the idea of anything passing through it, as water passes through a hose, seems quite impossible. The classic textbook definition of electricity, translated from electro-speak into plain English, states that electricity is the flow of electrons through a conductor from a negatively charged material into a positively charged material. Nature abhors a vacuum, and the positively charged material, which has been stripped of electrons by one of several generating processes, is just that. We have all felt the shock of static electricity after shuffling our bare feet across a wool rug: Electrons stripped off the rug by the friction of our feet build up in our body; then, when we grab the doorknob, the circuit is completed, the excess electrons rush back into the carpet, and we get a jolt (sometimes quite a strong jolt) of electricity.

Over the years many analogies have been contrived to explain the electricity phenomenon—none of which is entirely satisfactory. One such analogy compares electricity to a tank of water with a hose attached, and another compares it to a looped tube full of Ping-Pong balls that endlessly push each other around in a circle. Yet another uses horses galloping around a racetrack to try to help us visualize electrons racing around an electrical circuit. While all of these picturesque analogies help to explain some aspect of electricity (comparing a battery to a water tank, for example, works quite well), none does a good job of explaining them all.

In the following pages, we break electricity down into its fundamental elements; then, once an understanding of each of these elements has been estab-
lished, we put them together into the finished product. We proceed slowly and collect and study all the component parts; then, once we have a good understanding of them, we assemble them into a complete picture. Those readers who already have a good grasp of the basic principles of electricity will find some of the following to be repetitious, but bear with me—even those of us who work in marine electricity every day will benefit from a good review of the fundamentals. Let's start with a brief discussion of the most basic of all electrical components—the circuit.

## Electrical Circuits

Electrical circuits are just what they say they are—circles or loops of conductive material that allow an electrical impulse to flow around and around in an endless orbit. This conductive material is most often copper wire but it can actually be nearly any material. In an automobile the engine block and chassis are critical parts of many circuits. At home the very earth your house is sitting on is a part of the electrical circuit and is essential for the correct operation of your pop-up toaster and your television set. That's why one prong on all your electrical plugs is called the *ground*.

There are several types of electrical circuits with which we will want to become familiar. However, regardless of type, the essential elements of a circuit will always be the same.

▶ All circuits on a boat need a source of electrical power; it could be a battery, your municipal power through a shore-power connection, a generator, an engine-driven alternator, a solar panel, or a wind-driven turbine. It can even be (with catastrophic results) the chemical reaction between your aluminum outdrive and the bronze props on that big sportfisherman in the next slip.

▶ You'll also need an electrical conductor or a series of conductors so arranged that electrical energy can travel from the source to the place where it's needed (to the light bulb in the galley, for example), then back again to the source. As I mentioned above, nearly anything can serve as a conductor; even the air we breathe (normally an excellent insulator) serves as a conductor when the charge of electrical energy is massive enough—as anyone who has witnessed the flash of a lightning bolt can attest.

▶ Although they are not required to make an electrical circuit function, there is a practical requirement in most circuits for a fuse or circuit breaker. Circuit protectors defend circuits from destructive forces of excessive amperage, a subject we will deal with in some detail later on.

▶ Also not required but present in most circuits is some sort of switch to turn the electrical energy in the circuit on and off or to direct it to the place where we want it to go to work for us. Sometimes the circuit breaker serves as a switch, but there are many other types of switches that we will discuss later on.

▶ Finally, all functional electrical circuits need some sort of load or appliance. The circuit load is both the reason for the circuit's existence and the single most important element that makes it possible for the circuit to exist. The load can be a light bulb or the depth-sounder or the stereo system that converts the electrical energy flowing through the circuit into something useful—light, information for safe navigation, or pleasant and relaxing music. The load also serves to control the unrestricted flow of electrons that would otherwise destroy the circuit and even burn up your boat in the process.

Remember this one simple fact: whenever we have an electrical problem on board our boats, we can always trace the problem to a fault with one or sometimes more of these basic elements. Figure 1-1 shows the elements discussed above in a normal sequence as might be found on your own boat. When the switch we show here is turned on (referred to as *closed* in electro-speak), we can see the complete route that our friends the electrons have to follow. If you follow the guidelines in this book, like those electrons follow that circuit, you'll soon be tracing through all manner of circuits yourself, and when you develop trouble spots, you will, in all cases, be able to find them without difficulty.

## Circuits Found on Your Boat

In all of electrical engineering there are only two basic types of circuits common to boat use, and your boat, no matter how simple its electrical system might be, will use both in abundance. These are the *parallel* and *series circuits*. Actually, there is a third type, but it's really only a combination of the first two, called, appropriately enough, a *series-parallel circuit*. A clear understanding of what happens in each of the circuit types as electrons flow through them will go a long way toward helping us to think out problems which will undoubtedly arise later. Let's take a close look at these three types of circuits one at a time, but first we need to understand the differences between marine circuits and others, such as those found in your family car.

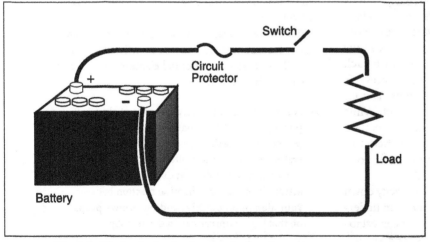

*Fig. 1-1. The basic circuit, showing the key elements.*

## Marine versus Automotive Circuits

One of the most common mistakes that many proud owners of new powerboats make is to try to save a few dollars by installing inexpensive automotive accessories in place of more expensive marine accessories. After all, it doesn't really matter if that new reading light in the forepeak is designed for a boat or an RV, does it? I mean, a light is a light, right? Wrong!

Even the best-made and most costly automotive accessories are not really appropriate for installation in boats, not so much because of the accessories as because of the circuits to which they will be attached. Most automotive equipment is made from mild steel or will have major components made from some highly corrosive material, but this is not what concerns us here. If you take a close look at that reading light, for example, you'll find that those designed for campers will have a single wire (usually referred to in electro-speak as a *lead*) and those designed for boats will have two.

Automobiles commonly use what are called *chassis ground* circuits where the metal frame of the car—the *chassis*—or the engine block serves as the second wire of the circuit and provides a path for the electrical current to flow back to the battery. On a boat this simply doesn't work. The fiberglass hull of the typical powerboat is a very poor conductor of electricity, and on steel and aluminum boats an electrical current passing through the hull causes all sorts of problems, the most important of which is severe corrosion. Thus, nearly all marine accessories will have two leads, and the second wire completes the circuit back to the battery. Also, the best marine accessories are heavily constructed of noncorrosive materials and are designed to function in the hostile marine environment.

OK, now that we understand the differences between boat stuff and car stuff (and have resolved to never put car stuff in our boat), let's get back to our three basic circuit types.

## Series Circuits

The simplest of circuit types is the series circuit, widely used on your boat to supply electricity to *single loads*, such as a cabin fan or bilge pump. With this circuit type, there is only one path for electrical current flow. Figure 1-2 depicts a simple series circuit. The inherent problem with this circuit type is that it cannot be used effectively on board to service more than one electrical appliance. Figure 1-3 on page 4 shows a series circuit with three cabin lights installed. As you can see, the electrical current must flow through one before it can get to the second, then through the second before it can get to the third. The problem with this circuit is that as electrical current flows through each load, it's doing work for us (making a light bulb glow, for example), and each of the loads in the series circuit must share the available power. So the available voltage at the source—in this case, the 12-volt battery—gets divided by each of the loads. In the example shown in figure 1-3, assuming that each of the light bulbs has the same wattage, the voltage drop across each bulb will be one third of the available 12 volts, or 4 volts each. Thus if the bulbs are engineered to run on a 12-volt source, each will glow more dimly than designed.

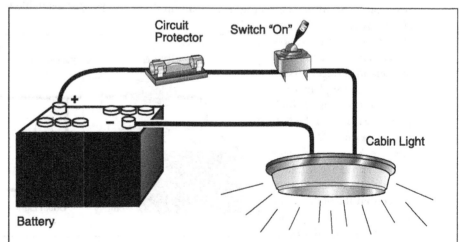

*Fig. 1-2. A simple series circuit with only one load.*

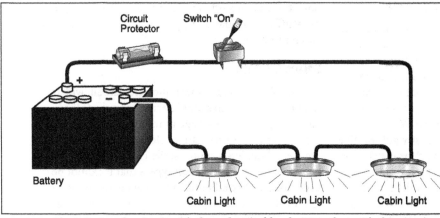

*Fig. 1-3. A series circuit with three electrical loads. Note that with this circuit type, there is only one path for electrical current flow.*

There is still another fundamental flaw in any series circuit that's expected to carry more than a single load: If any one of the electrical loads should fail in the open position (that is, break the circuit, as when a light bulb or a fuse blows), the flow of current through the circuit will cease, shutting all the other appliances down as well.

## Parallel Circuits

Parallel circuits, such as the one in figure 1-4, solve both problems we have with the series circuit by providing more than one path through which electrons can flow, which means that each load on the circuit receives the same voltage as all the others. This arrangement has three obvious advantages: first, it allows all the appliances on the circuit to share a single pair of leads from the battery and a single fuse or circuit breaker; second, each load or appliance will have direct access to battery voltage so that it can do its job with peak efficiency; and third, if one appliance on the circuit should fail in an open condition (electro-

speak for a broken circuit), the other appliances can carry on with their jobs.

Parallel circuits are clearly superior to series circuits any time multiple loads, such as several cabin lights or navigation lights, are served by one pair of wires and one main circuit protector.

## Series-Parallel Circuits

Series-parallel circuits are nothing more than complex (sometimes very complex) combinations of series and parallel circuits. In the real world of marine electrical systems, most of the circuits found on our boats are actually series-parallel circuits because they combine components wired in series, like switches and fuses, in the primary feed of the circuit, and at some other point loads are wired in parallel. Certain components (such as switches and fuses) of many actual circuits are usually wired in series regardless of the type of circuit they serve, while most appliances that share a circuit are wired in parallel. Figure 1-5 illustrates this arrangement.

The important thing to remember here is that the voltage available to the loads wired in the par-

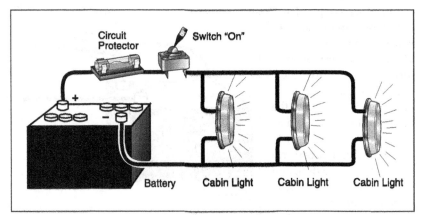

*Fig. 1-4. A typical parallel circuit. In a parallel circuit, there is more than one path for electrical current flow.*

allel section of the circuit will be quite close to the voltage at the beginning of the circuit. It's not too hard to see that by using series-parallel circuits, manufacturers can save a lot of money on switches, wire, and circuit protectors, but series-parallel circuits also greatly simplify a boat's overall electrical system, with no sacrifice in performance or safety.

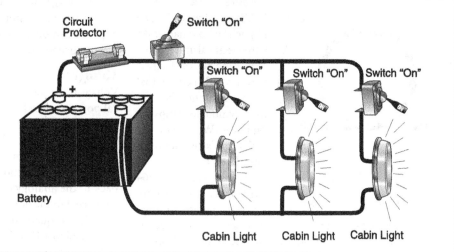

*Fig. 1-5. A series-parallel circuit as found on your boat.*

# Ohm's Law and What It Can Tell Us

Georg Simon Ohm (1787–1854), a German physicist, was one of the great early experimenters with electricity. He left us with the simple but oh-so-important mathematical formula that bears his name. Ohm's law helps us to understand the relationship between the measurable forces in electricity. Once we are armed with a clear understanding of the relationships between the different elements in this formula, we will have made a giant step forward in our ability to understand and locate electrical problems.

As we work with this invisible thing called electricity, we need to get used to dealing in an abstract way with the stuff. We'll be taking a lot of measurements with a multimeter, and we will learn to translate these measurements into meaningful information. Throughout the rest of this book I demonstrate the correct methods of obtaining accurate electrical measurements with a multimeter, and I try to provide an understanding of what these measurements mean. First, however, we must get the definitions of a few electrical terms clear in our heads, and then become completely familiar with this wonderful thing called Ohm's law.

## The Key Players

There are four terms that will continually crop up in any discussion of things electrical: *volts, amps, ohms,* and *watts.* Each of these terms represents an electrical value and is named after an early experimenter in electricity. These are the people who captured the concept of electricity and made it useful to people like you and me who own boats. There is a fifth term, also named after an early experimenter, that's gaining favor with the knowledgeable and trendy among us, the *joule.*

The unit of electrical resistance, the *ohm,* was named for Georg Ohm, the German scientist who gave us Ohm's law. The electrical symbol used to express the value for ohms is the Greek letter omega, shown in figure 1-6 on page 6. When used in Ohm's law, however, resistance is represented by a capital R.

Alessandro Volta (1745–1827) was an Italian physicist who gave us the unit of electrical force called the *volt.* The electrical symbol for volts is so simple that it doesn't need an illustration; it's just a capital V. However, when used in the formula for Ohm's law, voltage is represented by a capital P, which stands for *potential.*

*Fig. 1-6. The ohm symbol, the Greek omega.*

Andre-Marie Ampere (1775–1836) was a French physicist whose namesake is the electrical unit that describes the rate of electrical flow through a circuit that we call the *amp*. The electrical symbol for amps is a capital A. When working with Ohm's law, we use a capital I for amps.

James Watt (1736–1819) was a Scots mathematician credited with significant improvements of steam engines who coined the word "horsepower" to measure the amount of work a machine is doing. Horsepower is fine for measuring large amounts of energy, but it doesn't work for the small amounts that we have to measure while working with electricity, so, in honor of this ancient Scot, we call the electrical unit of power a *watt* and use a capital E to represent it. Watts aren't used in the formula for Ohm's law, but they are important in a corollary to Ohm's law, called the *pie* formula (because P × I = E, as we will soon see), that we will be using to calculate the size of wires and circuit protection.

James Joule (1818–1889) was an English chemist credited with the discovery that heat is a form of energy. Thus, a *joule* is a unit of electrical energy equal to the amount of work done (or heat generated) by a current of 1 amp acting for 1 second against a resistance of 1 ohm. The symbol for a joule is a J and it also is not used in Ohm's law calculations. Joules aren't really important for the work that we do throughout the rest of this book. I wouldn't even mention them here if it weren't for the fact that the joule is gradually replacing the watt in some areas of electricity (*joule* is also replacing *calorie* in the list of nutritional information on many food packages) and that you'll probably run into it in your other reading. When you do hear the term, you're fairly safe in assuming that 1 joule = 1 watt.

So you can see that our foundations of electricity are named after quite an interesting international rogues' gallery of electrical scientists.

Let's forget about joules for now and take a look at each of these other terms more closely, and perhaps we can begin to get a clearer picture of their importance to us.

## Voltage

Voltage is the measure of the potential that an electrical power source has for doing work for us. Thus, a fully charged 12-volt battery has the potential of producing 12 volts (actually closer to 13.5 volts) of power. In fact, the term *electrical potential* is often used instead of the word *voltage* and means the same thing. To refer back to the analogy of the water tank, where a hose connected to the bottom of a tank might measure 100 pounds per square inch (psi) of water pressure, a wire connected to a 12-volt battery (in a circuit, of course) will measure 13.5 volts of electrical potential. In both cases we are referring to the energy that's available to do work and nothing else; the voltage in the battery is exactly the same concept as the water pressure in the tank. Simply think of voltage as electrical pressure. The higher the voltage in the battery (or in any other source of electrical power), the more pressure is available to send electricity along its path in a circuit.

## Amperage

Amperage is often confused with voltage, and I think it's the most difficult of all our definitions to grasp. Think of amperage as the rate of electrical flow past a given point in a circuit. If you can think of voltage as electrical pressure, then it should be easy to think of amps as the volume of electrical energy flowing through a point in a circuit. Amperage is most important in my mind because too much of it in a circuit is what trips circuit breakers, blows fuses, melts wires and other components, and sometimes burns up boats. This stuff needs to be carefully controlled, and much of the rest of this book will be devoted to understanding how to do just that.

## Resistance

Resistance, as we said, is measured in ohms and is that invisible force that holds back electrical flow (amperage) and reduces the electrical potential (voltage) as electrical energy flows through a circuit. It's also the electrical unit that puts electricity to work for us. For example, it's the resistance in the element of a light bulb or the toaster in your kitchen that makes the element glow and give off light or toast your bread. And it is the rapidly fluctuating resistance in microscopic transistors (measured in tiny fractions of an ohm) that makes the wonderful world of marine electronics possible. In marine wiring, unwanted or excessive resistance is caused by such things as loose or corroded connections, wire that is too small in diameter, or wire runs that are too long.

One noticeable by-product of resistance to electrical flow is heat. In the case of the toaster, we have engineered a way to make this heat useful. In the case of a loose or corroded connection, the heat generated is sure to cause damage to the area around the connection; read melted switches and plug connections. Figure 1-7 illustrates Mr. Ohm's formula.

## Ohm's Law

No, you don't have to worry about going to jail for breaking Ohm's law. In fact, you can't break it (not without a nuclear particle accelerator that costs many millions of dollars), because it is, for all practical purposes, inviolate—you couldn't break it if you tried. Simply stated, Ohm's law is a mathematical formula we can use to calculate any one of the values we mention above as long as we know the value of any two of the first three. For example, if we know the amperage and resistance for a circuit, we can easily calculate the voltage, or if we know the voltage and amperage, Ohm's law gives us the resistance. Once we know the amperage and the voltage, we can calculate the wattage using a simple little formula, called the pie formula, that we will get to in a moment ("Working with the Numbers").

It's important to note here that various versions of the following formulas exist, assigning different letter designations to the elements of the formula (E for volts or sometimes watts, for example; the letter I is often used to designate amperage as well). The point is that it really doesn't matter what letter you use, as long as you know which value it's assigned to. For our purposes we'll keep it simple and use V for volts, A for amps, W for watts, and R for resistance or ohms. Figure 1-8 on page 8 shows the simple equation used to find watts, or amps if voltage and wattage are given.

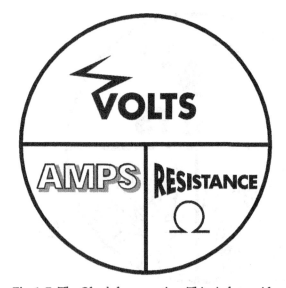

*Fig. 1-7. The Ohm's law equation. This circle provides a visual relationship between the key electrical players. If any two of the values are known, the third can be found by using either multiplication or division. By multiplying amps times ohms, voltage can be found. By dividing voltage by ohms, amperage can be found. Dividing volts by amps determines resistance (ohms). Notice that if voltage remains constant and if resistance increases, reduce amperage flow and vice versa. This explains mathematically why a short circuit to ground, before power reaches a load (resistance), is so dangerous. Amperage will go way up until either a fuse blows or a breaker trips, or something burns up! Conversely, it also explains why, if resistance increases (loose connections, too small a wire), amperage needed by the appliance won't be delivered.*

Ohm's law works out rather nicely for us as boaters because we will always be able to measure at least two of the values we need to calculate the third. Voltage (V) and amperage (A) are both easily measured using a basic multimeter, and we will learn how to do this later. With some circuits, ohms (R) are a little tricky to measure accurately, but we'll learn how to handle them also. For our purposes, wattage (W) is not measured but calculated from voltage and amperage, or information often provided by the appliance manufacturer.

*Fig. 1-8. The power formula. Like the Ohm's law equation, the power equation can be used to determine the third value if two are known. Multiply and divide just as with Ohm's law. This is the "pie formula," which is useful for determining AC amperage. All UL-rated (Underwriters Laboratory) appliances must have either volts and watts or volts and amps indicated on an attached sticker. The sticker is useful for sizing circuit breakers and wire size.*

## Working with the Numbers

A quick look at Ohm's law and the pie formula, presented above, and some brief experimentation with a few actual numbers illustrate the interrelationship of all the elements we have discussed so far. As with any algebraic formula, we can move and substitute values so that we can use the same formula, written different ways, to determine any of our electrical values as follows:

▶ $V = A \times R$, or volts equal amps multiplied by ohms.

▶ $A = V + R$, or amps equal volts divided by ohms.

▶ $R = V + A$, or ohms equal volts divided by amps.

With the pie formula we get the following three variations:

▶ $W = V \times A$, or watts equal volts multiplied by amps.

▶ $A = W + V$, or amps equal watts divided by volts.

▶ $V = W + A$, or volts equal watts divided by amps.

So, assuming a 13.5-volt constant (the normal voltage in a charged 12-volt battery), let's see what happens to amperage when the resistance in a circuit changes from, say, 5.5 ohms to 7.8 ohms. By dividing 13.5 volts by 5.5 ohms we see that the amperage draw through this circuit will be 2.6 amps. By increasing the circuit resistance to 7.8 ohms, we will end up with 1.73 amps.

If the resistance in a circuit is known or if it can be accurately measured, we can apply this simple formula as the first step in determining what size circuit breaker or fuse to use. (See chapter 4 for more detail on circuit protectors and how to select them.) As the resistance in a circuit goes up in value, the amperage goes down. Conversely, as resistance goes down, amperage goes up. This trade-off between amps and ohms is always valid, regardless of the amperage and resistance, as long as the voltage remains constant.

As for a practical application of the pie formula, it's quite useful when you're adding AC appliances to your boat. All Underwriters Laboratories (UL) approved appliances must have a tag or label affixed to them with the operating voltage and wattage of the appliance clearly stated. By applying the pie formula, and dividing the wattage by the voltage, we can determine how many amps the appliance will require for operation.

With DC appliances, determining the amperage used by the load is always the first step in determining the size of the fuse or circuit breaker we will need and the size of the wire we will use to supply the circuit.

## Voltage Drop

*Voltage drop* is simply the reduction of voltage in a circuit caused by amperage working to overcome resistance, and represents the conversion of electrical energy to some other form of energy. For example, when you turn on a bilge pump the current (amperage) used by the pump converts the power wattage to mechanical energy that turns the impeller of your pump and keeps your bilge dry. In another, less desirable example, when current encounters resistance (ohms) in a circuit caused by wiring that is too small or by corroded terminals, the wattage is converted to heat (wattage is more properly called joules here) that can blow fuses and trip circuit breakers. In extreme cases it can destroy your boat.

In both cases, the reduction in voltage from the beginning of the circuit at the positive terminal of the battery to the end of the circuit at the negative terminal is called the voltage drop. Normally, voltage drop is referred to as a percentage that we get by dividing the original voltage into the amount of the drop. Thus, a circuit measuring 13.5 volts at the positive terminal and 12 volts at the negative terminal (we will discover how to make these measurements later on) will be experiencing a 1.5-volt or 11.1 percent voltage drop.

## Putting It All Together

Some basic facts relative to what happens to resistance, voltage, and amperage as they are dispersed throughout the different circuit types are in order. In other words, it's time to assemble our monster.

Beginning with the series circuit, remember that there is only one path for electrons to flow throughout the circuit. Here's what happens: as amperage (which you'll recall is the volume of electrical energy flowing through a circuit) travels through the circuit, voltage (the electrical potential) is used up and reduced as the current (amperage) encounters resistance (ohms) and is converted to power (wattage). This reduction in voltage is referred to as voltage drop. The sum of the individual voltage drops measured at each component in a series circuit is equal to the original source voltage. The total circuit resistance in a series circuit is the sum of the individual resistance values of each load (resistance) in the circuit. The same amperage will flow through each resistance in a series circuit but the voltage is divided and shared by the loads in the circuit.

In the parallel circuit, there is more than one path for electrons to follow, and this changes the characteristics of the circuit considerably. First, having more than one path reduces the inherent circuit re-

sistance. The total circuit resistance in a parallel circuit will always be lower than the resistance for any single resistance in the circuit. Current (amperage) will vary as it feeds each individual resistance in the circuit to the extent that the resistance values are different. The total circuit current in amps will be the sum of the current drawn at each load in the circuit.

## Circuit Problems and How They Occur

In my years of listening to people talk about electricity, I've learned one thing for sure. To the uninitiated, every time anything goes wrong with their electrical system, it's described as a "short." Although this is certainly possible, the truth is that most problems that occur with electrical systems on boats are not short circuits. In fact, a more probable cause for electrical trouble on a boat is caused by the unwanted open or interrupted circuit, already mentioned. So, what are the common problems, and what are some of their causes and characteristics?

### Open Circuits

An *open circuit* is one that contains a break or *open* in the continuous path, or route, for electron flow described earlier. This can be caused by a break in the wiring, a connection that has come undone, or corrosion that accumulates to the point where the voltage drop is so great that current will no longer flow in the circuit. By comparison, a "wanted" open occurs when you switch off an electrical device. The switch effectively breaks the continuity through the circuit.

To pinpoint unwanted opens in a circuit you must attack them systematically with your multimeter, and we will learn just how to do this in a later chapter.

### Short Circuits

*Short circuits* are just that, circuits that have been shortened from their original design. *Shorts*, as they are commonly called, are almost always induced by human error and come in three varieties.

#### Shorts to Ground
The first of the three is the short circuit to ground. With this condition, the wire to the electrical load

(the feed) has somehow connected itself directly to ground before reaching the appliance. In a short to ground, the resistance in the circuit (which you'll remember is essential for a circuit to operate) has been circumvented. As Ohm's law will tell you if you work through the numbers, a lot of amperage will flow with only the resistance of the wire to stop it. The good news: If the circuit is designed correctly, the fuse or circuit breaker will trip. The bad news: Some wire and insulation may be burned before the circuit protection opens the circuit.

### Intercircuit Shorts

The second variety of short is what I refer to as the *intercircuit short*. With this type, two or more electrical circuits will be affected simultaneously. The cause? Drilling through a wiring harness to install new deck gear and then running a screw down through the deck into the harness, effectively connecting multiple circuit wires. This short circuit with a screw is quite common. Another frequent cause for this type of short is not thinking dynamically. Remember, our electrical system will change when the engine is running and while we are underway. Wiring harnesses that rub against moving pulleys, hot exhaust manifolds, and the like are electrical time bombs. Check to be sure all wiring is properly secured and clearance from moving machinery is adequate.

### Internal Shorts

The third and final short circuit type we will discuss is the *internal short*, a short circuit that can occur deep within the internal circuitry of the electrical appliance itself. This type of short circuit is the most harmless of the three because it doesn't usually threaten the safety of our boats. Internal shorts can, however, be expensive to correct because they often mean that expensive equipment will have to go into the repair shop or worse, into the dumpster. Often a short inside a piece of equipment will simply cause the equipment to stop functioning. At other times the fuse or circuit breaker will trip without the risk of burned wires or insulation (assuming the circuit protection is rated properly).

## Tools

Most of us will already have a good collection of basic tools. However, besides our regular collection of sockets, spanner wrenches, screwdrivers, pliers, and the like we'll need to acquire a few more specific items. Once we start working with electricity and begin performing serious electrical troubleshooting procedures and upgrades, we are going to need specialized equipment that will allow us to work safely and do a proper job.

Figure 1-9, a photo of my personal collection of tools, shows some of this equipment.

Technology has been good to us electricians in the last several years, and significant improvements in tools and equipment have been made, specifically in the areas of multimeters and crimping tools (we take a closer look at these in chapters 3 and 4). As you go through this book, you'll see these tools in use, with specific instructions for every test procedure you'll ever need on board your boat.

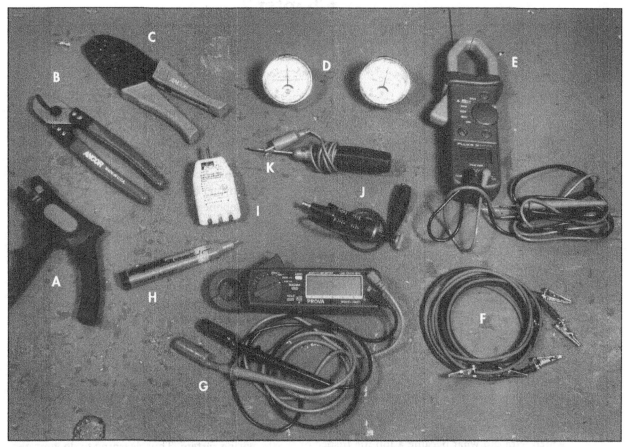

*Fig. 1-9. Some basic and not-so-basic electrical tools from my collection. Beginning at the lower left and moving clockwise are (A) wire stripper, (B) cable cutter, (C) ratcheting crimping tool, (D) inexpensive Snap-On inductive ammeters, (E) Fluke 36 high-amperage inductive multimeter (true RMS), (F) miscellaneous jumper leads used for various tests, (G) the Ancor/Prova inductive ammeter with frequency scale, (H) AC probe pen, (I) AC LED socket (outlet) tester, (J) Snap-On ignition spark tester, (K) 12 V test light/probe.*

# Chapter 2

# Working with Wiring Diagrams

## The Trouble with Boats

In chapter 1 I mentioned that I first started working with electricity in the automotive trade and it wasn't until later that I became involved with boats. One of the first things that I learned while working on cars was the value of a good wiring diagram. With a glance at a sheet of paper covered with lines and squiggles and a plethora of other arcane hieroglyphics, I could tell immediately what went where and how. When something went wrong, I could tell from a quick study of the diagram what the most likely cause of the problem might be and where to go to fix it. Naturally, when I switched to the marine field and started working on boats, the first thing I did was reach for the trusty wiring diagram.

Alas, there were no wiring diagrams, at least none that were comparable to those I had been accustomed to. Troubleshooting a defective electrical system, which had been so straightforward with automobiles, became a study in frustration and confusion. Just locating components and determining which wire did what became a job for Inspector Sherlock and his trusty Watson, or in this case, Inspector Sherman and his trusty multimeter.

Until only recently, boatbuilders generally have done a rather poor job of creating usable wiring diagrams for their products. Some supply only partial diagrams, while others don't supply any at all or simply pass on to the buyer the one provided by the engine builder. On the other hand, some builders go to the opposite extreme and provide diagrams that are masterpieces, but you have to be an electrical engineer to interpret them. They are far too complicated to be very useful for the occasional boater/electrician and can even be confusing for the professional.

An electrician working on a car with a decent wiring diagram can usually go directly to an electrical problem and fix it with a minimum of fuss and time. However, that same electrician working on a boat is quite likely to spend half or even more of his or her time just trying to figure out how the systems are wired. Manufacturers and boatbuilders outdo themselves, it seems, in the creative way they locate components in obscure lockers and hide wiring in unlikely places.

To further complicate the situation, many marine components, such as radios, radar, and navigation instruments, are installed by the distributor or dealer and not by the boatbuilder or manufacturer. If you're buying a used boat, you can bet that there are numerous components installed by the previous owner, who may or may not have known anything about electricity. You can also bet that even if your new boat came with a comprehensive wiring diagram, none of these aftermarket add-ons are ever noted on it.

With the cost of a boatyard electrician well past the $100-an-hour mark in some areas, it's easy to see why electrical repair bills can get so high. With every job done at the boatyard, a substantial portion of the bill goes toward paying the electrician to figure out the wiring system. Thus, learning to do your own electrical work is one of the most cost-effective ways that you, as a boatowner, can spend a few hours. Once you finish this book you'll be able to make your own basic repairs and additions. You may even pay for the book with your first job.

As a first step in becoming a competent marine electrician you should draw up your own wiring diagram for your boat, if you don't already have one. If you do have a wiring diagram, it's very likely that you can make significant improvements with just a few revisions and additions, and it's the purpose of this chapter to show you how to do this. Follow the advice given here and you'll be well on your way toward understanding what wiring diagrams are telling you, and you'll be able to properly upgrade your diagram as you add new equipment to your boat.

# Wiring Diagrams

A wiring diagram, sometimes referred to as a schematic diagram, is a wonderful tool often compared to a road map. Suppose you were to find yourself in Salt Lake City for the first time and you were trying to get your new Ranger bassboat to Lake Mead to give her a spin. The first thing you would be likely to do is reach for a road map. Salt Lake City would be clearly shown on the map with graphic symbols that might tell you not only its location but its relative size, elevation, and in special cases, things like its political and racial demographics. Lake Mead would likewise be shown with graphics that would contain a lot of information about the lake such as its size, shape, pool elevation, and anything else the mapmaker thought was important. The lines connecting the city to the lake would represent roads, of course, but you could also tell by the nature of the lines what the roads would be like: paved or dirt, straight or twisty, single-lane, double-lane, divided, or interstate. You would also see intersections, junctions, detours, and areas of potential trouble and congestion. To see what the various symbols and graphics mean you would look at the key or legend, which is usually provided on a corner or on the back of a map.

The wiring diagram you're going to develop or improve for your boat is just like that road map. It will provide us with the information to trace a route from start to finish, in this case the electrical flow through the circuits on your boat. The trouble is, unlike road maps, which are reasonably consistent in design and have that prominent key to tell you what the symbols mean, wiring diagrams come in a variety of designs and styles, and there is seldom a key to reference. Fortunately, most of the basic electrical symbols are fairly standard and the others that you'll need for our wiring diagram aren't too hard

to figure out. Before we do anything else, let's take a look at a few of the more common electrical symbols that you're likely to encounter on any standard wiring diagram.

# Common Symbols

Like road maps, wiring diagrams use a variety of symbols to indicate different components within an electrical circuit. Electrical engineers are trained to recognize several thousand of these symbols and to understand just what they mean. This gives wiring diagrams a certain consistency. To the untrained eye, however, these symbols can be as cryptic as an ancient Chinese manuscript.

Figure 2-1 illustrates some of the symbols most frequently used in marine wiring diagrams.

### Elements of a Good Wiring Diagram

A wiring diagram should be laid out just like a road map and will incorporate many of the features of a

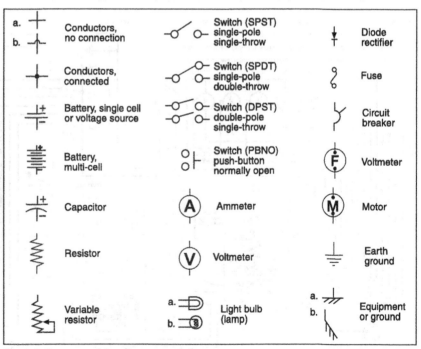

*Fig. 2-1. Common wiring diagram symbols.*

good map. Some of the most important elements of a good wiring diagram are as follows:

▶ Every wiring diagram for a small boat should be simple enough to be easily read and understood, even by those of us who don't have an engineering degree.

▶ The relative location of all electrical components on the boat must be shown.

▶ Each component of each circuit must be shown with all relevant specifications.

▶ The size and the type of the fuse or circuit breaker used in each circuit must be clearly indicated.

▶ Each wire to and from each component in the boat must be identified on the diagram by color and number or label, depending on how this marking is applied.

▶ The gauge of every wire in each circuit should be shown.

Figure 2-2 shows an example of a diagram with all the elements described above.

Figure 2-3 shows a far less descriptive diagram, which was the norm for years. (This one may look a lot like the one that came with your boat.)

## Component Identification

If you're new to marine electrical systems, one of the first things you should do is learn to identify the wiring and the major components of a circuit. Getting a positive ID on such items as bilge blowers, bilge pumps, and cabin lights is easy because you can tell what they do just by looking at them, but what about the other required components in the circuit? Where are they, and how can you begin to determine which wires feed what circuits as you look at the multitude of choices behind your distribution panel?

Figure 2-4 shows the back of a typical master distribution panel, with all the key components identified. For a further explanation of what these

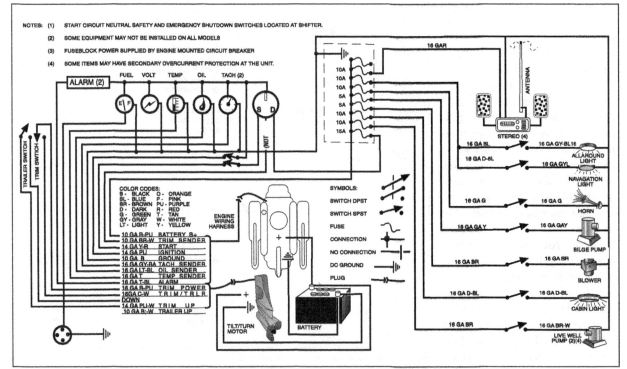

Fig. 2-2. A good wiring diagram with all of my listed key elements incorporated.

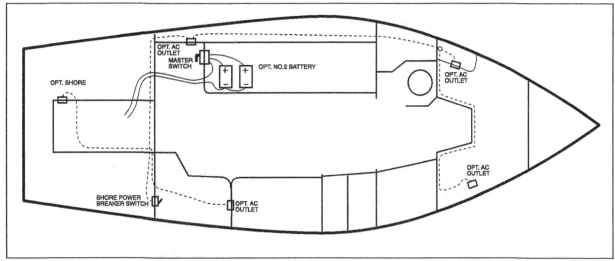

*Fig. 2-3. A typical, poor-quality diagram. This is all that came with a sailboat that I purchased in the early 1980s to describe the electrical installation. The problem is certainly not exclusive to sailboats!*

components do, refer to the glossary at the back of this book.

## Wire Identification and the ABYC Color Code

Identifying the wires that connect the various components illustrated by a wiring diagram can sometimes be a challenge when you first get started. The good news here, however, is that our friends at the ABYC have developed a standard color code for boat wiring that brings order to this previously mind-boggling task. This color-coding scheme, which has been around for twenty-odd years, is finally catching on.

The ABYC color code assigns a specific color of wire to each function in a properly wired marine electrical system. Thus, an electrician who is working on a boat wired to the ABYC standard and is confronted with a dark blue wire knows immediately that that wire is for the interior lights and nothing else. He or she also knows that the purple wire is for the ignition system, and that all those red and yellow wires are the DC-positive and -negative connectors. This standard makes it easy to identify a wire's function in the system on any boat, not just your own, even without the help of a wiring diagram.

*Fig. 2-4. A switch panel with key components identified.*

**WIRING COLOR CODE**

| Color | Use |
|---|---|
| Green, or green w/yellow stripe(s) | DC grounding conductors |
| Black, or yellow | DC negative conductors |
| Red | DC positive conductors |

**ENGINE AND ACCESSORY WIRING COLOR CODE**

| COLOR | ITEM | USE |
|---|---|---|
| Yellow w/red stripe (YR) | Starting circuit | Starting switch to solenoid |
| Brown/yellow stripe (BY) or Yellow (Y) - see note | Bilge blowers | Fuse or switch to blowers |
| Dark gray (Gy) | Navigation lights Tachometer | Fuse or switch to lights Tachometer sender to gauge |
| Brown (Br) | Generator armature Alternator charge light Pumps | Generator armature to regulator Generator Terminal/alternator Auxiliary terminal to light to regulator Fuse or switch to pumps |
| Orange (O) | Accessory feed | Ammeter to alternator or generator output and accessory fuses or switches. Distribution panel to accessory switch |
| Purple (Pu) | Ignition Instrument feed | Ignition switch to coil and electrical instruments. Distribution panel to electric instruments |
| Dark blue | Cabin and instrument lights | Fuse or switch to lights |
| Light blue (Lt Bl) | Oil pressure | Oil pressure sender to gauge |
| Tan | Water temperature | Water temperature sender to gauge |
| Pink (Pk) | Fuel gauge | Fuel gauge sender to gauge |
| Green/stripe (G/x) (Except G/Y) | Tilt down and/or trim in | Tilt and/or trim circuits |
| Blue/stripe (Bl/x) | Tilt up and/or trim out | Tilt and/or trim circuits |

**NOTE: If yellow is used for DC negative, blower must be brown with yellow stripe.**

*Fig. 2-5. ABYC-recommended color codes from their E-11 standard. (Courtesy ABYC)*

Figure 2-5 at left lists the ABYC's recommended color codes and the circuits (or parts of circuits) they serve, as found in *Standards and Technical Information Reports,* Standard E-11, tables 14 and 15. If your boat is wired to the ABYC's recommended standards, you can get a jump start in deciphering what you see behind your distribution panel by using this table.

By now you may be saying to yourself, "Hey, this is great—but wait, as I look behind my distribution panel I see 20 red wires and 20 yellow ones [or black ones on an older boat] and several each of about a dozen other colors. What do all these wires do and which one feeds which circuit?" All you know from the table above is that the yellow (or black) wires are supposed to be DC-negative conductors, the red ones should be DC-positive conductors, green ones are ground wires, and light blue ones are for the instruments. But as you sort through this spaghetti, how do you tell just exactly what each wire does? Your boat may not use the ABYC-recommended colors in its wiring, or it may only use some of them. Also, as with most changes, initial acceptance of the color-coding standard when first introduced was neither universal nor overwhelming. Most manufacturers have implemented the changes gradually as they updated their assembly procedures and as stocks of existing wire were depleted. Also, it's important to note that the ABYC standard allows for deviation from the recommended color scheme as long as all wiring is identified in some way. Many builders have adopted a numbering scheme that positively identifies any wire with numbered labels affixed to the wire; a wiring diagram for the boat then lists the numbers and identifies them. The standard also allows for color substitution as long as a wiring diagram is supplied to identify the wires positively.

If you own one of these older boats or a new one that doesn't comply with the ABYC color-coding standard, the only answer is to go through the entire electrical system and write down the color and function of each wire. This isn't as hard as it sounds, and I show you how to do it at the end of this chapter.

Fortunately, compliance with the standard is now nearly universal, and the odds are that if you're buying a new boat, both the boatbuilder and the engine manufacturer will have complied. This is good news,

> ### ► A Note on Engine-maker Compliance and the ABYC Color Code
>
> It's important to note that the ABYC standards are recommendations only, and should not be confused with the National Electric Code (NEC), the mandatory safety standards for land-based electrical installations developed and published by the National Fire Protection Association (NFPA). Mercury Marine is one of the few engine manufacturers that actually follows the ABYC-recommended color codes. But since all engine makers provide comprehensive wiring diagrams with their products, they are still compliant with ABYC standards.

of course, but even if your wiring system is in compliance with the ABYC recommendations and you have a comprehensive wiring diagram, you still don't know what all those multicolored wires in back of the distribution panel do. This brings us to circuit identification, a procedure that's a little different than wire identification.

## Circuit Identification

Circuit identification will help you to determine the specific function of each wire in back of your switch or circuit-breaker panel (which, for consistency, let's call the distribution panel) or any wire on the boat for that matter. There are several accepted methods for identifying circuits, but unless the manufacturer of your boat was unusually considerate, you'll have to come up with a system and install it yourself. The technique is called "wire chasing" in electro-speak, and it simply involves following a specific wire from one end to the other and placing some means of identification on the wire as you go.

First learn to concentrate on the circuit in question; forget about all those other wires for the time being. Fortunately, circuit identification is one of the easiest ways to become familiar with the details of your system. Here are a few methods you can use.

### Numbered Labels

On the off chance the manufacturer of your boat was unusually meticulous and provided circuit identification, this is the method they probably used to do it. Numbered circuit ID labels come in pads available in any electrical supply house. They are simply clear plastic peel-and-stick labels with white or black numbers printed on them (black for the white and light-colored wires, and white for the black and dark-colored wires). To use them, first identify the circuit you want to label by the nameplate on the front of the distribution panel adjacent to the switch or circuit breaker. (It will probably say something generic like "accessories.") There are usually five or six labels of each number in a set, so all you need do is place a number on the first wire behind the switch panel, then trace the wire to the fixtures that it operates. Place labels at strategic places along the wire as you go. Next, trace the yellow or black wire back to the common bus (which should be located somewhere near the distribution panel) and label it the same way. Now write that circuit number down someplace handy and move to the next circuit. If you already have a wiring diagram, you should also write the new circuit number on the corresponding circuit on the diagram.

Now you know that the circuit on the switch panel marked "accessories" is circuit number 32 and it feeds the light in the forepeak and the exhaust fan in the head. If either if these appliances should stop working, all you need do is trace wire number 32 until you find the problem.

## Named Labels

Several manufacturers make label sets that you can use just like the numbered labels. They simply state just what fixture or fixtures a specific circuit operates. Named labels have the advantage of not requiring a key to translate the number into a function, but they also have several disadvantages. For one thing, they are not as neat and tidy as the numbered labels, and most circuits will have more than one function, requiring more than one label. You can get around this last objection by simply writing your own labels on white electrical tape with a permanent marker and wrapping it around the wire, but it still is a bit messy, especially on large or complex systems. The labels also tend to fall off if exposed to solvents or fumes.

## Colored Heat-Shrink Tubing

A great way to identify circuits is to provide each one with its individual color code applied with heat-shrink tubing. By using two colors for each circuit,

you can ID up to 25 separate circuits with only five separate colors; if you use three colors for each circuit, the total number of circuits jumps to 125. The big drawback to this system is that each wire must be disconnected at both ends before the heat-shrink can be applied, so it's very labor-intensive when applied to an existing system. However, it's fine for additions to existing systems and when a boat must be completely rewired.

## Colored Tape and Wire Ties

You can, of course, apply the same color designation as described above using colored electrical tape, which is easy to apply without disconnecting any of the wires. The trouble with tape is that it isn't as permanent as heat-shrink and it's liable to wash off if exposed to fuel, solvents, or lubricants (such as WD-40). You can do the same thing using colored wire ties, which are a little bit messier but tend to be more permanent.

There are many other methods for wire identification that are acceptable and are often used by both boat builders and owners. The ABYC standard only states that some means of identifying the wires in each circuit should be employed. All of the above methods are quite acceptable and are good alternatives for any work you may do, such as adding on new equipment.

Whatever means of circuit identification you select—numbered or named labels, colored heat-shrink tubing or tape, or a new one that you think up for yourself—of this you can be sure: knowing what every wire on our boat does, where it goes, and where it comes from is going to make your boating life much simpler when problems crop up.

## Substituting Wire Colors

Before we leave this fascinating discussion of component identification, we need to cover one other situation that might arise while you're working on your new ABYC-compliant wiring system. What if you need to replace the 14-gauge brown wire that connects your generator to the alternator, and the only colors you have in your tool box are orange and yellow? This brown wire is only 3 feet long, and the electrical supply house which might or might not have it in stock is 45 minutes away. What do you do?

Often, one or more of the various colors for wiring to the ABYC recommendations may not be readily available at the time you perform a repair, and substitution may be the only practical solution. It's perfectly OK to use one of the other colors provided you code both ends of the replacement wire with the proper color and then make a prominent note on the wiring diagram. The best code medium in this case is colored heat-shrink tubing, but, of course, brown heat-shrink is less likely to be available than brown wire. In this case you could make do with a written label wrapped around the wire and protected with waterproof tape. When you substitute wire colors, circuit ID becomes doubly important.

## Expanding the Basic Circuit

Expanding the elements of the basic circuit to include the components shown in figure 2-6, you end up with something that looks very much as it might look if it were wired on your boat, even though this might be hard to see in this compressed state. In this diagram, I am illustrating what the wiring for a bilge blower circuit would look like if we backtracked to the master switch panel on the boat.

Figure 2-7 on page 20 illustrates what the power supply circuit to a master switch panel should look like, with a circuit protector (fuse or breaker) and battery master switch installed. I should point out, however, that many boats do not use a battery master switch, and many installations don't have the fuse or breaker installed either. The latest version of the ABYC's electrical standard E-11 states that "A battery switch shall be installed in the positive conductor or conductors from each battery or battery bank with a CCA rating greater than 800 amperes."

You'll have a lot more information on batteries and battery banks in chapter 5. For the moment, suffice to say that many small runabouts with only one small battery could easily fall below this 800-amp threshold, and would be exempt from the recommendation for a battery switch. I should also point out that even though switches are not recommended for these

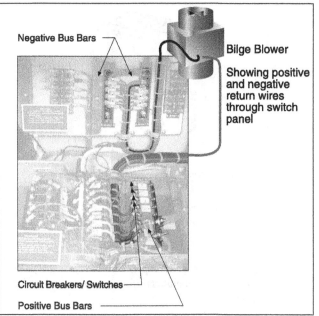

*Fig. 2-6. A bilge blower circuit highlighted on the switch panel, with the key components identified. When looking at large clusters of wires in an arrangement like this, it's important to focus on only the components and wires that are important to you at the moment. To begin your search, start at the wiring at the back of the switch or breaker labeled "blower" in this example and carefully tug on the wire to follow it through any bundling at the back of the panel. Once you've identified all the wiring behind the panel, locate the component in question on your boat. A good wiring diagram may indicate a relative component location on the boat, but don't count on it: usually you have to search on your own to find all the components in a given circuit.*

small batteries, 800 CCAs is more than enough current to start a fire and cause serious burns in the event of a short. Thus, a means of quickly disconnecting these small batteries is no less important than it is for the big guys, in my mind. All batteries, regardless of CCA rating, should have a master shut-off switch.

### Chasing Circuits

Remember that the distribution panel (or panels—sometimes there are more than one) on your boat is the point at which most of the circuits on your boat come together in close proximity, and the situation

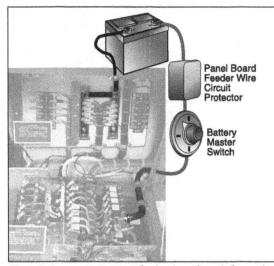

*Fig. 2-7. A proper power supply circuit to the switch panel showing the circuit protector (fuse or breaker) and the battery master switch.*

always looks a lot worse than it really is. Once you learn what a basic circuit looks like and develop the habit of ignoring everything but that one circuit you're working on, all that spaghetti will start to make sense, and everyday repairs will come easily and quickly.

For example, suppose one Sunday morning you decide to take the old Donzi for a run out to Block Island to buy the kids and some friends a pizza. It's a beautiful sunny day with a flat-calm sea and not a cloud in the sky. It's the perfect day for a family cruise—the kind of day you bought your boat for. You back the trailer down the ramp like an expert, slide the old girl off the trailer with the panache of long practice, lower the out-drives, and hit the blower switch to clear the engine compartment of any gasoline fumes prior to starting the engines. Nothing happens. Nada, zip, zero.

Without the blower you can't safely (or legally) start your engines. No engines, no Block Island. No Block Island, no pizza. You aren't going to be a very popular guy, and what has started out to be a perfect day on the water is rapidly deteriorating into a first-class disaster. What to do? Lucky for you, you bought this book and know exactly what to do.

The first thing you'll do, of course, is to check the state of the battery charge and all the terminals. Once you have determined that everything is as it should be here, move to the distribution panel and check the fuse or the circuit breaker for the bilge blower. Now move to the switch on the panel identified (hopefully) as the blower switch and trace the two wires from there to the connection on the distribution panel. Then trace the wires from the switch to the blower motor itself.

Aha! Look there—right where the blower leads emerge from the engine compartment bulkhead. See that white powder on the terminal block? It's copper oxide and it's a sure sign of corrosion. Sure enough, a close inspection shows a terminal that's completely engulfed in the stuff. First, make sure the blower switch is turned off. Then remove the terminal with a screwdriver, then a quick scrape with your trusty pocket knife takes care of the corrosion. Once the terminal is cleaned and reattached, the blower is as good as new, and you're soon blasting over the waves thinking of nothing but pepperoni, mushrooms, and mozzarella cheese. The day is saved, and instead of a schmuck you're a hero. Plus you probably saved yourself enough in repair bills to at least pay for the pizza.

Figure 2-6 on page 19 illustrates what you must focus on when confronted with an electrical problem of this magnitude. The highlighted areas of this drawing are the only things you should be thinking about as you try to troubleshoot a problem with this bilge blower circuit. Looking at figure 2-8, you can see what this might look like on a typical wiring diagram (the dotted line represents the proper circuit), with each element of the circuit identified. Track down and check out each of the basic elements described in chapter 1, and you'll quickly locate the trouble with any circuit.

## Locating Components

A common trick for boatbuilders, especially on mid- to larger-sized boats, is to install remote junction boxes for wiring. They really do this to simplify the electrical system and to save money on wiring, but it

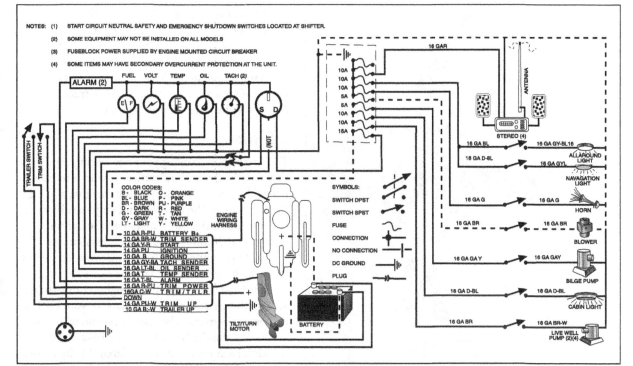

*Fig. 2-8. How the bilge blower circuit would look on a good-quality wiring diagram.*

often seems like they do it just to confound us poor electricians. The problem isn't with the use of the junction boxes—they usually make a lot of sense. The problem is where the boatbuilders choose to locate them. I have found them inside lockers, under floorboards, behind drawers and medicine cabinets, over headliners, and I even found one behind a holding tank where I couldn't get to it without a lot of unpleasant pumping. These terminals are often located in spots so obscure that you would never find them without the help of some kind of wiring diagram showing their exact location—even then, they can sometimes be hard to find.

Hidden junction boxes can often be the source of a loose or broken connection in a circuit and must be found before the faulty circuit can be put back into service.

The first thing you do once you find one of these lost junction boxes is to note its location on the wiring diagram for the future reference of the next poor slob who has to work on the boat. I don't have any way of telling how much time I have wasted over the years emptying out lockers and pulling up floorboards trying to find one of these elusive connection points, but I know that it's a lot.

Figure 2-9 shows one of these junctions, carefully hidden.

## Locating Wires

Another common problem you will encounter as a beginning marine electrician is the mysterious case of the vanishing wires. Often wires exit the distribution panel only to disappear behind a cosmetic bulkhead or cabinet. Worse yet, they vanish into a molded-in conduit on the inside of the hull, only to reappear at the component itself. The wiring can travel the entire length of the boat without leaving a single clue as to what may be going on between the distribution panel and the light fixture, or whatever other component is in question. This is another case where a good wiring

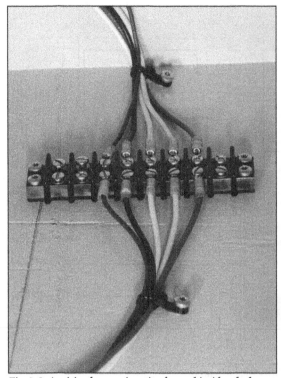

*Fig. 2-9. A wiring harness junction located inside a locker. Not only are these difficult to find at times, but many are uninsulated, as shown here. Don't pile all your tools into this one! A short circuit is sure to occur across the terminals.*

diagram can make all the difference in the world because it will show how the wiring for each circuit is routed through the boat. A comprehensive diagram will even indicate where any of those elusive hidden junction boxes may be located.

# Drawing Your Own Wiring Diagram

Now that you know how to chase wires and to identify components and devices, it's time to draw up an inclusive and detailed diagram of the electrical system on your boat. Drawing a new diagram is easier than you think, although it's time-consuming. If you have a large boat with a complex system it's best to divide the project up into several sessions of several hours each. If you don't like the way your drawing

comes out the first time, don't be afraid to do it over until you get it just the way you want it. Even if you have a good diagram already, it isn't a bad idea to make up a new one. There is no better way to learn firsthand about all the little intricacies and idiosyncrasies of your electrical system than to trace each circuit and write it down in a diagram.

## Subsystems

The first step in drawing your new wiring diagram is to mentally divide the electrical system into subsystems. These might logically be the charging and starting subsystem, the ignition and engine subsystem, the console-navigation subsystem, the lighting subsystem, and the house or utilities subsystem. Another way to do the same thing is to divide your boat physically with each division labeled as a subsystem so that the head, galley, forepeak, engine compartment, and anything else that's appropriate for your boat becomes a subsystem. The actual division will depend on the size and the kind of boat you have, but you get the idea. Next get three or four large (11- by 14-inch is ideal) sheets of graph paper for each of your subsystems (you'll be doing each one over several times) and a large clipboard or a piece of plywood to write on. Write the name of each subsystem on a separate sheet of the paper.

## The Rough Draft

For your first draft you're going to make a separate diagram for each subsystem. You'll put them back together for the final if you like, but for now it's a lot easier to keep the systems in order if you keep them separate in your mind's eye, hence the separate sheets of paper. As a logical first step, let's start with the charging and starting circuit; it's one of the simplest but also one of the most important.

First draw a sketch of the battery symbol as it's shown in figure 2-1 on page 13, for each of the batteries on your boat. Now label each battery with all the pertinent information you have available. This might include the cold-cranking amps and the amphours, if you know these things (much more about batteries will come later), but at a minimum it will be the nominal voltage—either 6 or 12 volts—for each. The next step is to draw in the battery cables just as they appear on your batteries. For now, just worry about the cables that connect the batteries to each other and ignore the others. Double-check to make sure you have the *polarity* right—that all the positive and negative terminals are labeled correctly. Now add to your drawing any battery isolators, isolation switches, or any other paraphernalia you find connected directly to the battery. If you find a mysterious component you can't identify, just make a little drawing of what it looks like and keep going. You'll have plenty of time to come back and fill in the blanks when you figure out just what that mystery contraption is.

Once you have drawn the batteries and the directly connected cables, move to your battery isolation switch and draw a rough sketch of it somewhere near the middle of your diagram. (If your drawing becomes too messy or you run out of room, simply trace the lines you want to keep onto a clean sheet of paper. Get used to the idea of redrawing your work—you'll be doing it many times.) A typical switch has four positions; label them on your diagram just as they appear on your switch, probably "No. 1," "No. 2," "both," and "off". (Complex systems might have two or more of these switches.) Now connect the switch to the battery on the diagram just as it's connected on your boat, and don't forget to include the fuses, using the fuse symbol shown in figure 2-1, that should be connected to the positive battery leads somewhere between the batteries and the switch.

Now that you have the positive side of your battery system drawn it's time to fill in the negative side. Find where all the negative battery cables are connected at a common point on your boat. This could be on a separate stud, on a heavy-duty terminal strip, or on an engine or transmission bolt. Draw this on your diagram roughly as you find it on your boat, once again sketching in any mysterious components that you find attached but can't identify.

The next step is to locate on your boat the starter motor, the alternator, and the voltage regulator. If you can't find a voltage regulator, you most likely have an alternator with an internal regulator. Draw

little pictures of these items on your diagram, making sure that you provide terminals for all the wires you see attached to each. Next draw a three-terminal switch that will represent your starter key switch. These little drawings needn't be fancy; just a little rectangle identified with a label will be fine.

Now that you have the alternator, the starter, the start switch, and perhaps the voltage regulator drawn on your diagram, follow each wire that's connected to each item on your boat and draw it on the diagram just as you find it. Don't forget to write down the color of the wire, the gauge, if you can tell what it is (sometimes the gauge is written on the wire; more on this later), and the circuit ID number or code, if your boat has one. Trace each wire for its entire length, and when you come to a switch, fuse, circuit breaker, or any other device that you may or may not be able to identify, draw that in too. When you encounter wires that leave this particular subsystem and go to another, such as the ones connected to the accessory position on your starter switch, show them going off the page and label their destination ("to radio," "to alarm system," or whatever is appropriate). If you can't tell where one of these wires goes, just label it with a question mark for now.

You may not believe this, but you now have a rough draft of your wiring diagram for your starter and charging subsystem. Once you redraw it, it should look something like the one in figure 2-2. If it still doesn't look like much, don't worry as long as you can look at the drawing and relate all your little sketches and symbols to actual components on your boat.

Now that you understand how the process works, you can work your way through each of the subsystems on your boat. If you have a large or an unusually complex boat, this will take a lot of time, but keep at it. Eventually you'll have a complete, albeit crude, drawing of each of your subsystems. Go through these drawings one at a time and make sure you have at least a tentative understanding of what you have done. Convert any of your rough sketches of components to the proper symbols as shown in figure 2-1 if you can, but the important thing is that you know what your figures represent. If you find one or two that are still confusing, just retrace the wires on your boat (it will be much easier the second time around) until you understand what you have written down. It's now time to put it all together in a final drawing.

## The Final Draft

If you have done a good job with your rough draft, the final draft is optional. A well-done rough drawing is often more than adequate for use as a working wiring diagram and more than enough for most working electricians. Any professional electrician working on your boat will love you forever for your efforts in drawing up the rough draft just because you have made his or her life so much easier. There is also an advantage to keeping all your subsystems on separate sheets, because as you make additions and changes to your boat you can redraw each subsystem as it becomes necessary.

If, however, you're the fastidious type and would like a more professional and finished look for your diagram, there are several ways to accomplish this. The easiest approach is to buy an electrical engineer's stencil at any well-equipped art supply store and use it to render your rough sketches into a finished drawing. These stencils come in a myriad of styles and have hundreds of electrical symbols on them. Either the stencil for basic DC systems or one designed for

automotive applications will do just fine. Once you have the stencil, it's a simple though time-consuming matter of converting your crude sketches into a polished drawing with all the proper symbols. Still another method, which most true professionals are using today, is to use a computer graphics program to acomplish the same task. The only problem with this approach is that unless you're using a sophisticated program such as AutoCAD, which has a substantial symbols library, you'll find yourself having to create your own symbols. These don't have to be complicated, however; as long as they're properly labeled, any unique shape will suffice.

If you want to carry the finished copy of your electrical diagram to a ridiculous extreme, you can take your roughs to an electrical engineering firm. If you promise to leave a substantial portion of your material wealth with them, they will have your sketches rendered into a computer-generated schematic that will be worthy of framing and hanging over your fireplace. They might even review your work and point out your mistakes. Better yet, if you happen to know a friendly electrical engineer or someone proficient with electronic drafting, perhaps you can trade a weekend of chasing bluefish off Fire Island for a finished set of drawings. After all, that would be fun, and isn't having fun what powerboating is all about?

# Chapter 3

# Selecting and Using a Multimeter

## Multimeters

A multimeter is a highly versatile measuring and testing tool that will be essential for performing a great many of the tests and procedures that we will be covering in the rest of this book. It's one of the first tools that you as an aspiring marine electrician will need to buy, and it's by far the most important. With your multimeter you'll be able to make quick and accurate measurements of all elements of your electrical system, and you'll rarely approach any electrical task without it in hand.

Back when I first started in electrical work, a good (and expensive) multimeter was already one of the most important tools in my toolbox. However, there are profound differences between the cumbersome multimeters of only a few years ago and the sleek digital marvels we have today. My first meter was a 4-inch-thick, 6- by 8-inch black box, festooned with knobs and terminals and a large white dial with some six or eight scales printed on its face. In those days the better and more expensive a meter was, the larger it was, simply because a large analog scale is much more accurate and easier to read than a small one. To use this beast I would select the range of the scale I wanted, set the function, zero or calibrate the meter needle, connect the probes, and say a short prayer that I had set the dials and connected the probes properly. Any mistakes, and the meter would make a little crackling sound, emit a puff of white smoke, and I would be holding a handful of useless junk.

This is a bit of an exaggeration, of course, but the point is that the multimeters of just a few years ago were unwieldy, expensive, delicate, and hard to read and interpret. That expensive analog monster I used in my early days as an electrician was not nearly as versatile and accurate as the most inexpensive digital meter is today.

What a difference a few years makes! Huge advances in multimeter technology and design have brought us meters that are compact (the smallest is about the same size as and only slightly thicker than a credit card), rugged, reliable, and so easy to read that a novice can be using one with only a few minutes of study. They are also cheaper than they used to be: now a perfectly usable meter with somewhat limited capabilities can be had for less than $20 at any Radio Shack, about two-thirds what an inexpensive meter cost 20 years ago. Back when I bought my first multimeter, there were perhaps a dozen different models from which to choose; today there are hundreds of different makes and models available to the beginning electrician. In fact, there are so many different multimeters on the market that selecting the right one can be a bit daunting, and if you make the wrong choice it can be an expensive mistake. Let's take a little time to review the selection process so you get just the right one for you.

## Selecting a Multimeter

Without a doubt, the most important decision you'll make as you equip yourself for the electrical troubleshooting procedures we will visit in the forthcoming chapters is which multimeter to buy. Even an inexpensive meter with limited capabilities will make working on your electrical system much easier than trying to do the job without one. In fact, many of the tests we will be discussing are impossible without at least a basic multimeter. However, if you spend just a little more money and buy a meter with a few more advanced features, you can expand your capabilities considerably, allowing you to test for more things. But it's just as easy to buy too much meter as it is to buy an inadequate one. The current crop of multimeters range from under $20 to over several thousand dollars in price. If you aren't careful, you can spend a lot of money on fancy features that you don't need and will never use.

## Digital versus Analog Meters

The first decision you'll have to make is between a multimeter with a digital display and one with an analog display. There are still inexpensive (as well as expensive) analog meters available for those few of us who still prefer them. However, for general marine work a good digital meter is so far superior to the analog models that the latter aren't really worth considering, regardless of any cost considerations.

The trouble with the inexpensive versions of the analog meters is that they often have no internal circuit protection, making it easy to destroy the meter if you connect it improperly. Further, many of these meters suffer from low *impedance*, or internal resistance, which reduces the sensitivity of the meter. Meter sensitivity is an important consideration for many of the procedures outlined in this book.

Even with an expensive analog meter that's connected correctly, it's easy for a novice to make a mistake in measurement because the analog dial is difficult to read. These meters have adjustable scales that can be confusing to use and require the user to interpolate values if the needle falls between two lines on the scale. Incorrect readings that are easy to make with an analog meter are all but impossible to make with a digital meter, even for a beginner.

There is a huge selection of digital multimeters available. The simple-to-follow specifications listed here will help you to narrow down the field to exactly what you need.

## Digital Features You Need

You must make sure that the multimeter you select has all the features you need for boat work. Be particularly wary of some meters sold at the major home-supply stores, such as Home Depot, and residential electrical supply houses. After a recent tour of several of these stores to see what multimeters were available, I discovered that some of the meters they sell are designed just for home use. They are just fine for work with AC current at home, but they are limited in their DC measurement capability, a defect that renders them useless for onboard work. A typical multimeter suitable for marine use will have a capacity of 600 to 1,000

amps in both the AC and DC modes, and it will have resistance values up to 10,000 or 20,000 ohms or even more.

### Root-Mean-Square (RMS) Multimeters

Most of the desirable features of your new multimeter we will be discussing here apply to DC measurements, because that's where you'll be doing most of your work. There is one important feature, however, that applies only to alternating current, and that's in the way the multimeter reads AC voltage. Less-expensive meters, called *average-responding multimeters*, read AC voltage by averaging the peaks of the wave form (don't worry, we discuss alternating current thoroughly in chapter 11), which can give erroneous readings. *Root-mean-square (RMS) meters* use a formula that compensates for the valleys and peaks of the wave form (the root mean square of the maximum amplitude of the wave) and gives a reading that's much closer to the actual usable voltage in the circuit.

Average-responding meters will work just fine as long as you're measuring linear loads such as those found on incandescent lights, toaster ovens, and the like. The problem comes when you try to measure current on a non-linear load. In effect, this is any AC load that has some sort of solid-state control. Many air conditioners and refrigeration systems fall into this category. Depending upon the AC feed (shore power, inverter, or generator), the error can be as much as 40 percent on the low side. This error has serious safety implications when you're trying to determine wire gauge and circuit-protection ratings. The simple solution, if you can afford it, is to buy the RMS meter if you're going to be working around AC current supplied by anything other than a shore-power connection.

If your boat is equipped with shore power and has no inverter or generator, the less-expensive average-responding meters will give adequate results. (The difference between the AC power created by an inverter or a generator versus a shore-power connection will be discussed in chapter 11.)

### Self-Scaling

No, the self-scaling feature doesn't have anything to do with cleaning fish (if they ever bring out a multimeter that will do that, I will be first in line to buy one). *Self-scaling* (also called *auto-ranging*) simply means that once you select a function on your meter, the meter will sense the magnitude of the function and set the scale accordingly. This important feature takes the guesswork out of selecting the correct voltage, resistance, or amperage to work with. For example, if you wanted to measure the value of a resistor with a meter that did not have self-scaling and you set the meter to the wrong scale, you would get a grossly incorrect reading. For certain functions, such as amperage and voltage, if you set the scale incorrectly you might blow a fuse in the meter or even damage or destroy the meter. With self-scaling, the danger of selecting the wrong scale is greatly reduced, even though you must still be careful selecting the function.

## *Diode Checking*

The diode-check function, as found on most of the better multimeters, is really only an ultrasensitive and highly selective section of the resistance scale, but it's a useful feature that adds virtually no cost to the meter. Although it's possible to check some diodes with a meter that does not have specific diode-checking capability by setting the meter to the lowest ohms scale, the reading that results should never be counted on as accurate. To check a diode with a diode-checking meter, you test for continuity (see below) in one direction, then reverse the probes and check again in the other direction. If the diode is working properly you'll have continuity in one direction and not in the other. Diodes need a certain amount of current flowing through them to function, and the internal batteries of many meters without a diode-check function don't provide enough current in the ohms scale to close the diode. Often when a diode being checked with a meter using the regular ohms scale shows no continuity in both directions, the diode is fine but the meter just isn't up to testing diodes. The problem is that you don't have any way of telling if the fault is with the diode or the meter. If you can only afford one meter, make sure that it has diode-checking capability.

The diode scale will work with nearly any diode you may encounter in marine work. The most common diodes you'll need to check are in your battery isolators, in your alternator, and on any solar panels you might be using to keep your batteries topped up. We will talk more about diodes in a later chapter.

## *Continuity Alarm*

Be sure to select a meter that has an audible alarm to indicate continuity on the ohms scale. This alarm usually consists of a high-pitched beep that signals the user that the meter is reading a resistance value lower than infinity. This simple feature really comes in handy when you're in a tight spot where you can barely connect two wires and can't see the face of your meter. Make sure that you can actually hear the signal. Some of the alarms use such a high pitch that those of us whose hearing isn't perfect can't detect it.

The alarm is used while checking for continuity through a circuit where the actual resistance in ohms is of minor concern. Knowing for a fact that the circuit you're testing doesn't have a break in it is all the information you're after. An encouraging beep from your meter will give you that assurance.

## *Adequate Amperage*

One essential difference among multimeters is in their capability to read amperage on the DC scale on a magnitude normally encountered in marine electronics. Many expensive meters are capable of reading amperage in tiny fractions of an amp. Some of these will read in milliamps (1 milliamp = 1/1,000 of an amp) but will balk at reading anything over an amp. Most marine electrical gear, however, operates at between half an amp (500 milliamps) and about 8 amps, so it's important that your meter be able to read in this range.

I consider the amperage-reading capability of a multimeter to be extremely high on the list of essential features. Circuit breakers and fuses are both rated by amps, and you need the capability of checking them. Selecting the correct wire gauge for a new piece of equipment will involve an accurate measurement of both amps and volts. Excessive amperage in an undersized, improperly protected circuit is what burns boats to the waterline.

For most of the electrical components on which you'll be working, a meter that reads to 10 amps will do the job. However, there are certain items on some boats that will require a meter that reads much higher amperage. Anchor winches, starter motors, and alternators all require a meter that measures in the hundreds of amps. When I am working on any of these components I prefer the capability of measuring amperage to values as high as 600 amperes.

The less-expensive meters that only read amperage in the milliamp range, usually up to about 500 milliamps, are fine for electronic work, but they are useless for onboard amperage readings. Slightly more expensive meters will often read 10 or sometimes as high as 20 amps, but they require that the circuit be broken for connection of the meter (more on that later).

Some meters that have a limited amperage scale can read higher amperage using a shunt, a large, low-value resistor that bleeds a tiny amount of current off a high-amp circuit so that a low-amp meter can read it. Shunt meters are complicated to use and difficult to read, and so they aren't really a consideration for us. However, you're likely to find shunts permanently wired to the alternator circuit on boats that use amp gauges with high-amperage alternators.

### Inductive Pickups

If you'll be working a lot with high-amperage DC circuits such as on a starter motor, electric windlass, or alternator, you'll need a meter with an inductive pickup. These look just like a normal meter with a huge crab-claw–like clamp on one end.

To measure voltage and resistance with an inductive-pickup meter, you use probes just like on a regular meter. The only difference is in the way you measure amperage. With a regular meter, you must break the circuit on which you want to measure the amperage, hook the probes up in series, and hope that the amperage doesn't exceed the capacity of the meter. If it does, there will likely be some fireworks (either a blown fuse or a blown meter). With the inductive meter, simply clamp the crab claw around a wire, making sure the wire is centered and oriented properly (if you get it back-

wards, you get a negative reading) and read the amperage off the scale—no hassles disconnecting wires, and no fireworks.

A few of the better (more expensive) meters, such as those made by Fluke, have an optional clamp that plugs right into your existing meter, converting it to the inductive-pickup type. These are fine meters, but the adapters often cost more than the meter itself. By the time you add up your total investment, you would be better off buying a separate meter with a built-in clamp. Keep it simple; to read big amps, get a meter designed to handle the task right out of the box.

In summary, for most basic circuit checks on your boat, a meter with a 10- to 20-amp capability will do the job. However, if you wish to check alternator output in amps, starter current, and anchor-windlass loads, you'll need the higher-amperage capabilities of some of the better meters. There are many multimeters available, and the one you select will depend on your budget, your boat's equipment, and the intensity of your desire to do it all.

### The Multiple-Multimeter Solution

I have found that the best solution to this dilemma of which multimeter to buy is to combine several relatively inexpensive instruments rather than to buy one meter that does everything. A basic digital multimeter with a 10- or 20-amp capability will be just fine for testing most of the lighting and small-motor circuits on your boat. For measuring any circuits drawing over 20 amps, Snap-On makes an inexpensive pair of inductive-pickup analog amp gauges (Snap-On part number MT1009), which read to 100 amps in DC and to 500 amps in AC. In this case the analog scale is fine because with high-amperage tests we don't need to measure tiny fractions of an amp; a reading in whole amps is plenty. These gauges will serve your needs well for everything but shore-power or AC generator work.

Figure 3-1 shows one of my inexpensive 20-amp multimeters and the MT1009 Snap-On gauge set. This combination of instruments can be bought for under $100 and will measure current up to 500 amps.

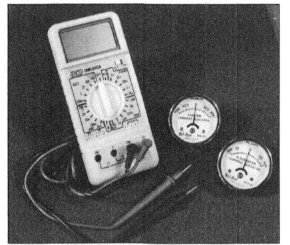

*Fig. 3-1. A 20-amp multimeter with Snap-On inductive meter set offers a fairly economical solution for measuring amperage up to 500 amps. The combination can be purchased for under $100.*

The ideal situation for general marine work would be two meters in your toolbox: one medium-priced general-purpose meter with a diode-check feature and a 10- to 20-amp capacity, and one inductive-pickup meter with at least a 600-amp capacity. Most working marine electricians have several meters that they use regularly, and it's not unusual for some gadget hounds to own four or five different meters.

## A Few Specific Recommendations

There are a few inductive meters with which I am personally familiar and can recommend as good choices for your first meter.

### Ancor 702070

One excellent general-purpose meter is the latest Ancor-brand pocket meter (see figure 3-2, page 30) with built-in inductive pickup. This meter doesn't quite reach my ideal of a 600-amp capability, but on measurements of up to 200 amps in both AC and DC it does a fine job. It also has the usual ability to measure volts and resistance and the less-usual ability to measure frequency (we discuss frequency, or Hertz, in chapter 11). Frequency measurements are useful for checking the output of shore-power outlets,

### ► A Word about Inductive Pickups

*Induction* is the phenomenon whereby an electrical current flowing through any material creates a magnetic field around the material. For example, a lightning bolt passing through the atmosphere can generate a huge magnetic field around it, and every time Wile E. Coyote grabs the wrong wire as he is trying to electrocute the Road Runner, it's the induction-induced magnetic field that makes his fur stand on end. Because of induction, any wire that has electrical current flowing through it will have a magnetic field surrounding it, regardless of the insulation used and the strength of the current. The intensity of the magnetic field increases in direct proportion to the current flowing through the wire. Thus, the higher the current, the stronger the magnetism.

Inductive-pickup meters measure this magnetic force and convert the reading into amperes. Meters with an inductive pickup can save a lot of time, and they are much easier and safer to use than those that measure amperage with probes. Just clamp the meter around the wire from which you want to take a reading, and, if you have the thing turned on and set properly, the meter does the rest.

Also, meters with an inductive pickup will have a small arrow embossed on the inside of the clamp jaws. This arrow should point toward the power source in the circuit, not toward the electrical load. (If you get it backward, you'll get a negative reading.) Finally, to ensure an accurate reading when using an inductive meter, it's important to keep the jaws as close as possible to 90 degrees in relation to the conductor you're checking.

The inductive meters are a great choice for most of us, but they do have their drawbacks. An inductive meter can measure the amperage on only a single wire at a time, so bundled wires or wires enclosed in insulation can be difficult to measure on occasion. Also, on circuits drawing less than 1 amp of current, some inductive meters may not be sensitive enough to get a reading. In this case a less-expensive conventional meter may be a better choice. This is a point worth checking before spending several hundred dollars on a clamp-type meter if you'll be working with many circuits with less than 1 amp of current. However, most onboard electrical equipment will use 1 amp or more. The most common exceptions are electronic equipment in standby mode and some small fluorescent lights.

generators, and inverters, to make sure they are running properly.

The Ancor meter does not have a diode-test function, and in actual use I have found that it will not effectively test some diodes commonly used in

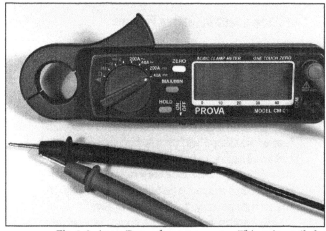

Fig. 3-2. Ancor/Prova clamp-type meter. This unit retails for around $300 and offers amperage reading capability up to 200 amps and a frequency-checking function, useful for some AC tests. Made by Prova, marketed in the United States by Ancor.

Fig. 3-3. Fluke Model 336 clamp-type meter. This is a true RMS (root-mean-square) meter that can read up to 600 AC or DC amps. This is an excellent choice if you do a lot of AC work. Its shortcoming is that its ohms scale is not as sensitive as other meters I've used. This model sells for about $275.

marine applications, such as those used in battery isolators. It does work for testing most alternators, but it may not be adequate for many inboard or inboard-outboard starter-current tests. The Ancor (part number 702070) is available through major marine retailers such as Defender Industries and West Marine for about $300.

### Fluke Model 336

If you're the type that simply has to have the best, Fluke Corporation makes what I consider to be some of the finest multimeters available anywhere. There are other fine meters, of course, but Fluke's top-of-the-line Model 336 offers one additional feature that will be useful if your boat is equipped with extensive AC circuitry such as a generator, inverter, or air-conditioning and refrigeration systems. This meter will measure up to 600 amps DC and 600 amps AC, far beyond what most boaters need. It does not have a diode-test function, however, nor will it measure AC frequency.

Figure 3-3 shows a Fluke Model 336 true RMS clamp-type inductive meter. It's available through all the major marine supply houses in the United States for about $275.

Both of these meters come with fairly easy-to-read instructions, but be warned that the meter companies in general assume that you know how to attach the meters to the circuit correctly for the measurement you're making. Reading the sections that follow will assure that you do!

## Using Your Multimeter

There are literally hundreds of checks and tests that you'll be able to carry out with your new multimeter. However, at least 90 percent of everything you'll ever need to do will involve some form of the following four basic procedures: voltage measurement, voltage drop, amperage measurement, and resistance measurement. These procedures are so important that we discuss each in detail. Measuring voltage is the easiest, so let's cover that one first.

### Measuring Voltage

To test for voltage, first make sure that your meter is turned on and that the leads are inserted into the correct sockets (the leads that came with your new meter probably have spike-like probes on the ends,

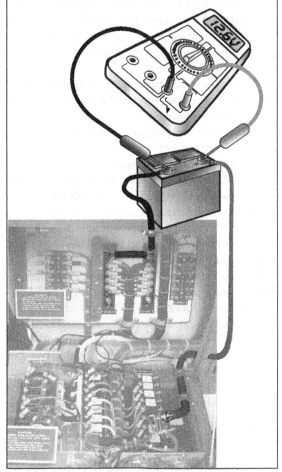

*Fig. 3-4. Meter on a volts scale hooked in parallel across a battery. A fully charged battery would read between 12.6 and 13.5 volts.*

although a rare few might have alligator clips). The black lead goes into the socket that's probably marked "COM," and the red one goes into the socket marked "DCV" or something similar. If you do not have a self-scaling meter, also double-check to make sure that your meter is set to the proper range (20 volts for a 12-volt system). Now go to one of your boat's 12-volt batteries and touch the black probe to the negative terminal and the red probe to the positive terminal. You should be able to read the battery voltage on your meter's digital readout. If your bat-

tery has a full charge, this reading will be between 12.6 and 13.5 volts. A negative sign in front of the voltage means that you have the probes connected backwards.

That's all there is to a voltage check. Once you have your meter set up properly, any time you touch the red probe to a hot positive terminal or bare wire and the black probe to a negative terminal or wire (or to ground), your meter will tell you the voltage at the point the red probe is touching. In other words, whenever your meter leads are connected to the circuit in parallel, as is explained in chapter 1, with some sort of load between them, you get a voltage reading.

Inexperienced meter users often make simple mistakes and become puzzled when their new meter shows no reading at all. This absence of a reading can be dangerous because it can lead the novice to believe the circuit is turned off when it's in fact still live or *hot*.

Figure 3-5 on page 32 illustrates a multimeter properly connected to a 12-volt circuit to check for adequate voltage at a cabin light. The red meter lead is connected to the positive terminal on the light, and the black lead is connected to the negative connection.

Many beginners get confused when they try to check voltage at points throughout a circuit and can't figure out what to do with the black lead. This lead should always be connected to the yellow (or black on older boats) lead of the circuit you're testing or to a good ground connection.

Figure 3-6 on page 33 shows this same circuit with a meter hooked up in parallel to the switch activating the circuit. In effect, both meter leads are connected to a positive feed with no load between them. This hookup is incorrect and will not show a voltage reading under any circumstances.

## Testing for Voltage Drop

Voltage drop, as we discovered in chapter 1, is the natural and unavoidable loss in voltage as amperage works to overcome resistance in a circuit. The drop is the amount of source voltage loss caused by the inherent resistance to electrical flow through the wiring in the circuit and any connections where wires and circuit components are installed.

Virtually all circuits contain some resistance. Thus, there is always some voltage drop in every circuit. This is true in AC circuits as well as in DC circuits. However, because of the trade-off between voltage and amperage (as voltage in a circuit goes up, the amperage required to do the same amount of work goes down), the drop in a 120-volt AC circuit is of little consequence. With low-voltage DC circuits, however, voltage drop is a major concern and you'll need to know how to measure it.

So how much voltage drop is acceptable? Once again our friends at the ABYC offer some guidelines. Section E-11 of the *Standards and Technical Information Reports* talks about critical and noncritical circuits. Certain fixtures such as navigation lights, bilge pumps, and navigation equipment are required for safety, and their efficient operation is critical. However, the brightness of a cabin light or the speed of a fan in the galley just isn't that important. Thus, the standards allow only a 3 percent maximum voltage drop for critical equipment and up to a maximum of 10 percent voltage drop for noncritical equipment. In a perfect world, and certainly in any electrical work you perform, it's really best to shoot for 0 percent voltage drop as an ideal, but in the real world some voltage drop will always be present, especially in long wire runs.

There are several simple math problems that may help you to get a feel for what the ABYC maximum voltage drop figures mean.

Assume a 12-volt system. If a noncritical circuit is allowed a 10 percent maximum voltage drop, you need to know what 10 percent of the system voltage for your 12-volt circuit equals. In practice the actual numbers will be slightly different. A fully charged 12-volt battery will have a voltage of between 12.6 and 13.5 volts. The actual voltage would change the following numbers slightly, but we will use the 12-volt figure to simplify the math.

To find the allowable voltage drop, turn the percentage into a decimal and multiply it by 12 (the system voltage in this example). The problem looks like this: $0.10 \times 12 = 1.2$. The maximum allowable voltage loss would be 1.2 volts, so by subtracting 1.2 volts from the original 12 volts, you end up with 10.8 volts as a minimum allowable voltage at any point in the circuit. Applying this same math to the 3 percent criteria, multiplying $0.03 \times 12$ gives a maximum allowable voltage drop of 0.36 volt, which means that 11.64 volts would be the minimum allowed at the appliance.

## Measuring Voltage Drop: Method 1

So, now that you have an understanding of the voltage drop that's allowed in critical and noncritical circuits, how can you actually measure it with your multimeter? There are two methods. The first method is probably the simplest to understand, but it won't always give the best results when you're trying to isolate the exact spot in the circuit that's causing a problem.

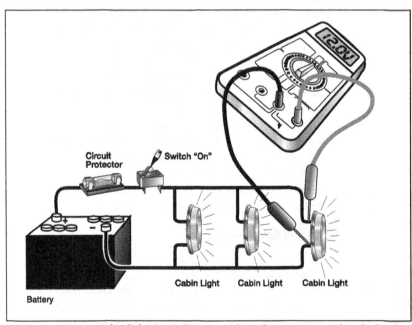

*Fig. 3-5. Cabin light circuit diagram with a voltmeter connected to check voltage going to one of the light fixtures.*

Circuit Protector

Switch "On"

Cabin Light    Cabin Light    Cabin Light

Battery

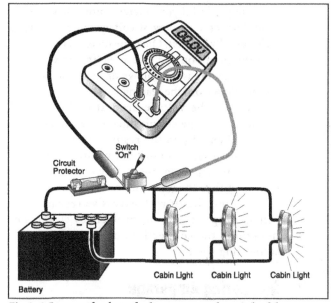

*Fig. 3-6. Incorrect hookup of voltmeter across the switch of the same cabin light circuit. When the meter is connected in this manner, the source voltage cannot be measured. The only reading you would get here is the* voltage drop *through the switch.*

Let's assume you're checking voltage drop at the light fixture in the head. First make sure that all DC circuits on board your boat except the one you're checking are turned off. Battery voltage must be kept as stable as possible for this test, and any circuits that are turned on will drain the battery, if only slightly; this slight drain can alter your readings. Now check the voltage at your battery as described above. If you're checking voltage at the distribution panel, connect your meter with the red lead attached to the positive bus at the back of the panel and the black lead attached to the negative bus. Record your reading to at least two decimal places. Fractions of a volt count here!

Next, go to the light socket and check the voltage. Again, the red test lead probe should be attached to the positive side of the fixture and the black probe to the negative side. You may have to disassemble the fixture to get access to the contacts for the light bulb. Put the red probe on one contact and the black to the other and take a direct reading. Make sure the

circuit is on and the bulb is lit. If you're working with one of the more modern bayonet bulb holders, connect the red probe to the left-side bulb clamp and the black probe to the right side and take a direct reading.

If the reading you get is the same as the reading at the battery or distribution panel, great! No voltage drop is present. If the reading is lower than the source voltage, as it usually is, there is a voltage drop present. To measure it, subtract your reading from the source voltage. The difference between the two readings is the voltage drop between the power source and the appliance.

Record the reading. To determine the percentage of drop, subtract the light-socket reading from the source-voltage reading and divide the result by the original source voltage. Shift your decimal point two places to the right, and you'll have found the percentage of drop in that particular circuit. Depending upon which category the circuit falls into, the drop must be less than 3 percent or less than 10 percent. If you get more than the 3 percent or 10 percent limit, the circuit has excessive voltage drop, which is probably caused by wiring that's too small for the length of the circuit or a loose or corroded connection. You must now trace the exact fault.

The next voltage-drop test will isolate the drop between the positive conductor and the negative conductor of the circuit.

Figure 3-7 on page 34 shows voltage being checked at the back of a typical distribution panel. Figure 3-8 on page 34 shows the meter connections at your multimeter, and correct meter attachment at a variety of typical bulb holders.

### Measuring Voltage Drop: Method 2
The second method for checking voltage drop is sometimes difficult for the beginner to understand. The meter will be connected in parallel, but you won't attach your lead probes to separate positive or negative conductors. Instead, attach both your probes to the same conductor or between a terminal in the circuit and a terminal on the appliance you're

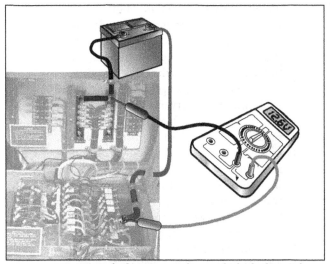

*Fig. 3-7. In checking source voltage at the back of a switch panel, remember to always verify your power source first when tracing circuits.*

testing. Sometimes you'll be testing directly across switches and relays or from one end of a wire to the other, even though I said earlier that you shouldn't do this.

Figures 3-9, 3-10, 3-11, and 3-12 illustrate the various meter-connection possibilities for this test.

Begin with the circuit you're measuring turned off. The meter should be turned on, set to measure

DC voltage, and if your meter is not self-scaling it should be set to the lowest voltage on the DC volts scale (usually 2 volts). Once the meter is connected, turn the circuit on and take a reading on your meter. The reading is the voltage drop at that point in the circuit. Record the reading.

Measure the voltage drop at each wire and connection in the circuit, including the negative return, then add up the results. The total of all these measurements must fall within either the 3 percent or 10 percent limit. Any reading that's a lot higher than the others in the circuit indicates a point in the circuit with excessive resistance or voltage drop. Correct any problem by cleaning or tightening the connection, or by replacing the connecting wire.

# Measuring Amperage

As already discussed there are two methods used to test amperage. One method uses meter leads and requires the disconnection of the DC power lead for the circuit you're testing (I discuss AC in more detail in chapter 11); the other uses a clamp-type inductive meter.

## *Using Meter Leads*

Unlike voltage checks, amperage checks with a basic multimeter require that the meter be connected in

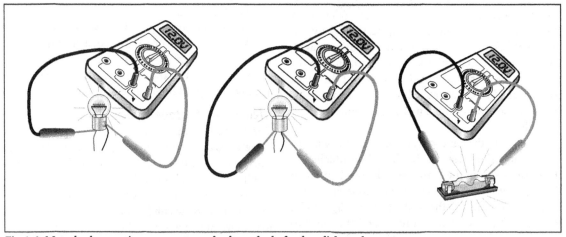

*Fig. 3-8. Meter lead connections on a meter and voltage checks for three light-socket types.*

*Figs. 3-9, 3-10, 3-11, 3-12. Various hookups for checking voltage drop. In figure 3-12, the meter leads are shown as you would trace through a circuit looking for voltage drop at various points in the circuit.*

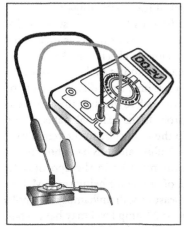

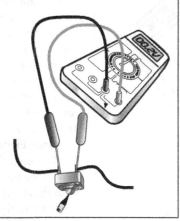

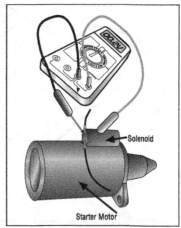

*Fig. 3-9. Measuring the actual voltage drop between the stud and the terminal. Remember, the circuit must be turned on to get any reading. The 0.2-V reading indicates either a loose or corroded connection that requires repair. Although less than 3% of 12V, 0.2 V at any point in a circuit spells trouble at that point.*

*Fig. 3-10. Checking the voltage drop at the switch. Again, the circuit must be "on." If the connections were clean and tight, the 0.2-V reading shown would indicate a fault (probably corrosion) inside the switch.*

*Fig. 3-11. Checking the integrity of the starter solenoid. Excessive voltage drop here necessitates removing the starter to replace the solenoid.*

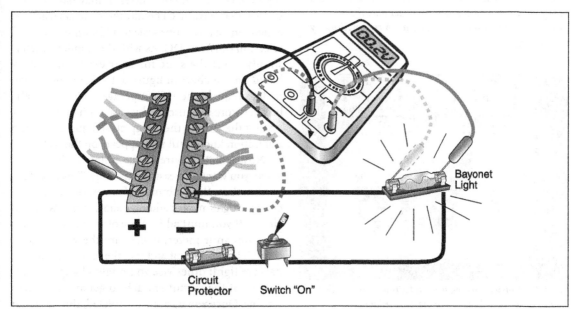

*Fig. 3-12. The solid leads measure the voltage drop in the positive feed wire to the light. The dotted leads check the negative return. A high meter reading indicates undersized wiring.*

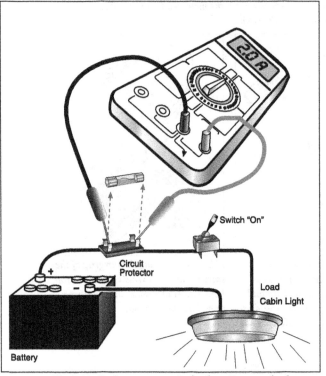

*Fig. 3-13. Basic ammeter series hookup. Remove the fuse and attach the meter leads as shown; all the circuit's power supply must then flow through the meter once the circuit is turned on. Here the meter measures a 2 A current draw by the cabin light.*

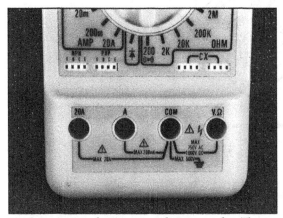

*Fig. 3-14. A meter showing a 1- and 20-amp socket. The 1-amp socket would be used to measure milliamps.*

series with the circuit. (If you have probes on your meter leads, you'll find this test much easier if you go out and buy a set of leads with alligator clips on the working end of the leads.) First make sure the circuit is turned off and that your meter is turned on and set up properly. Double-check to make sure that the red lead is plugged into the socket for 10 or 20 amps, if your meter has one. Now disconnect a wire at the point where you wish to measure the amperage and clip the black probe to the terminal that is closest to the battery. Clip the red probe to the remaining terminal. Figure 3-13 illustrates this basic hookup.

The meter's leads must be in the appropriate socket for the level of amperage being read. Meters with the ability to measure both milliamps and whole amps up to the 10- or 20-amp level may have separate sockets for the red test lead as shown in figure 3-14. The black lead will remain in the "COM" socket. If your meter is self-scaling, you'll have to select between AC and DC only. If the meter is not self-scaling, you'll have to select a scale appropriate for your expected reading. Figure 3-15 shows some typical current values for the equipment on your boat.

### Using an Inductive Pickup

If you have an inductive meter, it may have several scales to select from. Generally these meters will have a high- and a low-amps scale in addition to the usual selection of AC or DC. As with the standard meter, simply select the scale for your expected reading based on the chart in figure 3-15. Some inductive meters require the DC amperage scale to be calibrated before each use. In this case, with the meter set up and the jaws of the clamp closed, just rotate the calibration knob until zero appears on the scale.

Now isolate a wire at the point in the circuit where you want to measure amperage. This might involve unbundling a bunch of wires, or in extreme cases it might involve adding a short run of wire to a circuit. If you must add a piece of wire to get a place to clamp your meter, make sure the wire is large enough for the circuit and that the temporary terminals are tight; otherwise you might change the dynamics of the circuit enough to get an inaccurate reading. Once you have a wire isolated, simply clamp

## Typical DC Amperage Draws for On-Board Equipment

| Equipment Load | Amperage Draw (range, depending on unit) |
| --- | --- |
| anchor light | .1–3 A |
| anchor windlass | .75–300 A |
| autopilot | .1–30 A |
| bilge blower | .1–3 A |
| bilge pump | 1.5–5 A |
| cabin fan | .1–2 A |
| cabin light (incandescent) | .1–4 A |
| fish-finder | 0.1–1.0 A |
| fluorescent light | 0.7–2 A |
| freshwater pump | .4–5 A |
| knotmeter | 0.1–1.0 A |
| Loran/GPS | .1–2 A |
| macerator pump | .15–20 A |
| masthead light | .1–2 A |
| radar | .4–8 A |
| refrigeration (DC) | .5–8 A |
| running lights | .3–6 A |
| SSB radio (transmit 25–30 A) | .1–2 A |
| stereo/tape deck/CD | .1–2 A |
| VHF radio (transmit 5.0–6.0 A) | 0.7–1.5 A |
| washdown pump | 2.5–5 A |
| wiper motor (each) | 1.5–5 A |

*Fig. 3-15. A table showing typical current draws for power-boat equipment. Remember that these values are approximate and your equipment may vary from these values. Always confirm the draw for your own equipment.*

the meter around the wire with the equipment on the circuit turned on, make sure the meter is oriented properly, and read the amperage off the scale.

Ammeter use will be illustrated in a variety of tests throughout this book, so if you're still uncertain about how to use your meter, the photos and diagrams that follow should set you straight.

## Measuring Resistance and Continuity

All circuits and the components within them have some resistance to electrical flow. However, if any current at all is flowing through a circuit, you have a closed circuit and what is called *continuity*. When doing a continuity check, you won't really care what the actual resistance might be. Any resistance reading lower than infinity will indicate continuity. You'll usually use a continuity check to look for an open or broken circuit.

Suppose, for example, that light in the head we were working on earlier were to suddenly stop working. The first thing you would check is the condition of the bulb. Then you would check to make sure that the switch was on and the circuit breaker or fuse was in good order. Still no light? It's time for a continuity check.

First set up your meter to read ohms. You'll now be using it as an ohmmeter. The scale isn't that important, but it's best to set non-self-scaling meters to the lowest scale. If your meter has a continuity alarm, touch the probes together and listen for the beep. Also check for a zero reading on the face of the meter indicating zero ohms. If you don't get a beep or if the meter doesn't read zero, the internal battery for your meter is probably low and will need replacing. Next disconnect the wire for the light fixture at the distribution panel and at the light itself and connect one probe to each end of the wire. It doesn't matter which probe goes on which end.

Like the amperage test above, the continuity test is usually much easier if you have a set of meter leads that use alligator clips in place of spike probes. It's also unlikely that your leads are long enough to reach from the distribution panel to the light fixture so you'll need a jumper wire. Any piece of wire that is the correct size and length will do fine. Just add an insulated alligator clip to each end, and you're in business.

Now clip one end of your jumper wire to the wire you disconnected at the distribution panel and the other end to either meter lead. Clip the other meter lead to the wire you disconnected at the light fixture and listen for the beep. If you don't hear a beep, you either have the meter connected improperly or you don't have continuity. If you don't have a continuity alarm, check for a reading on the meter. Any reading but OL (overload) is fine. Zero means no resistance at all. OL means infinite resistance and a break in the circuit.

A common mistake made by beginners (and more than a few of us pros) is to pinch the probes of the meter leads onto the ends of the wire with bare fingers. If you try this and there is a lack of continuity in the wire, the current from the meter can take a detour through your body and your meter will beep and show continuity when none exists. Any time you're using your meter it's best not to touch the probes, but when you're checking continuity or resistance it's

critical to keep your hands away from them.

Whenever you're using the ohms scale on your meter, the wiring you're working with must not be live. The switch for the circuit must be off. The ohms scale and the diode-check function use a tiny amount of calibrated current from the meter's internal battery. Even a small amount of external current can distort your reading or even damage the meter. Failure to turn off the circuit will trip your meter's internal fuse or, in the case of some inexpensive meters without internal protection, you'll burn the meter out.

Figure 3-16 shows an ohmmeter battery test being performed and what your meter's screen should indicate.

## What Do the Numbers on My Ohmmeter Tell Me?

Proper interpretation of your multimeter's ohm readings is important; otherwise, misdiagnosis of problems can occur. Unlike the direct readings on the volts and amps scales, resistance values are a bit more cryptic for the newcomer to electrical testing.

If you're using a digital meter, the letters OL on your screen stand for overload, which replaces the symbol for infinity familiar to analog instrument users and is shown in figure 3-17. OL means that the resistance being read by the meter is higher than its ability to read it and usually indicates a break in the circuit, or an open circuit. If your meter is reading a string of zeros, perfect continuity is indicated with no perceptible resistance. Any numbers shown on your meter (including zeros) show the resistance in ohms and indicate a complete circuit.

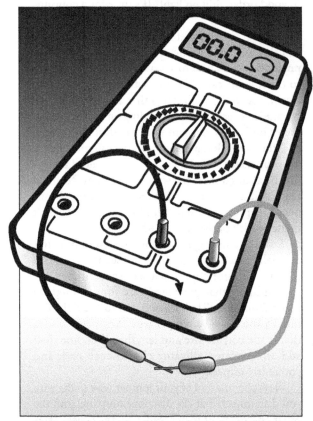

Fig. 3-16. Checking the ohmmeter battery by touching the leads together. Some meters also have a "BAT" indicator on the face that indicates when power from the unit's internal battery is too low.

Fig. 3-17. OL (overload) shown on the face of a digital multimeter.

Specific resistance is not too important for general circuit checks. Specifications are never given, and general assumptions really can't be made considering the variety of equipment available. For example, if you checked for continuity through a circuit for your stern light and you got a resistance reading, it would indicate that all is well through the circuit. The resistance you're reading is in the light bulb filament. (Typically, bulbs of this type will show several hundred ohms of resistance.) But suppose you check the same circuit and you see an OL reading on your meter. This indicates an open circuit, and most probably the bulb is blown and needs replacement.

An ohm reading near zero would indicate a short circuit between the positive conductor and ground. If this circuit has been blowing fuses or tripping the circuit breaker, you'll know you're on to something—the first step in tracing a short circuit!

Figures 3-18, 3-19, and 3-20 show the three possible meter readings, and what is happening in the circuit to give these readings.

On some components, like ignition coils and spark-plug wires, resistance values are given in workshop manuals so you have a specification to work with. In these cases, use your ohmmeter to test for faults within the components by matching readings to the specifications. On non-self-scaling meters, you'll have to select the appropriate ohms scales.

Even self-scaling (auto-ranging) models can be a bit confusing. Some meters give a direct reading with the decimal point placed exactly as it should be, but others have a high or low scale and require some minor interpretation to place the decimal. Read your multimeter's instructions carefully to be certain you have a clear understanding of how this scaling works on your meter.

Actual tests on ignition components as well as other ohmmeter tests where specific resistance values are important will be illustrated in chapter 7.

*Figs. 3-18, 3-19, 3-20. Sequence diagram showing a circuit with continuity and some resistance on a meter, the same circuit showing a break or open and the "OL" reading on the meter, and the same circuit showing a short and a typical meter reading.*

*Fig. 3-18. Continuity.*

*Fig. 3-19. Open circuit and no continuity.*

*Fig. 3-20. Continuity and possible short circuit.*

So, as we close out chapter 3, remember the tips given here and carefully select the best multimeter you can afford. Your meter is a long-term investment, and, unlike today's computer, it will never be obsolete. Volts, amps, and ohms haven't changed one bit in over a century! However, some of the latest developments in this area utilize software and PC uploads from some of the newest high-end meters for tracking voltage, amperage, and resistance changes over time. Rest assured, I'll be adding this capability to my arsenal of electrical test equipment in the not-too-distant future!

# Chapter 4

# Wire and Circuit Protection Standards and Repair Procedures

## Order Out of Chaos

If you were to study the development of the American pleasure-boating industry from the turn of the twentieth century to the early 1970s, you would notice a curious phenomenon. While other developing industries gradually evolved a more-or-less uniform set of standards that dictated the minimum safety and performance parameters for their products, the recreational marine industry had none. For many industries, such as automobiles, aircraft, food, and health, the government dictated the standards. In other less critical industries, and particularly in recreational industries, the standards were imposed by the industry itself or by the marketplace.

Take golf, for example, which, overlooking the differences in accident rates, is remarkably similar demographically and statistically to pleasure boating. Golfing gradually developed a set of rules and standards for course construction and equipment design that industries involved in the sport violated at their peril: If a golf course is not laid out just right, nobody will play on it, and if a golf club isn't built just so, no one will buy it.

Remarkably, no such basic standards ever developed for the people and companies that built pleasure boats. It's true that industry leaders like Chris-Craft, Owens, Penn Yan, and many others built quality products to their own standards that were an excellent value for their customers. However, some builders produced shamefully shoddy boats that were not only a poor value but dangerous as well. One New England manufacturer of open fishing boats, for example, built hundreds of boats with particleboard decks and transoms that literally melted once water penetrated the paint job. Another company, in California, became famous for building boats with fiberglass hulls that were so thin that you could read a newspaper through them.

The U.S. Coast Guard has a long list of safety regulations that apply to recreational boating, but few of these standards applied to the construction of the boat. That bassboat with the particleboard decks, for example, had a legal limit on the number of people it could carry and the horsepower of the outboard it could use, but not a word was ever said about the integrity of the basic construction.

Finally, out of frustration with fly-by-night builders and a growing accident and fatality rate that was giving recreational boating an increasingly tarnished image, the industry banded together. Organizations like the National Marine Manufacturers Association (NMMA) and the American Boat & Yacht Council (ABYC—for contact information see the sidebar on page x)—were formed with the stated purpose of bringing order out of chaos by establishing a binding set of minimum standards for the construction of pleasure boats. One of the remarkable results of the formation of organizations like these has been a steady decrease in the number of fatal boating accidents.

## ABYC Standards and Recommendations

The ABYC standards and recommendations to which I refer throughout this book do not just apply to boatbuilders, however. They apply to you and to me and to everyone who works on boats. In fact, recent certification programs for marine technicians initiated by the ABYC drive home the point that the standards are as useful for repairing and modifying boats in the field as they are for building boats in the factories. These standards are an invaluable tool for weekend boaters who decide to make their own repairs and perform some of their own installations. Much of this chapter addresses the points you should consider when selecting wire, circuit breakers, and fuses. We will even discuss a few basic electrical repairs you can make on your boat.

If you own a boat that's more than a few years old, it may not comply with all of the standards outlined in the ABYC's *Recommended Standards and Technical Information Reports.* This is not a cause for immediate concern. These standards have evolved over the years and have been revised as new materials and technology became available. The tables, charts, and recommendations in this chapter and in the rest of this book reflect the recommendations of the ABYC at the time this book was written. Wire types and circuit-protection ratings are not likely to change in the foreseeable future. On the other hand, there could be breakthroughs in insulation technology as newer and better materials are developed, and a technological advance might create a new circuit breaker that will be better than the ones we use today. If either of these events should transpire, rest assured that the ABYC will take a close look and make appropriate recommendations based on what they see.

## Basic Wiring

The ABYC electrical standards go into great detail on the minimum criteria for both DC and AC circuits used on boats. Basic considerations include the length of the wire, nominal voltage, amperage, routing of the wire, insulation temperature rating, and the chemical environment to which the insulation is likely to be exposed. One additional consideration is the conductive material used in the wire.

### Wire Types

Electrical wire comes in a variety of types and conductor materials, but by far the most common conductors are made of copper. Aluminum is used in some automotive applications, but aluminum conductors of any type, including terminal strips and studs, are strictly prohibited in the ABYC electrical standards. The soft aluminum used in wiring corrodes easily (unlike the hard aluminum used in boat hulls), and it can become brittle and break when subjected to the constant vibration and flexing of a typical boat underway. It also isn't as good a conductor

as copper, and the added resistance means that it gets hotter quicker than copper. Don't ever use aluminum wire on your boat, and if you find any already installed, immediately remove it and replace it with copper wire.

In addition, solid wire, especially the solid-copper Romex that's used in house wiring, is never acceptable on boats. This precludes the use of many wiring types found in hardware stores or in home-supply houses. Solid-copper residential wiring breaks easily under vibration, and it was never intended to withstand the exposure to moisture or oil and gas fumes found on today's boats.

According to the ABYC specifications, the only acceptable material that may be used for boat wiring is stranded copper. Although not specifically mentioned in the standards, good-quality boat cable today is often tinned as well. This means that every strand of copper in the wire is coated with a thin layer of tin (solder, actually) that impedes the formation of corrosion. Copper doesn't corrode in the same way as such materials as aluminum and steel, but forms a thin layer of oxidation that's highly resistant to electricity. The tinning slows and reduces the formation of this oxide layer and greatly reduces the incidence of problems caused by corroded wires. It's also much easier to solder than untinned wire.

Tinned copper wire will pay off in the long run. Initially it may seem a bit expensive compared to stranded copper without tinning, but on a boat, where corrosion is a constant battle, the tinned wire will hold up far longer than would untinned wire. The tinning does a great job of resisting corrosion at terminals as well as preventing oxidation from migrating up the wire under the insulation, a common problem with untinned wire.

Stranded copper wire is available in several types. The chart in figure 4-1 on page 42 is taken from section E-11 of the ABYC's *Recommended Standards and Practices* and illustrates several additional points. Notice that the American Wire Gauge (AWG) standard is used to designate wire size. You may encounter wires on your boat that carry the Society of Automotive Engineers (SAE) designation. Quality marine-grade wire with an AWG-size is often larger in

| CONDUCTOR GAUGE | MINIMUM ACCEPTABLE CM AREA AWG | MINIMUM ACCEPTABLE CM AREA SAE | MINIMUM NUMBER OF STRANDS | | |
|---|---|---|---|---|---|
| | | | TYPE 1* | TYPE 2** | TYPE 3*** |
| 18 | 1,620 | 1,537 | - | 16 | - |
| 16 | 2,580 | 2,336 | - | 19 | 26 |
| 14 | 4,110 | 3,702 | - | 19 | 41 |
| 12 | 6,530 | 5,833 | - | 19 | 65 |
| 10 | 10,380 | 9,343 | - | 19 | 105 |
| 8 | 16,510 | 14,810 | - | 19 | 168 |
| 6 | 26,240 | 24,538 | - | 37 | 266 |
| 4 | 41,740 | 37,360 | - | 49 | 420 |
| 2 | 66,360 | 62,450 | - | 127 | 665 |
| 1 | 83,690 | 77,790 | - | 127 | 836 |
| 0 | 105,600 | 98,980 | - | 127 | 1064 |
| 00 | 133,100 | 125,100 | - | 127 | 1323 |
| 000 | 167,800 | 158,600 | - | 259 | 1666 |
| 0000 | 211,600 | 205,500 | - | 418 | 2107 |

*Type 1 - Solid conductor and stranding less than that indicated under Type 2 shall not be used

**Type 2 - Conductors with at least Type 2 stranding shall be used for general purpose boat wiring.

***Type 3 - Conductors with Type 3 stranding shall be used for any wiring where frequent flexing is involved in normal use.

NOTE:   1.   Metric wire sizes may be used if of equivalent circular mil area. If the circular mil area of the metric conductor is less than that listed, the wire ampacity shall be corrected based on the ratio of the circular mil areas. For comparison of conductor cross sections (AWG and ISO) (See AP TABLE 2 )

2.          The circular mil area given is equal to the mathematical square of the diameter of the AWG standard solid copper conductor measured in one thousandths of an inch.

The area in square inches $= \dfrac{pi(circular\ mils)}{4(1,000,000)}$

The circular mil area of the stranded conductors may differ from the tabulated values and is the sum of the circular mil areas of the wires (strands) in the conductor.

Fig. 4-1. Table XII from the ABYC electrical standards, section E-11, comparing wire types and stranding. (© ABYC)

10-gauge Type 2 wire will contain 19 strands of wire, whereas an AWG 10-gauge Type 3 wire will have 105 strands. Type 3 wire will also have a slightly lower resistance for a given gauge than a Type 2 wire.

## Wire Size

Once you have determined the type of wire to use on your project (and in nearly all cases this will be Type 3 tinned copper wire), you must decide which size. Important considerations here are the length of the wire, the voltage (usually 12 volts, but if your boat is over 35 feet long you might have a 24-volt system), and the amperage the circuit is expected to carry (sometimes called *ampacity*). This information is usually supplied by manufacturers of the equipment you intend to install on the circuit. If it isn't contained in the instruction manual or printed on the side of the equipment itself, you may have to perform the following test to determine what these values are.

diameter than the equivalent SAE designation. Stick to AWG-rated wires, prefereably those marked "boat cable" on the insulation.

As the wire-gauge numbers get smaller, the wire gets progressively bigger in diameter, and the minimum circular cross-sectional area of the wire, indicated by circular mils (CM), gets larger. Next, the chart shows the minimum number of strands for both Type 2 and Type 3 wire. The finer the strands, the more strands there are in a wire of a given size and the more flexible the wire will be. It's easy to identify the two wire types, because Type 3 wire has a lot more strands than Type 2. For example, an AWG

To test for amperage, connect the equipment you want to test to your boat's battery (or any 12-volt battery) with a set of automotive jumper cables. Hook the positive lead to the battery first and the negative lead next. Be careful not to let the clamps at the other end of the cables touch and arc. Next, set up your multimeter to measure DC amps.

When you're uncertain of the amount of current a piece of equipment will require, it's best to perform this check with your meter's 10- or 20-amp setup. An over reading on the wrong scale (with the meter's leads in the incorrect sockets) will blow the meter's internal fuse. Make sure that the jumper leads are connected to the DC positive and negative terminals on the piece of equipment in question. Clip the leads in series with the load and take the amperage reading once the equipment is running. With an inductive clamp meter, simply get the equipment running, clamp onto either of the leads of the jumper cables, and take a reading.

Figure 4-2 shows the hookup for making this basic test. For a look at the typical amperage for common items of equipment you might find on your boat, refer to figure 3-15 on page 37.

Once you have established the amperage for the equipment you're testing, selecting the correct size of wire to use is simply a matter of working the numbers found in figures 4-3 and 4-4 on pages 44 and 45.

Let's try out figure 4-3. You've decided that you're dealing with a critical circuit and will use the 3 percent maximum voltage drop value. Yours is a 12-volt boat, and you know that the pump in question draws 5 amps and that 20 feet of wire separates it from the panel board supplying the pump. A two-way run would mean a total conductor length of 40 feet. Find the 40-foot column on the chart and correlate it with the 5-amp row in the 12-volt section. You should find a 10-gauge wire size recommendation.

Keep in mind that these two charts are designed for sizing wires based on the ABYC acceptable voltage drops described earlier. Don't confuse the 3 percent and 10 percent specifications. And most important, remember that the length of the wire is the total of the positive and negative sides of the circuit. For example, if a component is 12 feet from your distribution panel, the length of the run will be 24 feet. The column that most closely matches that on either of these tables is labeled 25 feet. When a number falls between any two values, always round up to the next highest number.

## Wire Insulation

Quality wire has a rather lengthy story written right on the insulation. The writing on the wire can help you decide the wire's suitability for certain applications: the maximum voltage for the wire and insulation; resistance of the insulation to oil, moisture, and fuels; and temperature ratings of the insulation; are all explained in cryptic notation. Again, our friends at the ABYC come

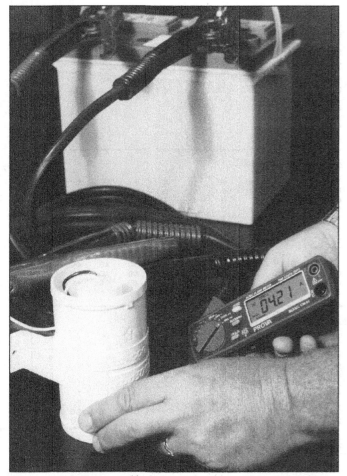

*Fig. 4-2. Battery jumper cables being used to determine amperage draw for a new electrical installation. In this case, I'm checking the actual draw for a new bilge blower.*

*(continued on page 46)*

## CONDUCTORS SIZED FOR 3 PERCENT DROP IN VOLTAGE

*NOTE:* **In the event of a conflict between the voltage drop table and the ampacity table, use the larger wire size.**

Length of Conductor from Source of Current to Device and Back to Source - Feet

**12 Volts - 3% Drop Wire Sizes (gauge) - Based on Minimum CM Area**

| TOTAL CURRENT ON CIRCUIT IN AMPS. | 10 | 15 | 20 | 25 | 30 | 40 | 50 | 60 | 70 | 80 | 90 | 100 | 110 | 120 | 130 | 140 | 150 | 160 | 170 |
|---|---|---|---|---|---|---|---|---|---|---|---|---|---|---|---|---|---|---|---|
| 5 | 18 | 16 | 14 | 12 | 12 | 10 | 10 | 10 | 8 | 8 | 8 | 6 | 6 | 6 | 6 | 6 | 6 | 6 | 6 |
| 10 | 14 | 12 | 10 | 10 | 10 | 8 | 6 | 6 | 6 | 6 | 4 | 4 | 4 | 4 | 2 | 2 | 2 | 2 | 2 |
| 15 | 12 | 10 | 10 | 8 | 8 | 6 | 6 | 6 | 4 | 4 | 2 | 2 | 2 | 2 | 2 | 1 | 1 | 1 | 1 |
| 20 | 10 | 10 | 8 | 6 | 6 | 6 | 4 | 4 | 2 | 2 | 2 | 2 | 1 | 1 | 1 | 0 | 0 | 0 | 2/0 |
| 25 | 10 | 8 | 6 | 6 | 6 | 4 | 4 | 2 | 2 | 2 | 1 | 1 | 0 | 0 | 0 | 2/0 | 2/0 | 2/0 | 3/0 |
| 30 | 10 | 8 | 6 | 6 | 4 | 4 | 2 | 2 | 1 | 1 | 0 | 0 | 0 | 2/0 | 2/0 | 3/0 | 3/0 | 3/0 | 3/0 |
| 40 | 8 | 6 | 6 | 4 | 4 | 2 | 2 | 1 | 0 | 0 | 2/0 | 2/0 | 3/0 | 3/0 | 3/0 | 4/0 | 4/0 | 4/0 | 4/0 |
| 50 | 6 | 6 | 4 | 4 | 2 | 2 | 1 | 0 | 2/0 | 2/0 | 3/0 | 3/0 | 4/0 | 4/0 | 4/0 | | | | |
| 60 | 6 | 4 | 4 | 2 | 2 | 1 | 0 | 2/0 | 3/0 | 3/0 | 4/0 | 4/0 | 4/0 | | | | | | |
| 70 | 6 | 4 | 2 | 2 | 1 | 0 | 2/0 | 3/0 | 3/0 | 4/0 | 4/0 | | | | | | | | |
| 80 | 6 | 4 | 2 | 2 | 1 | 0 | 3/0 | 3/0 | 4/0 | 4/0 | | | | | | | | | |
| 90 | 4 | 2 | 2 | 1 | 0 | 2/0 | 3/0 | 4/0 | 4/0 | | | | | | | | | | |
| 100 | 4 | 2 | 2 | 1 | 0 | 2/0 | 3/0 | 4/0 | | | | | | | | | | | |

**24 Volts - 3% Drop Wire Sizes (gauge) - Based on Minimum CM Area**

| Amps | 10 | 15 | 20 | 25 | 30 | 40 | 50 | 60 | 70 | 80 | 90 | 100 | 110 | 120 | 130 | 140 | 150 | 160 | 170 |
|---|---|---|---|---|---|---|---|---|---|---|---|---|---|---|---|---|---|---|---|
| 5 | 18 | 18 | 18 | 16 | 16 | 14 | 12 | 12 | 12 | 10 | 10 | 10 | 10 | 10 | 8 | 8 | 8 | 8 | 8 |
| 10 | 18 | 16 | 14 | 12 | 12 | 10 | 10 | 10 | 8 | 8 | 8 | 6 | 6 | 6 | 6 | 6 | 6 | 6 | 6 |
| 15 | 16 | 14 | 12 | 12 | 10 | 10 | 8 | 8 | 6 | 6 | 6 | 6 | 6 | 4 | 4 | 4 | 4 | 4 | 2 |
| 20 | 14 | 12 | 10 | 10 | 10 | 8 | 6 | 6 | 6 | 6 | 4 | 4 | 4 | 4 | 2 | 2 | 2 | 2 | 2 |
| 25 | 12 | 12 | 10 | 10 | 8 | 6 | 6 | 6 | 4 | 4 | 4 | 4 | 2 | 2 | 2 | 2 | 2 | 2 | 1 |
| 30 | 12 | 10 | 10 | 8 | 8 | 6 | 6 | 4 | 4 | 4 | 2 | 2 | 2 | 2 | 2 | 1 | 1 | 1 | 1 |
| 40 | 10 | 10 | 8 | 6 | 6 | 6 | 4 | 4 | 2 | 2 | 2 | 2 | 1 | 1 | 1 | 0 | 0 | 0 | 2/0 |
| 50 | 10 | 8 | 6 | 6 | 6 | 4 | 4 | 2 | 2 | 2 | 1 | 1 | 0 | 0 | 0 | 2/0 | 2/0 | 2/0 | 3/0 |
| 60 | 10 | 8 | 6 | 6 | 4 | 4 | 2 | 2 | 1 | 1 | 0 | 0 | 0 | 2/0 | 2/0 | 3/0 | 3/0 | 3/0 | 3/0 |
| 70 | 8 | 6 | 6 | 4 | 4 | 2 | 2 | 1 | 1 | 0 | 0 | 2/0 | 2/0 | 3/0 | 3/0 | 3/0 | 3/0 | 4/0 | 4/0 |
| 80 | 8 | 6 | 6 | 4 | 4 | 2 | 2 | 1 | 0 | 0 | 2/0 | 2/0 | 3/0 | 3/0 | 3/0 | 4/0 | 4/0 | 4/0 | 4/0 |
| 90 | 8 | 6 | 4 | 4 | 2 | 2 | 1 | 0 | 0 | 2/0 | 2/0 | 3/0 | 3/0 | 4/0 | 4/0 | 4/0 | 4/0 | 4/0 | |
| 100 | 6 | 6 | 4 | 4 | 2 | 2 | 1 | 0 | 2/0 | 2/0 | 3/0 | 3/0 | 4/0 | 4/0 | 4/0 | | | | |

**32 Volts - 3% Drop Wire Sizes (gauge) - Based on Minimum CM Area**

| Amps | 10 | 15 | 20 | 25 | 30 | 40 | 50 | 60 | 70 | 80 | 90 | 100 | 110 | 120 | 130 | 140 | 150 | 160 | 170 |
|---|---|---|---|---|---|---|---|---|---|---|---|---|---|---|---|---|---|---|---|
| 5 | 18 | 18 | 18 | 18 | 16 | 16 | 14 | 14 | 12 | 12 | 12 | 12 | 10 | 10 | 10 | 10 | 10 | 10 | 8 |
| 10 | 18 | 16 | 16 | 14 | 14 | 12 | 12 | 10 | 10 | 10 | 8 | 8 | 8 | 8 | 8 | 6 | 6 | 6 | 6 |
| 15 | 16 | 14 | 14 | 12 | 12 | 10 | 10 | 8 | 8 | 8 | 6 | 6 | 6 | 6 | 6 | 6 | 6 | 4 | 4 |
| 20 | 16 | 14 | 12 | 12 | 10 | 10 | 8 | 8 | 6 | 6 | 6 | 6 | 6 | 4 | 4 | 4 | 4 | 4 | 2 |
| 25 | 14 | 12 | 12 | 10 | 10 | 8 | 8 | 6 | 6 | 6 | 6 | 4 | 4 | 4 | 4 | 2 | 2 | 2 | 2 |
| 30 | 14 | 12 | 10 | 10 | 8 | 8 | 6 | 6 | 6 | 4 | 4 | 4 | 4 | 2 | 2 | 2 | 1 | 1 | 1 |
| 40 | 12 | 10 | 10 | 8 | 8 | 6 | 6 | 4 | 4 | 4 | 2 | 2 | 2 | 2 | 2 | 1 | 1 | 1 | 1 |
| 50 | 12 | 10 | 8 | 8 | 6 | 6 | 4 | 4 | 2 | 2 | 2 | 2 | 1 | 1 | 0 | 0 | 0 | 0 | 0 |
| 60 | 10 | 8 | 8 | 6 | 6 | 4 | 4 | 2 | 2 | 2 | 2 | 1 | 1 | 0 | 0 | 0 | 2/0 | 2/0 | 2/0 |
| 70 | 10 | 8 | 6 | 6 | 6 | 4 | 2 | 2 | 2 | 1 | 1 | 0 | 0 | 0 | 2/0 | 2/0 | 2/0 | 3/0 | 3/0 |
| 80 | 10 | 8 | 6 | 6 | 4 | 4 | 2 | 2 | 1 | 1 | 0 | 0 | 0 | 2/0 | 2/0 | 3/0 | 3/0 | 3/0 | 4/0 |
| 90 | 8 | 6 | 6 | 6 | 4 | 2 | 2 | 2 | 1 | 0 | 0 | 2/0 | 2/0 | 2/0 | 3/0 | 3/0 | 3/0 | 4/0 | 4/0 |
| 100 | 8 | 6 | 6 | 4 | 4 | 2 | 2 | 1 | 0 | 0 | 2/0 | 2/0 | 2/0 | 3/0 | 3/0 | 3/0 | 4/0 | 4/0 | 4/0 |

*Fig. 4-3. The ABYC's Table X from section E-11, showing conductor sizes for a 3 percent drop in voltage. (© ABYC)*

CONDUCTORS SIZED FOR 10 % VOLTAGE DROP

*NOTE:  In the event of a conflict between the voltage drop table and the ampacity table, use the larger wire size.*

Length of Conductor from Source of Current to Device and Back to Source - Feet

| TOTAL CURRENT ON CIRCUIT IN AMPS | 10 | 15 | 20 | 25 | 30 | 40 | 50 | 60 | 70 | 80 | 90 | 100 | 110 | 120 | 130 | 140 | 150 | 160 | 170 |
|---|---|---|---|---|---|---|---|---|---|---|---|---|---|---|---|---|---|---|---|
| **12 Volts - 10% Drop Wire Sizes (gauge) - Based on Minimum CM Area** | | | | | | | | | | | | | | | | | | | |
| 5 | 18 | 18 | 18 | 18 | 18 | 16 | 16 | 14 | 14 | 14 | 12 | 12 | 12 | 12 | 12 | 10 | 10 | 10 | 10 |
| 10 | 18 | 18 | 16 | 16 | 14 | 14 | 12 | 12 | 10 | 10 | 10 | 10 | 8 | 8 | 8 | 8 | 8 | 8 | 6 |
| 15 | 18 | 16 | 14 | 14 | 12 | 12 | 10 | 10 | 8 | 8 | 8 | 8 | 6 | 6 | 6 | 6 | 6 | 6 | 6 |
| 20 | 16 | 14 | 14 | 12 | 12 | 10 | 10 | 8 | 8 | 8 | 6 | 6 | 6 | 6 | 6 | 6 | 4 | 4 | 4 |
| 25 | 16 | 14 | 12 | 12 | 10 | 10 | 8 | 8 | 6 | 6 | 6 | 6 | 6 | 4 | 4 | 4 | 4 | 4 | 2 |
| 30 | 14 | 12 | 12 | 10 | 10 | 8 | 8 | 6 | 6 | 6 | 6 | 4 | 4 | 4 | 4 | 2 | 2 | 2 | 2 |
| 40 | 14 | 12 | 10 | 10 | 8 | 8 | 6 | 6 | 6 | 4 | 4 | 4 | 2 | 2 | 2 | 2 | 2 | 2 | 2 |
| 50 | 12 | 10 | 10 | 8 | 8 | 6 | 6 | 4 | 4 | 4 | 2 | 2 | 2 | 2 | 2 | 1 | 1 | 1 | 1 |
| 60 | 12 | 10 | 8 | 8 | 6 | 6 | 4 | 4 | 2 | 2 | 2 | 2 | 2 | 1 | 1 | 1 | 0 | 0 | 0 |
| 70 | 10 | 8 | 8 | 6 | 6 | 6 | 4 | 2 | 2 | 2 | 2 | 1 | 1 | 1 | 0 | 0 | 0 | 2/0 | 2/0 |
| 80 | 10 | 8 | 8 | 6 | 6 | 4 | 4 | 2 | 2 | 2 | 1 | 1 | 0 | 0 | 0 | 2/0 | 2/0 | 2/0 | 2/0 |
| 90 | 10 | 8 | 6 | 6 | 6 | 4 | 2 | 2 | 2 | 1 | 1 | 0 | 0 | 0 | 2/0 | 2/0 | 2/0 | 3/0 | 3/0 |
| 100 | 10 | 8 | 6 | 6 | 4 | 4 | 2 | 2 | 1 | 1 | 0 | 0 | 0 | 2/0 | 2/0 | 2/0 | 3/0 | 3/0 | 3/0 |
| **24 Volts - 10% Drop Wire Sizes (gauge) - Based on Minimum CM Area** | | | | | | | | | | | | | | | | | | | |
| 5 | 18 | 18 | 18 | 18 | 18 | 18 | 18 | 18 | 16 | 16 | 16 | 16 | 14 | 14 | 14 | 14 | 14 | 14 | 12 |
| 10 | 18 | 18 | 18 | 18 | 18 | 16 | 16 | 14 | 14 | 14 | 12 | 12 | 12 | 12 | 12 | 10 | 10 | 10 | 10 |
| 15 | 18 | 18 | 18 | 16 | 16 | 14 | 14 | 12 | 12 | 12 | 10 | 10 | 10 | 10 | 10 | 8 | 8 | 8 | 8 |
| 20 | 18 | 18 | 16 | 16 | 14 | 14 | 12 | 12 | 10 | 10 | 10 | 10 | 8 | 8 | 8 | 8 | 8 | 8 | 6 |
| 25 | 18 | 16 | 16 | 14 | 14 | 12 | 12 | 10 | 10 | 10 | 8 | 8 | 8 | 8 | 8 | 6 | 6 | 6 | 6 |
| 30 | 18 | 16 | 14 | 14 | 12 | 12 | 10 | 10 | 8 | 8 | 8 | 8 | 8 | 6 | 6 | 6 | 6 | 6 | 6 |
| 40 | 16 | 14 | 14 | 12 | 12 | 10 | 10 | 8 | 8 | 8 | 6 | 6 | 6 | 6 | 6 | 6 | 4 | 4 | 4 |
| 50 | 16 | 14 | 12 | 12 | 10 | 10 | 8 | 8 | 6 | 6 | 6 | 6 | 4 | 4 | 4 | 4 | 4 | 4 | 2 |
| 60 | 14 | 12 | 12 | 10 | 10 | 8 | 8 | 6 | 6 | 6 | 6 | 4 | 4 | 4 | 4 | 2 | 2 | 2 | 2 |
| 70 | 14 | 12 | 12 | 10 | 8 | 8 | 6 | 6 | 6 | 6 | 4 | 4 | 4 | 2 | 2 | 2 | 2 | 2 | 2 |
| 80 | 14 | 12 | 10 | 10 | 8 | 8 | 6 | 6 | 6 | 4 | 4 | 4 | 2 | 2 | 2 | 2 | 2 | 2 | 2 |
| 90 | 12 | 10 | 10 | 8 | 8 | 6 | 6 | 6 | 4 | 4 | 4 | 2 | 2 | 2 | 2 | 2 | 2 | 1 | 1 |
| 100 | 12 | 10 | 10 | 8 | 8 | 6 | 6 | 4 | 4 | 4 | 2 | 2 | 2 | 2 | 2 | 1 | 1 | 1 | 1 |
| **32 Volts - 10% Drop Wire Sizes (gauge) - Based on Minimum CM Area** | | | | | | | | | | | | | | | | | | | |
| 5 | 18 | 18 | 18 | 18 | 18 | 18 | 18 | 18 | 18 | 18 | 18 | 16 | 16 | 16 | 16 | 14 | 14 | 14 | 14 |
| 10 | 18 | 18 | 18 | 18 | 18 | 16 | 16 | 14 | 14 | 14 | 14 | 14 | 12 | 12 | 12 | 12 | 12 | 12 | 12 |
| 15 | 18 | 18 | 18 | 18 | 18 | 16 | 14 | 14 | 14 | 12 | 12 | 12 | 12 | 10 | 10 | 10 | 10 | 10 | 10 |
| 20 | 18 | 18 | 18 | 16 | 16 | 14 | 14 | 12 | 12 | 12 | 10 | 10 | 10 | 10 | 8 | 8 | 8 | 8 | 8 |
| 25 | 18 | 18 | 16 | 16 | 14 | 14 | 12 | 12 | 10 | 10 | 10 | 10 | 10 | 8 | 8 | 8 | 8 | 6 | 6 |
| 30 | 18 | 18 | 16 | 14 | 14 | 12 | 12 | 10 | 10 | 10 | 10 | 8 | 8 | 8 | 8 | 6 | 6 | 6 | 6 |
| 40 | 18 | 16 | 14 | 14 | 12 | 12 | 10 | 10 | 8 | 8 | 8 | 8 | 8 | 6 | 6 | 6 | 6 | 6 | 6 |
| 50 | 16 | 14 | 14 | 12 | 12 | 10 | 10 | 8 | 8 | 8 | 6 | 6 | 6 | 6 | 6 | 6 | 4 | 4 | 4 |
| 60 | 16 | 14 | 12 | 12 | 10 | 10 | 8 | 8 | 8 | 6 | 6 | 6 | 6 | 6 | 6 | 4 | 4 | 4 | 4 |
| 70 | 14 | 14 | 12 | 10 | 10 | 8 | 8 | 6 | 6 | 6 | 6 | 6 | 6 | 4 | 4 | 4 | 2 | 2 | 2 |
| 80 | 14 | 12 | 12 | 10 | 10 | 8 | 8 | 6 | 6 | 6 | 6 | 4 | 4 | 4 | 4 | 2 | 2 | 2 | 2 |
| 90 | 14 | 12 | 10 | 10 | 10 | 8 | 6 | 6 | 6 | 6 | 4 | 4 | 4 | 4 | 2 | 2 | 2 | 2 | 2 |
| 100 | 14 | 12 | 10 | 10 | 8 | 8 | 6 | 6 | 6 | 4 | 4 | 4 | 4 | 2 | 2 | 2 | 2 | 2 | 2 |

*Fig. 4-4. Table XI from section E-11, showing conductor sizes for a 10 percent drop in voltage. (© ABYC)*

*(continued from page 43)* through with several tables to help decipher these secret codes. From ABYC section E-11 we see temperature-rating codes for flexible cords in figure 4-5, and insulation characteristics and temperature ratings for typical wiring conductors in figure 4-6.

Another table, shown in figure 4-7 on page 48, shows the allowable amperage for various sizes of wires used inside and outside engine-room spaces. Notice that the amperage decreases inside engine rooms where expected temperatures are greater than outside temperatures. Use this table to determine the size of conductors for low-voltage DC systems only; AC wiring uses different criteria. The information on this chart must be compared to the information in the charts shown in figures 4-3 and 4-4. Always use the largest wire gauge indicated by the two charts for a given amperage based on the length of the wire run.

All wire used in DC circuitry should have a minimum rating of 50 volts stamped on the insulation. Most quality wire will have the AWG gauge embossed on the insulation as well. In general, wire sold as marine grade at the major supply houses will have a 105°C rating for the insulation, but it pays to check.

## Fuses and Circuit Breakers

Depending upon when your boat was built and who built it, you may have any combination of circuit breakers or fuses of different types used as circuit-protection devices. All such devices used on pleasure boats work on one of three basic principles, two of which depend on heat generated by resistance and a third that works on current-induced magnetism. Since fuses are easier than circuit breakers to understand, let's take them first.

| FLEXIBLE CORDS | | |
| --- | --- | --- |
| TYPE | DESCRIPTION | AVAILABLE INSULATION TEMPERATURE RATING |
| SO, SOW | Hard service cord, oil resistant compound | 60° C (140° F), 75° C (167° F) & higher |
| ST, STW | Hard service cord, thermoplastic | 60° C (140° F), 75° C (167° F) & higher |
| STO, STOW, SEO, SEOW | Hard service cord, oil resistant thermoplastic | 60° C (140° F), 75° C (167° F) & higher |
| SJO, SJOW | Junior hard service cord, oil resistant compound | 60° C (140° F), 75° C (167° F) & higher |
| SJT, SJTW | Junior hard service cord, thermoplastic | 60° C (140° F), 75° C (167° F) & higher |
| SJTO, SJTOW | Junior hard service cord, oil resistant thermoplastic | 60° C (140° F), 75° C (167° F) & higher |

*Fig. 4-5. Table VIII from section E-11, showing insulation markings and temperature ratings for insulation on flexible cords as used on board. (© ABYC)*

## Fuses

If you were ever foolish enough to connect the positive and negative terminals of any 12-volt battery with a length of wire with no intervening load to slow the flow of electrons, the wire would immediately become red-hot and melt. This is how an unfused short circuit can quickly destroy a boat, and it's how a fuse works. If you interpose a short piece of smaller-gauge wire into this ultrasimple circuit, the smaller wire will self-destruct and stop the flow of electrons before the heat builds up enough to damage the larger wire.

You have, in effect, built yourself a fuse in the form of the smaller wire.

You might recall that in chapter 1 I noted that a by-product of resistance is heat. Well, a fuse is designed with an element that will carry a certain amount of current and then heat up to a point where it melts, opening the circuit it's designed to protect. The trick is to select a fuse that will allow sufficient amperage to flow freely through the circuit to run all the equipment on the circuit but will self-destruct just before the current reaches the point where it can

| CONDUCTORS | | |
|---|---|---|
| TYPES (SEE NOTE) | DESCRIPTION | AVAILABLE INSULATION TEMPERATURE RATING |
| THW | Moisture and heat-resistant, thermoplastic | 75° C (167° F) |
| TW | Moisture-resistant, thermoplastic | 60° C (140° F) |
| HWN | Moisture and heat-resistant, thermoplastic | 75° C (167° F) |
| XHHW | Moisture and heat-resistant, cross linked synthetic polymer | 90° C (194° F) |
| MTW | Moisture, heat and oil resistant, thermoplastic | 90° C (194° F) |
| AWM | Style Nos. 1230, moisture, heat and oil resistant, 1231-1232, 1275 thermoplastic, thermosetting 1344-1346 | 105° C (221° F) |
| UL 1426 | Boat cable | See UL 1426 |

**NOTE: Some of the listed types are not commonly available in stranded construction for sizes smaller than 8 AWG.**

*Fig. 4-6. Table IX from section E-11, showing insulation markings for typical wiring conductors found on board (exclusive of flexible cables). (© ABYC)*

## ALLOWABLE AMPERAGE OF CONDUCTORS FOR SYSTEMS UNDER 50 VOLTS

| Conductor Size | Temperature Rating of Conductor Insulation | | | | | | | | | | | | |
|---|---|---|---|---|---|---|---|---|---|---|---|---|---|
| | 60° C (140° F) | | 75° C (167° F) | | 80° C (176° F) | | 90° C (194° F) | | 105° C (221° F) | | 125° C (257° F) | | 200° C (392° F) |
| English (Metric) see **Table VIII** | OS$_1$ | IS$_2$ | OS$_1$ | IS$_2$ | OS$_1$ | IS$_2$ | OS$_1$ | IS$_2$ | OS$_1$ | IS$_2$ | OS$_1$ | IS$_2$ | OS$_1$ OR IS$_2$ |
| 18 (0.8) | 10 | 5.8 | 10 | 7.5 | 15 | 11.7 | 20 | 16.4 | 20 | 17.0 | 25 | 22.3 | 25 |
| 16 (1) | 15 | 8.7 | 15 | 11.3 | 20 | 15.6 | 25 | 20.5 | 25 | 21.3 | 30 | 25.7 | 35 |
| 14 (2) | 20 | 11.6 | 20 | 15.0 | 25 | 19.5 | 30 | 24.6 | 35 | 29.8 | 40 | 35.6 | 45 |
| 12 (3) | 25 | 14.5 | 25 | 18.8 | 35 | 27.3 | 40 | 32.8 | 45 | 38.3 | 50 | 44.5 | 55 |
| 10 (5) | 40 | 23.2 | 40 | 30.0 | 50 | 39.0 | 55 | 45.1 | 60 | 51.0 | 70 | 62.3 | 70 |
| 8 (8) | 55 | 31.9 | 65 | 48.8 | 70 | 54.6 | 70 | 57.4 | 80 | 68.0 | 90 | 80.1 | 100 |
| 6 (13) | 80 | 46.4 | 95 | 71.3 | 100 | 78.0 | 100 | 82.0 | 120 | 102 | 125 | 111 | 135 |
| 4 (19) | 105 | 60.9 | 125 | 93.8 | 130 | 101 | 135 | 110 | 160 | 136 | 170 | 151 | 180 |
| 2 (32) | 140 | 81.2 | 170 | 127 | 175 | 138 | 180 | 147 | 210 | 178 | 225 | 200 | 240 |
| 1 (40) | 165 | 95.7 | 195 | 146 | 210 | 163 | 210 | 172 | 245 | 208 | 265 | 235 | 280 |
| 0 (50) | 195 | 113 | 230 | 172 | 245 | 191 | 245 | 200 | 285 | 242 | 305 | 271 | 325 |
| 00 (62) | 225 | 130 | 265 | 198 | 285 | 222 | 285 | 233 | 330 | 280 | 355 | 316 | 370 |
| 000 (81) | 260 | 150 | 310 | 232 | 330 | 257 | 330 | 270 | 385 | 327 | 410 | 384 | 430 |
| 0000 (103) | 300 | 174 | 380 | 270 | 385 | 300 | 385 | 315 | 445 | 378 | 475 | 422 | 510 |

$_1$Outside engine spaces (OS)

$_2$Inside engine spaces (IS)

NOTE: Cross reference with voltage drop tables in figures 4-3 and 4-4.

*Fig. 4-7. Table IV from section E-11, showing the allowable amperage of conductors for DC systems under 50 volts. (© ABYC)*

damage anything. Fuses are simple devices, but to avoid problems with them there are some important things you should know.

### Fuse Types and Ratings

Popular fuse types shown in figure 4-8 include the cylindrical glass bus-type fuse designated as AGC, the newer and increasingly popular blade-type fuse designated as ATO, and a heavy-duty slow-blow fuse designated MDL, or type T. There are many fuse designations other than AGC, ATO, and MDL, but these three are the most common and will do for our purposes.

The most important specification to look for when selecting a fuse is the amperage. When selecting a fuse for a circuit, base the size of the fuse on the current-carrying capability of the smallest wire in the circuit. For example, if you select a 14-gauge AWG wire to get power from your distribution panel to a new depth-sounder but the leads built into the sounder are only 16 AWG, the fuse must be rated for the 16 AWG leads, even if they are only a few inches long.

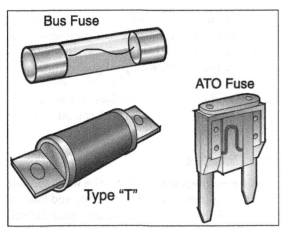

Bus Fuse

ATO Fuse

Type "T"

*Fig. 4-8. Bus-type glass fuse, slow-blow cylindrical fuse, ATO blade-type fuse.*

## AGC and MDL Fuses

AGC fuses (often generically called bus fuses) are the popular 1.25-inch glass-barrel fuses with tinned-copper end caps that have been around since the beginning of time. They are by far the most common type of fuse used to protect individual pieces of equipment and circuits on boats today, and are the type most often supplied with a piece of equipment when you buy it. Many bilge pumps, just to name one item, will have an AGC fuse in an in-line fuse holder wired right into the positive lead of the pump. At least one manufacturer (PAR) voids the warranty on the pump if this fuse is tampered with.

As you examine an AGC fuse, you may notice that it has a voltage rating embossed on the metal end cap. Usually this will be a fairly high number like 250 volts. Since you're using these fuses for DC circuits, this rating is completely irrelevant and can be disregarded. If you blow a 10-volt fuse, for example, it's perfectly OK to replace it with a 250-volt fuse, or vice versa. However, you would never replace a 10-amp fuse with anything other than another 10-amp fuse. We aren't quite done yet, though. Some motors and inverters require what is called a *slow-blow fuse.*

Motors and certain other devices require as much as five or six times more amperage to get started as they will use when they are up and running. Inverters

that supply AC loads to motorized equipment like electric drills will experience a surge of current whenever the AC motor starts up because AC output is proportional to DC input. Obviously, if you tried to protect any of these circuits with a regular AGC fuse, you would stay pretty busy changing fuses. A slow-blow (MDL) fuse allows a substantial amount of extra current to flow for a specified length of time before it blows and opens the circuit, and is just the thing for this situation.

Never make assumptions about the amperage of an AGC or MDL fuse based on a visual inspection of the element. Manufacturers use different materials for these elements with varying sizes and current-handling capabilities. Two fuses with elements that appear to be the same size could have entirely different ratings. You need to read the amperage specification embossed into the end caps of the fuse itself to be sure.

## ATO Fuses

An increasingly popular fuse being used by many of the large production boatbuilders is the ATO type, commonly referred to as a *blade-type fuse.* ATO fuses work in exactly the same way as the barrel-type AGC fuses mentioned above (the heat from excessive amperage melts the element and opens the circuit), but they offer several advantages over AGC fuses. They are color coded, for one thing, and the colors match the amperage ratings, as shown in the table in figure 4-9 on page 50. With AGC fuses you must remove the fuse to read the amperage; however, ATO fuses have the amperage embossed on the end of the fuse where it's always visible, even when the fuse is installed. ATO fuses have transparent plastic cases that allow you to see the entire element, so there is never a question about whether it's burned out or not. ATO fuses are also slightly easier to remove and replace than are AGC fuses.

A disadvantage to ATO fuses is that many of them use aluminum elements and blades. Using these fuses flies in the face of the ABYC directive for not using aluminum wiring or connections on boats. I have seen aluminum ATO fuses literally rot from corrosion when they were exposed to salt spray. Always use

ATO in-line-blade fuse holders with rubber covers as shown in figure 4-10.

If you find any aluminum fuses or fuse holders of any type on your boat, you should immediately re-move them and replace them with tinned copper or brass fuses and holders. If there is a question of what material an ATC fuse is made from, simply scrape one of the fuse blades with your pocketknife. Aluminum easily flakes away and reveals a shiny silver coloration right through the blade. Tinned copper or brass will show a yellow or pink coloration as the tin coating gets scraped away.

## ATO Fuses, Color and Amperage Rating

| Amp Rating | Color |
| --- | --- |
| 1 | Black |
| 2 | Gray |
| 3 | Violet |
| 4 | Pink |
| 5 | Tan |
| 7½ | Brown |
| 10 | Red |
| 11 | Blue |
| 12 | Yellow |
| 13 | Clear |
| 14 | Green |
| 15 | Orange |

Fig. 4-9. ATO fuses, color versus amperage rating.

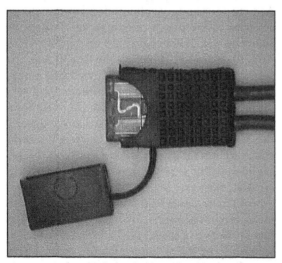

Fig. 4-10. In-line-blade fuse holder with rubber waterproof cap attached.

## Circuit Breakers

Fuses are an inexpensive and effective way to protect most circuits from too much amperage, and they are practically fool-proof if you pay attention and match the fuse to the circuit you want to protect. They do have several important disadvantages, though. For one thing, once they blow they are useless and must be replaced. This isn't an economic problem because both AGC and ATO fuses cost only a few cents apiece, but it can be a nuisance if you blow a fuse and find that you don't have a replacement. If this should happen with a critical piece of navigation equipment when you're caught offshore in a storm, it could even be dangerous. Another danger is that many of us faced with not having the correct size of replacement fuse will be tempted to use a fuse of a higher amperage or, even worse, to jump the holder with a piece of wire. (Actually, a chewing-gum wrapper is the fuse jumper's tool of choice.)

Another, less dangerous drawback to fuses is that they tend to be awkward to remove so that deactivating a circuit is sometimes inconvenient. This is especially true when the boatbuilder has located the fuse holder in the back of some obscure locker, as often happens. Here again, those among us who are easily led astray might be tempted to work on a circuit while it's live instead of taking the trouble of removing the fuse. The answer to all these problems is to have a reusable fuse that incorporates a switch so the circuit can be easily shut down, and this is just what a circuit breaker does.

Circuit breakers are available in only a limited range of sizes, the most common being 5, 10, 15, 20, 25, 30, 40, and 50 amps. AGC, MDL, and ATO fuses, however, are available in increments of 1-amp, and even fractions of an amp. This means that nearly all circuits on a boat need a combination of circuit breakers and fuses. In most cases a circuit breaker will be used to protect the circuit, and fuses will be used to protect each piece of equipment on the circuit. A typical lighting circuit, for example, might have five separate 25-watt light fixtures wired in parallel, with a 15-amp circuit breaker protecting the circuit and a separate 3-amp fuse protecting each of the five lights. If a problem were to develop causing a current surge at any one of the light fixtures, the fuse for that fixture would blow, leaving the others still working. A dead short in the main circuit, however, would trip the circuit breaker and extinguish all the lights.

## Ampere-Interrupting Capacity

The amperage rating of a circuit breaker is calculated as a percentage of the current-carrying capability of the smallest wire in the circuit. There is an additional rating, known as the ampere-interrupting capacity (AIC), that is a peak rating taking extreme situations such as catastrophic short-circuits and other surges into account. As a user, you need not worry about the AIC rating, as all the reputable producers of marine circuit breakers take these values into account.

## Trip-Free Breakers

ABYC specifications state that all circuit breakers used in pleasure craft be of the trip-free type, defined as "a resettable overcurrent-protection device, designed so that the means of resetting cannot override the overcurrent protection mechanism." This is an elaborate way of saying that they don't want you to be able to override the breaker by holding it closed once it has tripped. With trip-free breakers, the problem that caused the breaker to trip in the first place must be located and repaired before the circuit can be reactivated.

## Types of Circuit Breakers

There are two kinds of circuit breakers commonly used on today's boats. *Bimetallic breakers* sense resistance-generated heat, and *magnetic breakers* sense the magnetism induced by current flow. Let's look at them one at a time.

### Bimetallic Circuit Breakers

Bimetallic circuit breakers use two dissimilar metals, such as copper and stainless steel, fused together into a thin strip. In a normal state this metal strip connects the circuit inside the breaker. As current flows through the breaker, heat is generated, and since the two metals have different rates of thermal expansion, one metal expands more than the other, bending the strip. When the bending reaches a preselected critical point, the contacts inside the breaker separate and open the circuit.

### Magnetic Circuit Breakers

We already know, from our reading in chapter 3, that any conductor with current flowing through it will be surrounded by a magnetic field. Our second type of circuit breaker senses this magnetism, and when the magnetism reaches a critical magnitude, the circuit breaker trips and opens the circuit.

Either of these two types of circuit breaker works just fine in most marine circuit-breaker panels, and it's perfectly OK to mix them. In fact, since they both function in exactly the same manner with no significant external differences, it isn't important that you know which type you have. Just be certain that whatever breaker you select is designed for marine use, and you'll be all set.

### Removing Circuit Breakers

A big problem with many of the circuit breakers I've seen lately is in their labeling. Circuit breakers essentially all look alike, and the only way to be certain of their ratings is to read the label affixed to them. The problem is, some of these labels are located on the side of the breaker, requiring removal of the breaker from the switch panel to be certain of the amperage rating. These labels are typically glued-on paper labels that after a few years in the marine environment dry up and fall off or become very hard if not impossible to read.

Fortunately, removing a circuit breaker from its holder is a straightforward procedure. First be sure to turn off the master switch feeding the distribution panel to avoid arcing any wiring as you remove the breaker. Next, back out the one or two screws adjacent to the switch handle on the face of the panel and slide the breaker out from the back. Figure 4-11 shows the screws on the face of the panel holding the breaker in place, and figure 4-12 shows the breaker, with the specification label showing the unit's ratings, removed.

## Ignition Protection

Electrical ignition-protection regulations for gasoline-powered recreational watercraft go beyond the ABYC's voluntary standards and are enforced by the United States Coast Guard. ABYC section E-11 defines ignition protection in these official words: "Ignition Protection—The design and construction of a device such that under design operating conditions

▶ it will not ignite a flammable hydrocarbon mixture surrounding the device when an ignition source causes an internal explosion, or

▶ it is incapable of releasing sufficient electrical or thermal energy to ignite a hydrocarbon mixture, or

▶ the source of ignition is hermetically sealed."

What this means to me and you is that on gasoline-powered craft we can't have electrical stuff below decks that will ignite fuel fumes and blow up our boats. To this end, two important classifications need to be considered: the Society of Automotive Engineers (SAE) designation J 1171 and the Underwriters Laboratory (UL) designation UL 1500. These specifications state that the equipment to which they apply has been tested and approved for operation in explosive atmospheres. Approved equipment will have the fact that it meets the ignition-protection standards written right on the specification plate. Ignition-protected circuit breakers will have the statement "ign. protected" on the case. Figure 4-13 shows this labeling on the back of a circuit breaker. Make sure the components you use meet these standards.

These ignition-protection regulations apply to all areas below decks except for accommodation spaces and well-ventilated areas specified in section A-1.6

Fig. 4-11. Screws mounting a circuit breaker in place on a typical panelboard. Turn counterclockwise to remove. Also, make sure the main switch to the panel is turned off before moving breakers out of place.

Fig. 4-12. Circuit breaker removed, showing paper label. After a few years, you can count on these labels being unreadable and even coming unglued and disappearing altogether.

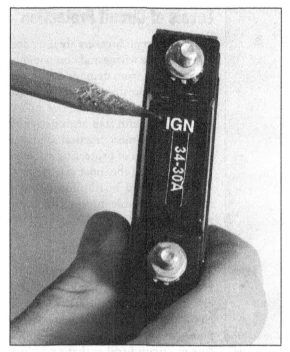

*Fig. 4-13. "Ign. protected" label on a protected breaker. This is the only breaker type that should be used in an engine room or compartment where CNG or LPG are stored.*

of the ABYC standards. There are exceptions to the rules for diesel-fueled boats, but on countless occasions I have seen jerricans of gasoline stored in diesel engine rooms. This circumvents the intent of the regulations, and one foolish move by the owner of these boats could cause a disaster. An improperly stored LPG (liquid propane gas) tank is also a time bomb.

# Testing Fuses and Circuit Breakers

One of the very first things you should check when a circuit of any type becomes inoperative is the condition of the fuses and circuit breakers, so it's important that you know how to verify that they are working properly. You might be saying to yourself, "Hey, my boat has all glass bus-type fuses. All I need to do is look at a fuse and I can tell if it's blown or not." This is not necessarily true. Often these AGC

fuses will fail under the end caps where the break in the element is out of sight. When some brands of circuit breakers trip, the reset lever remains in the "on" position and they give no visual clues as to their condition; this is especially true of the trip-free breakers required on boats. Fortunately it's easy to test circuit breakers and fuses using your multimeter.

## Testing Fuses

First, be sure the boat's battery master switch is turned on. Now set your meter to the appropriate DC voltage and attach the black probe to the DC negative bus on the back of your distribution panel or to any good ground. Touch the probe of your red lead to the positive side of the fuse holder and take a reading of your battery voltage. If you don't get a reading, you have a problem in the feed to the fuse from the positive bus bar. If you do get a reading of battery voltage, move your red probe to the terminal at the other end of the fuse and see if you get the same reading on your meter. If the reading is the same as the battery voltage, the fuse is working. If you don't get a reading, the fuse is blown and needs to be replaced. If you get a reading but it's lower than the battery voltage, you have a voltage drop that's probably caused by a corroded fuse holder. Remove the fuse and clean it and the holder. Replace the fuse and measure again. The reading should be the same on both sides of the fuse.

## Testing Circuit Breakers

To check for electrical continuity through a circuit breaker, first switch the breaker on and make sure that the terminals are clean and tight. With one meter lead attached to a known good ground, take a reading on the positive side of the breaker the same way you did for a fuse. If you get an identical reading at the adjacent terminal on the breaker, the breaker is working fine and any problems you may be having with the circuit have nothing to do with the circuit protection. If you do not get an identical reading on both sides of the breaker, it's faulty and will require replacement. Make sure to match the rating of the new breaker with the old one. Figures 4-14a and 4-14b on page 54 show this test.

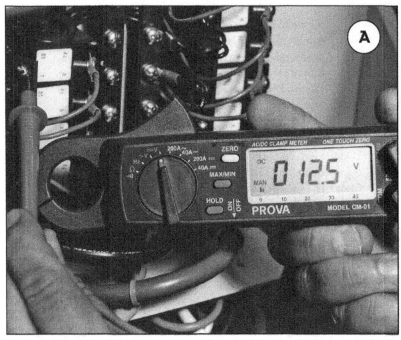

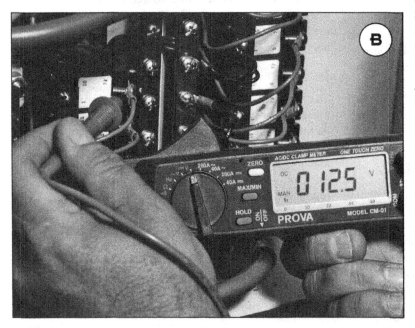

Figs. 4-14a, b. Meter test sequence for a circuit breaker. With one meter lead attached to a known good ground, check the feed side of the breaker for 12 volts. With the breaker turned on, you should have 12 volts at the adjacent terminal on the breaker. If not, the breaker is faulty and must be replaced.

# Levels of Circuit Protection

Fuses and circuit breakers are intended to protect the wiring and components in the circuit from damage due to excess current flowing through any part of the circuit at any time. The ABYC has come up with standards designed to provide the most practical solutions to the problem of protecting circuits. However, even the most experienced electricians and boatbuilders sometimes have trouble interpreting these standards.

## The 100–150 Percent Rule

The 100–150 percent rule contains the standards for the rating of fuses and circuit breakers for different types of circuits under differing circumstances. Some circuits must be protected with a fuse or circuit breaker that's no more than 100 percent of the total amperage-handling limits of all the components on a circuit, and other circuits may have a fuse or circuit breaker rated as high as 150 percent of the total amperage. One such division of standards is between motor circuits and nonmotor circuits.

### Motor Circuits

Motor circuits fall into a unique category. Starter-motor circuits on boats are the only circuits that are exempt from the requirement for circuit protection. The protection ratings for other DC motors fall into a gray area. In a perfect world, these motors would have a circuit breaker built in, as in most AC motors you may be familiar with. (The little red reset button on the side of the motor is actually a circuit breaker.) However, most of the DC motors you'll run into on board your boat do not have this type of protection. So, why are motors different from anything else electrical found on board?

The answer to this question lies in the two major differences between motor circuits and other circuits. First, as already mentioned, motors will draw a considerable amount of additional current when they first start up. Once the motor is running, the current tapers off to a more reasonable and considerably lower level. This start-up current must be accounted for, but a more serious possibility is a locked-rotor condition that occurs when the motor is getting power but the armature is prevented from turning. This can be caused by corrosion in the motor housing or bearings, or it can happen when a bilge-pump motor gets a piece of debris jammed in the pickup or impeller of the pump. When this happens, the flow of electrons increases dramatically.

The ABYC standards provide that the circuit protection preclude a fire hazard if the motor circuit is energized for seven hours under any conditions of overload, including locked rotor. The best way to make sure you're complying with this rule is to carefully follow the installation recommendations provided by the manufacturer. If you don't have the printed recommendations for the motor, call the company and ask for them. The only alternative is to test amperage drawn by the motor while it's in a locked-rotor condition, and this is not a very practical solution for the average boater.

## Nonmotor Circuits

The ABYC standards address circuit protection for nonmotor loads more clearly than they do protection for motor circuits. Basically, the rating of the fuse or circuit breaker used on a nonmotor circuit must not exceed 150 percent of the maximum amperage of the smallest conductor feeding the appliance. Odds are good that when you determine the current of an appliance, you'll discover that you can't buy a fuse or breaker that falls at exactly the 150 percent value. The key words here are *must not exceed*. I generally work in the range of fuses and breakers that are between 115 to 150 percent of the total amperage-handling capabilities of the circuit I am trying to protect and can always find a match.

## Distribution Panels

Distribution panels and switchboards fall into a slightly different category than regular on-board equipment. The protection ratings for distribution panels that supply multiple branch circuits are designed to protect not only the panel but also the primary-feed conductor to the board. This may be an important consideration if your boat's original distribution panel has blank sockets where more equipment could be added.

In general, in order to save money and weight, boatbuilders try to use the smallest wire sizes that they can get away with. If your boat came through with, let's say, three blank holes in the distribution panel where additional circuit breakers or fuses could be installed, you could have a problem. The boatbuilder may have rated the wire going from the battery to the panel for the loads he installed without any consideration for reserve capacity. As soon as you add anything to the panel, you risk exceeding the capacity of the feed wire.

The ABYC recommendations for dealing with this situation are clear: "A trip-free circuit breaker or a fuse shall be installed at the source of power for panelboards and switchboards, and shall not exceed 100 percent of the load capacity of that panel, or 100 percent of the current-carrying capacity of the feeders." There is an exception to this rule that will apply to many newer boats: the fuse or circuit breaker for the wire that connects the battery to the distribution panel may be rated at up to 150 percent of the capacity of the wire if the panel is equipped with a submain circuit breaker rated at no more than 100 percent of the load on the panel. Figures 4-15 and 4-16 on page 56 show these possibilities and the allowable ratings.

# Acceptable Locations for Fuses and Circuit Breakers

The next consideration you'll need to make if you're adding electrical equipment to your boat is where to locate the fuse or circuit breaker. Not all fuses and breakers are mounted on the main distribution panel, so some rules for placement of these devices are needed.

POWERBOATER'S GUIDE TO ELECTRICAL SYSTEMS

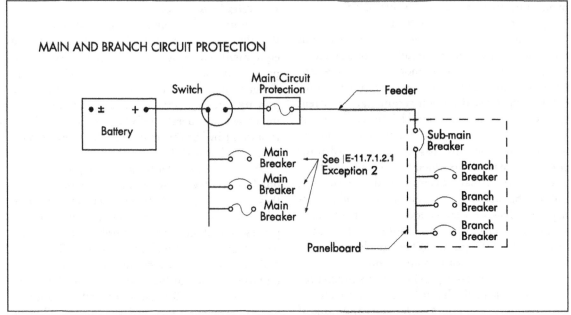

Fig. 4-15. With this installation (submain breaker installed) the main circuit protector can be rated up to 150 percent of the feeder wire ampacity. (© ABYC)

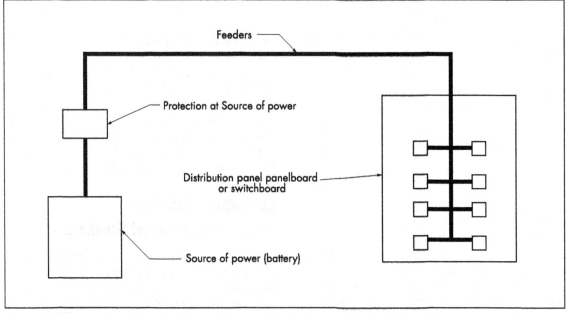

Fig. 4-16. Without a submain breaker (this panel has none), the feeder protection should be rated at no more than 100 percent of the feeder ampacity. (© ABYC)

56

## The 7–40–72 Rule

The 7–40–72 rule of the ABYC's standard E-11 is entitled *Overcurrent Protection* and states: "Ungrounded conductors (positive power feed conductor) shall be provided with overcurrent protection within a distance of 7 inches (175 mm) of the point at which the conductor is connected to the source of power measured along the conductor." That means that the fuse or circuit breaker must be located no more than 7 inches from the battery. There are some exceptions to the 7–40–72 rule, as follows:

▶ Starter motor circuits are exempted from circuit-protection requirements, and as already stated, these are the only circuits on board that are exempted.

▶ If a wire is connected directly to a battery terminal and is contained throughout its entire length in a sheath or enclosure (such as a conduit, junction box, control box, or enclosed panel), the fuse or circuit breaker should be placed as close as practical to the battery but no farther than 72 inches (1.83 m) away. A common question that arises over this exception is just what constitutes a *sheath*. The black corrugated-plastic tubing used by most production boatbuilders fills the bill for sheathing and is a good, inexpensive choice.

▶ A wire not connected directly to the battery terminal can be protected with a fuse or a circuit breaker mounted as far as 40 inches (1.02 m) from the point of connection as long as the wire is contained in a sheath. For example, a large stud on the starter-motor solenoid is commonly used to connect various components on the engine. Wires so connected can have fuses or circuit breakers located as far away as 40 inches from the stud as long as the wire is in a sheath—hence the 7–40–72 rule.

▶ Battery chargers (covered in chapter 6) add a degree of complexity to the basic rule. Built-in battery chargers, engine-driven alternators, and even solar panels are all considered battery chargers, and the rules go like this: "Each ungrounded (DC positive) conductor connected to a battery charger, alternator, or other charging source shall be provided with overcurrent protection within a distance of 7 inches (175 mm) of the point of connection to the DC electrical system or to the battery." This means that if the charger is connected to the battery and sheathed or enclosed, the fuse or circuit breaker can be as far as 72 inches away (1.83 m) from the battery. If the wire is sheathed, the 40-inch rule applies as long as the wire is not connected directly to the battery.

▶ One additional exception that applies to many newer powerboats is that no fuse or circuit breaker is required on self-limiting alternators. This applies to most alternators with internal voltage regulators as long as the connection is not at the battery, the conductor is in a sheath, and the wire is no more than 40 inches long. The protection rating must be based on the maximum rated output of the alternator. Figures 4-17, 4-18, and 4-19 on page 58 illustrate the various allowable protection locations and the exceptions.

The above recommendations are intended to minimize the chance of an electrical fire on your boat. But following these recommendations won't do anything to protect the equipment itself. That's why many electrical appliances will also have a built-in fuse. However, just because the device has a fuse built in doesn't mean you can wire it into your boat without supplying an additional fuse or circuit breaker as close to the battery as you can get it.

## Wire Routing and Support

The wire routing and support standards of the ABYC are intended to keep electrical wires from getting burned, chafed, or soaked by bilge water. It's important to think dynamically when installing any new wiring or repairing old wiring. Conditions change dramatically when your boat is underway in a rough sea with engine parts spinning away and exhaust at full temperature. Improperly routed wires and bundles of wire collected into harnesses can be damaged by spinning pulleys and shafts; harnesses without a little slack to allow for flexing of the engine mounts can be pulled apart; and the insulation on wires and

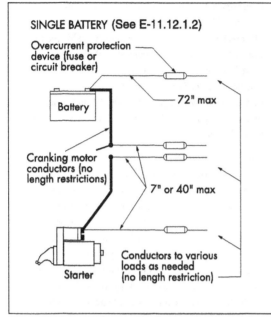

Fig. 4-17. Figure 15 from section E-11 on battery supply circuits, showing the location of overcurrent protection. (© ABYC)

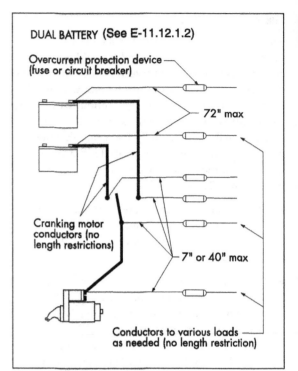

Fig. 4-19. Circuit protection in a dual battery installation. (© ABYC)

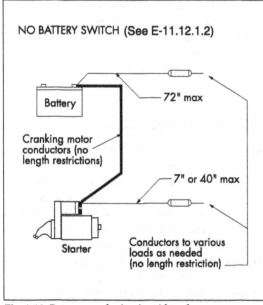

Fig. 4-18. Battery supply circuits with no battery master switch installed. (© ABYC)

cables near a hot exhaust manifold can melt away from the heat.

The rules for routing wires are simple, and common sense will go a long way toward keeping things right.

► Harnesses, unless they run through a conduit or built-in channel, need to be supported at least every 18 inches (45.7 cm).

► AC and DC conductors should never be bundled together unless separated by sheathing.

► Grommets must be used when running wires through cutouts in bulkheads and fiberglass panels. Some acceptable types are illustrated in figure 4-20.

► Wires must be kept as high above the bilge as possible, and those wires that must live there (such as the bilge pump wiring) should have waterproof

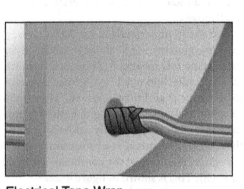

Electrical Tape Wrap

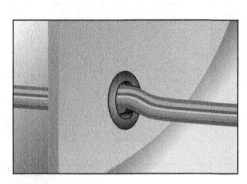

Grommet

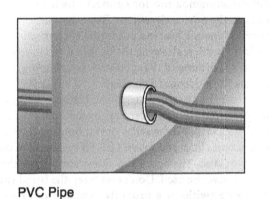

PVC Pipe

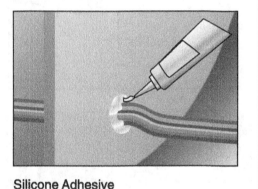

Silicone Adhesive

*Fig. 4-20. Acceptable methods of providing abrasion protection through bulkheads.*

connections. Sealing heat-shrink tubing works well in these cases. (See the circuit-repair section of this chapter.) All wiring should be routed at least 2 inches (50.8 mm) from wet-exhaust-system components and 9 inches (22.9 cm) from dry-exhaust components.

Methods of securing wire can be as simple as using nylon wire ties with screw holes for attachment. The recommended method of securing wires running above or near moving machinery is to use the plastic-dipped or rubber-insulated metal fasteners commonly found on standard engine installations. Figure 4-21 on page 60 shows a variety of acceptable wire-securing devices.

# Connecting the Dots: Making Wiring and Connection Repairs

In making repairs to existing wiring or building a new circuit for the latest electrical appliance you've purchased, proper techniques and components can make all the difference in the world when it comes to preventing problems later. Take the time to do the job right and do it once.

## Soldering Terminals

Over the years there has been some controversy and discussion among electricians regarding soldering versus crimp-type connectors used in electrical wiring on boats. For years I labored over each con-

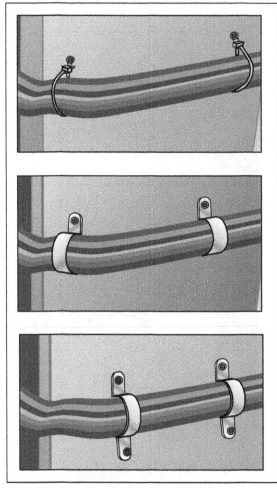

Fig. 4-21. *Tie-wraps and other acceptable clamps for securing wiring harnesses.*

practical than soldering them. It's certainly a lot more time-effective.

Once again, our friends at the ABYC have provided some guidance. In their view, solder must not be used as the sole means of connecting terminals to wire. The connection must first be mechanically fastened (crimped) and then soldered. They do make an exception, however, relating to battery terminals: Battery terminals may use only solder as long as the cable enters the terminal at a minimum distance of 1.5 times the diameter of the conductor (the battery cable itself). This is shown in figure 4-22.

The reasoning behind the ABYC's crimp-plus-solder recommendation for connections may not be clear to the novice electrician. Excessive current can generate enough heat in a poor-quality connection to melt the solder, allowing the terminal to come undone. I recommend that you stick to crimping, following the guidelines given here.

First select the correct terminal. Figure 4-23 shows the preferred types, all "captive" by definition. "Captive" means that if the screw or nut holding them in place comes loose, they won't fall off the shank of the screw or stud. The figure also shows some types that should never be used. Don't ever wrap the bared end of a wire (without a properly attached terminal) around a screw and tighten it in place. With stranded wire (the only type you should be using) it's quite easy to have some of the strands squeeze out, and they can end up touching an adjacent terminal, causing a short circuit.

nection, carefully soldering each lead. I considered crimp-on terminals to be the easy way out and inferior to soldered terminals. Well, times have changed and so has my view of the proper way to attach terminals to the ends of wires. In fact, I no longer use solder for any of my connections. Crimp technology has improved significantly so that if the crimps are applied correctly, you won't have any problems with them at all. Premier boatbuilders are using crimp connections exclusively with no problems, and I'm now convinced that crimping connectors is more

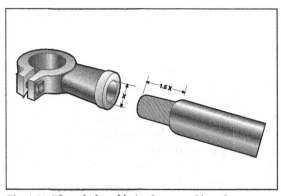

Fig. 4-22. *The rule for soldering battery cable ends.*

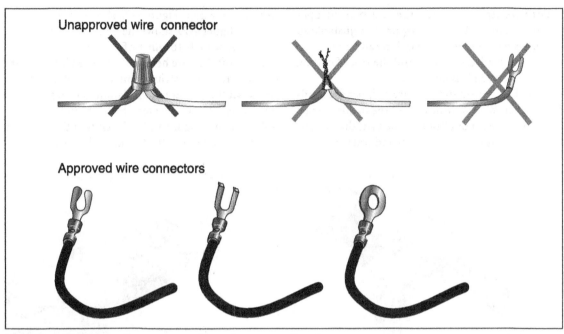

Unapproved wire connector

Approved wire connectors

*Fig. 4-23. Preferred types of connectors, and types that are not allowed.*

When selecting terminals, refer to the color codes and match the terminal color to the appropriate wire gauge. The colors are as follows:

| Red | 18–16 | gauge |
|---|---|---|
| Blue | 16–14 | gauge |
| Yellow | 12–10 | gauge |
| Burgundy | 8 | gauge |

Never crimp a wire into a larger terminal that's not the correct size. Either the connection will not hold or you'll lose some of the strands in the wire, creating an increase in resistance.

Crimping tools have changed over the last few years. Today's ratcheting crimping tools do a fine job and take away the big question, did I squeeze the pliers hard enough? These crimpers are easy to use; all you do is squeeze the handles until the ratchet snaps, and you can be sure the connection has been squeezed hard enough.

One disadvantage to these new crimpers is that manufacturers have designed them to use only their own terminals. Thus, you can only be certain of the

integrity of the crimp if you use terminals designed to match the crimper. This is not a huge problem if you buy your supplies at the same place you bought the crimper, but be aware that the crimper you buy may not be compatible with all brands of terminals. Figure 4-24 shows my crimper, made by Ancor.

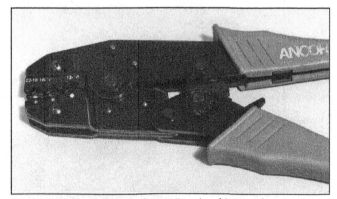

*Fig. 4-24. Ancor ratcheting crimper. By using this type of crimper, you can be assured that all your connections will be crimped properly as long as you use the tool correctly.*

For wire stripping, I use the end-type stripper shown in figure 4-25. This stripper is adjustable so that the exact amount of insulation can be removed from multiple pieces of wire, and the risk of cutting into the wire strands is minimized.

Both the crimper and the wire stripper are available through West Marine and all the major marine supply stores. At about $140 for the pair, this combination is a really good investment and will make your work much easier. Figure 4-26 shows the stripper in use, and figure 4-27 shows the crimper in use.

About ¼ inch (6 mm) of insulation should be stripped off the wire before it's inserted into the terminal ferrule. The stripper mentioned above allows you to set the amount of insulation to be removed in millimeters. The correct match of wire and connector is illustrated in figure 4-28. The ends of the wire just barely protrude from the ferrule of the terminal.

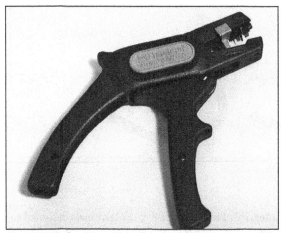

Fig. 4-25. End stripper. I love these tools because you can adjust the amount of insulation to remove for a really good match to the crimp connector. One drawback is that they only work on wire up to 10 AWG.

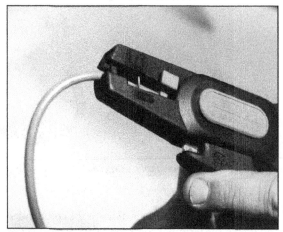

Fig. 4-26. End stripper in use.

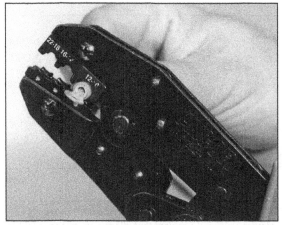

Fig. 4-27. Ratcheting crimper in use.

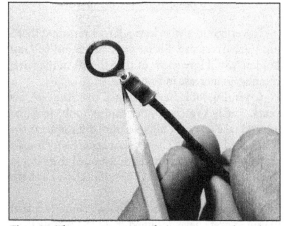

Fig. 4-28. The correct amount of wire protrusion through the barrel of the connector.

Make sure the crimper is in proper orientation with the terminal. For all but the butt-type connector, the handles of the crimping tool must be in the same plane as the ring or blade of the terminal, as shown in figure 4-29. For butt connectors, this really doesn't matter, but be sure both crimps align in the same plane. Always test your crimps by pulling on the wire hard enough to be sure they'll hold.

The newest variety of crimp terminals comes with heat-shrink casings preinstalled. After you crimp the terminal to the wire, heat the terminal with a heat gun, and the insulation will shrink tight around the terminal and seal it against moisture. This is a superior method of applying a terminal to a wire, but these terminals cost approximately a dollar each at this time.

When splicing a group of wires in a harness, it's a good idea to stagger the butt connectors so you don't end up with a bunch of them in one spot. Figure 4-30 illustrates what can happen. A better approach is shown in figure 4-31.

At some point you may find yourself having to repair or replace a gang plug. There are many types of these plugs available, and it's usually best to replace the entire plug assembly rather than to replace a single connector within the assembly. Replacing only a part of the plug rarely works and the watertight integrity of the plug is almost always ruined. Duplex and triplex assemblies are available at the major supply houses, and repairing these may also require replacing both the male and female ends of the plug.

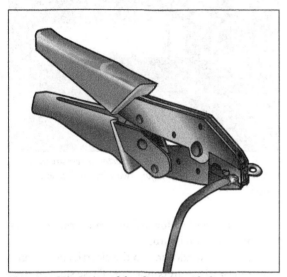

*Fig. 4-29. Orientation of the plier jaws with the connector to make a proper crimp.*

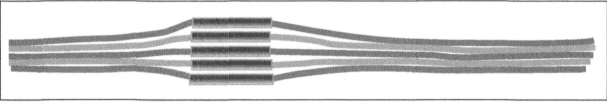

*Fig. 4-30. A "bunch" of butt connectors at a harness repair point. Taped and wrapped as it should be, this would look like a snake trying to swallow a rat!*

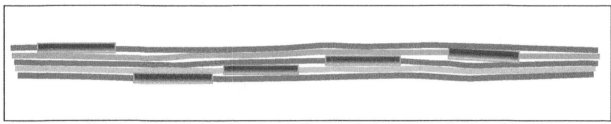

*Fig. 4-31. Staggered butt connectors at a harness repair point. Using this approach to harness repair will give a much neater job.*

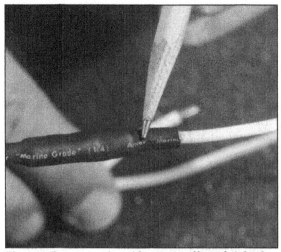

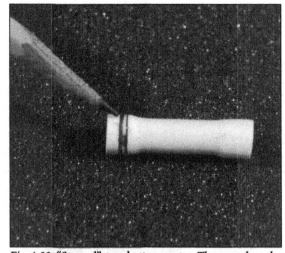

*Fig. 4-32. Butt connection with waterproof heat-shrink tubing. This is the highly recommended method for joining two wires together, especially in the area of the bilge.*

*Fig. 4-33. "Stepped"-type butt connector. These are the only way to go when you need to join two wires of different gauges.*

Finally, whenever you join two wires with butt connectors, I strongly recommend that you seal them with a length of heat-shrink tubing to make a watertight connection. These terminals are famous for trapping water and corroding. Figure 4-32 shows a butt connector that has been crimped and sealed with heat-shrink. Heat-shrink tubing is now available with

a sealer that's perfect for making waterproof connections anywhere on board.

Another new addition to the electrician's arsenal is the dual-gauge butt connector. These stepped connectors provide a solution to the age-old problem of connecting a smaller wire to a larger one. Figure 4-33 shows one of these new connectors.

# Chapter 5

# Batteries and Battery Systems

Of all the modern inventions that make life as we know it possible and, more important, make it possible for us to spend our weekends and holidays whizzing around various bodies of water in our powerboats, the 12-volt battery has to be one of the most important. Without that little plastic box full of acid and lead sitting in the bilge and the flow of electrons within it in a direct current path, our boats and boating wouldn't even vaguely resemble the sport we love and enjoy. All but the smallest dinghies and skiffs with hand-crank motors rely on batteries for everything from starting the motors to keeping the beer cold. Without that battery, you and I would be rowing, and as much as I admire healthful exercise, that idea lacks pragmatic appeal.

Oars worked just fine for great-granddaddy, but I enjoy flipping switches. With a flip of the first switch the out-drives lower into the water; with a flip of another switch the exhaust fans clear the bilge of fumes. Flipping the next switch turns on the VHF for the latest weather report. Finally, with a twist of the starter switches the engines rumble to life and I am away for a day on the water. None of this would happen without the boat's batteries, so let's take a close look at this most extraordinary and complicated contrivance.

## How Batteries Work: The Basics

In direct defiance of the wishes of one of my editors, I have decided to avoid a long dissertation on the chemistry that boils between the plates of your boat's batteries. For one thing, battery chemistry is a complicated subject that would take many pages to properly discuss. And for another thing, it's not what this book is about. I want you to know how the electrical system on your boat works and what to do when it doesn't. The internal chemistry of the battery just isn't that important. However, for you technophiles who do want to delve deeper into the chemical mysteries of the modern voltaic storage battery, I would refer you to your public library and the *Encyclopedia Britannica* where you'll find an exhaustive (and exhausting) article on the subject.

## Basic Chemistry

Unfortunately, I am not going to be able to avoid chemistry altogether, and there are a few underlying principles with which you should be familiar. For our purposes it's enough to know that the several types of storage batteries you might find on your boat all work on the same system. Batteries are divided into cells with plates of two dissimilar metals surrounded by an *electrolyte*. An electrolyte can be any electrically conductive material (electrolytes are an important component in popular energy drinks like Gatorade), and when any two metals are suspended in it they will produce an electrical voltage between them. (Voltage, you'll remember, is the potential to produce electrical current, and thus, is the only electrical value that's static.) The magnitude of the voltage will always be different for different combinations of metals and electrolytes.

The electrolyte used in your boat's batteries (as well as in your car batteries) is sulfuric acid, and the dissimilar metals are lead dioxide in the positive plate (or *cathode*) and *sponge lead* (a porous form of pure lead) in the negative plate (or *anode*). Thus, all such batteries are called "lead-acid" batteries.

As a lead-acid battery is discharged, the acid electrolyte is chemically converted to water (this explains why batteries can freeze and why the specific gravity changes, all of which we will cover later), and the plate material is converted to lead sulfate. To recharge a battery, you pass through it a 12-volt charge that converts the three active materials back into their original state. The actual chemical formula for this process when set in 10-point type is some 4 inches long, which is why I decided not to go into it any deeper than we have just done.

The only other ingredients in your boat's batteries are the *grid*, an inert (plastic) frame on which the solid active ingredients are suspended in the electrolyte, and the *case*. Lead dioxide, sponge lead, and lead sulfate are all very soft and fragile. The grid gives the plates the support they need to stand up to vibration and shock. The case, of course, contains the entire contraption and insulates one cell from the next.

The voltage from a single cell in a fully charged lead-acid battery will always be approximately 2.1 volts (called the *galvanic potential*), regardless of the size of the battery. A lead-acid cell the size of your house is going to produce the same voltage as one the size of a peanut. Thus, when six of these cells are strapped together in series (positive to negative and negative to positive), you have a standard 12-volt battery.

Recent engineering innovations have allowed manufacturers to produce plates that are slightly thinner than their predecessors but just as electrically capable. And due to advances in material technology, the new plates are much stronger than the old ones. Figure 5-1 shows the construction of a typical 12-volt battery with cell dividers and internal plates.

## Types of Lead-Acid Batteries

There have been enormous advances in battery technology in the past few years, and the result is a large and growing assortment of batteries that you can use on your boat. The days of the massive black case with gooey sealer and exposed lead cell-connecting bars are fading into history. Many of the heavy-duty commercial batteries are still constructed in the traditional manner, but even here things are changing fast. We now have low-maintenance, no-maintenance, cranking, deep-cycle, gel-cell, AGM (absorbed glass mat), standard automotive, and even special golf-cart batteries.

Which is just the right choice for you and for your boat? Well, that depends on what you're going to do with the battery once you buy it. Many boats today will have at least two types of batteries on board, and some will have more than that.

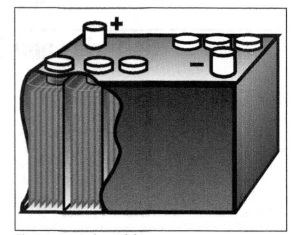

Fig. 5-1. A typical 12-volt battery.

To start, we can eliminate the standard automotive battery from all but incidental marine applications. These batteries might look just like their marine counterparts, but they are very different. Automotive batteries, even the so-called heavy-duty ones, are lightly constructed with thin plates hung on fragile grids; even the cases are thin plastic. This is because your automobile just doesn't need a big, heavy battery. Your boat, however, does need a big, heavy battery, and car batteries wouldn't last very long in the marine environment. Marine batteries must stand up to the vibration and deep states of discharge common on boats, and they must be able to withstand levels of neglect and abuse to which you would never subject your car battery.

The difference between batteries is not only in the physical construction but in the ratios of lead peroxide and other materials such as antimony and a calcium alloy used in constructing the battery's plates, and in the amount of material used in the plates. These variations affect the number of times a battery can be *cycled* (the number of times a battery can be discharged and then recharged) and still come back to useful life.

The construction of a battery also affects how long it can remain discharged before the lead sulfate hardens to the extent that recharging can't reverse the chemical reaction. When this happens, the battery is said to be *sulfated* and must be replaced. These chemical and construction variations in battery types also explain why some batteries have a tendency to produce more hydrogen (a process called *gassing*) than others.

Engineers have been able to reduce gassing to almost nothing by adding antimony into the plate material. Less gassing means less water loss, and hence the evolution to the sealed batteries which are becoming the norm today. We now enjoy modern gel-cell or absorbed-glass-mat (AGM) technologies that keep the sulfuric acid in either a gelled state or absorbed in a mat material, much like conventional dry-cell batteries.

The first basic choice you'll have to make as you try to pick out a battery for your boat is between the old-technology wet-cell batteries, the new gel-cell batteries, and the even newer absorbed-glass-mat (AGM) batteries, so let's take a close look at each of these three.

## Wet-Cell Batteries

Wet-cell battery technology has been around since the days of the first electric-start automobiles. This is the type of battery with the removable cell caps (generally, but not always) with which we are all familiar, because it's the type still found under the hood of the family car. Wet-cells have the lead plates suspended in liquid electrolyte, and the durability of the individual batteries depends on the robust construction of the case and grids as well as the amount of material in the plates.

Even today, wet-cell batteries offer some important advantages over gel-cell and AGM batteries, the new kids on the block. They are usually the cheapest to buy initially and, as we will see below, they are by far the cheapest to use over the long haul—provided, of course, that you don't neglect regular maintenance. They also stand up well to abuse such as over- and undercharging.

The disadvantages of wet-cells are that they require more elaborate ventilated battery compartments. They will not hold a charge as long as the newer gel-cells and AGMs, which means that they can't be left unattended for as long. They must be kept upright at all times, and they require regular topping-up with distilled water.

## Gel-Cell Batteries

Gel-cell batteries work on the same principles as wet-cells, and the materials are basically the same. The big differences are that the electrolyte is rendered into a paste about the consistency of grape jelly, and the plates (which have a slightly different composition, to reduce gassing) are suspended in this goo. Since there is no liquid to top up, there is no need for the familiar caps, and the cells are, for all practical purposes, sealed.

There are several important advantages to gel-cell batteries. You don't have to worry about spilling the electrolyte by tipping the case over, for one thing. In fact, gel-cells work just fine on their sides or even upside down. They hold a charge much better than wet-cells and can be left unattended for longer periods of time—and, of course, you don't have to worry about topping-up the electrolyte.

The disadvantages of gel-cells, besides the cost (which we will go into below), are that they cannot be overcharged without suffering permanent and often terminal damage. Also, because the electrolyte can't circulate between the plates the way it can in a wet-cell battery, gel-cell plates must be kept thin enough to accept a charge in a reasonable length of time.

Generally, over the last few years, gel-cells have developed quite a bad reputation for not living up to the claims made for them by manufacturers. Moreover, gel-cells have charging needs that differ from both the AGM (which we will discuss next) and wet-cell batteries. Traditional constant-rate ferro-resonant battery chargers, which are found on all older boats and on new high-production boats (Sea Ray and Bayliner, to name two), have destroyed many gel-cell batteries. Gel-cell batteries must be charged using a three-stage smart charger (covered in chapter 6) with the voltage set for gelled electrolyte.

## Absorbed-Glass-Mat Batteries

Absorbed-glass-mat batteries are also of the no-maintenance type. They have a sealed case, just like their gel-cell cousins: you couldn't add water to these batteries if you wanted to. The primary difference between AGM batteries and gel-cells is in the way the electrolyte is supported. AGMs have a fiberglass mat between the cells that further supports the electrolyte. There are other important differences, though. Tests have shown that AGMs are less sensitive to charge rates than gel-cells, perhaps making them a better choice if you own an older boat with a constant-rate charger. (More on chargers in the next chapter.)

## No-Maintenance Batteries

Beware of batteries sold by some chain stores such as Sears and Wal-Mart that purport to be no-maintenance batteries and lack a filler cap just like gel-cells and AGMs. These are often wet-cell automobile batteries that have an internal reservoir of electrolyte that's gradually used up as the battery is recharged. Once this reservoir is gone, the batteries are junk. These might be fine for your car, but they have no more business on your boat than any other automobile battery. A few may even be marketed as marine batteries, so be extra careful when buying from discount stores. The best policy is to buy your batteries from a reputable supplier who specializes in batteries for boats.

## Battery Life

But what about charging cycles? How many times on average can the different types of batteries be discharged and recharged before they need to be replaced? This is a difficult question, because the number of charging cycles that you can expect out of a battery depends upon the rate and depth of discharge, the recharging method, and the quality of the battery construction. Also, batteries of the same nominal size will often have different amp-hour capacities, and the real concern is cost per amp-hour. The Typical Battery Charging Cycles table above represents the average number of times top-quality batteries of each type can be discharged and recharged. Cheap substitutes will provide a much lower average number of cycles.

## Cost Comparisons

Conventional wet-cell batteries are the least expensive of the three types we have discussed, no matter

## Typical Battery Charging Cycles

| Battery Type | Cycles |
| --- | --- |
| Conventional wet-cell | 800–4,500 cycles (2,650 avg.) |
| Gel-cell | 800–2,000 cycles (1,400 avg.) |
| AGM | 1,000–5,000 cycles (3,000 avg.) |

Note: The above averages are based on manufacturer's claims under ideal conditions. Actual averages will be considerably lower in the less-than-ideal conditions found on your boat.

which way the cost is measured. The question is, if I buy the new gel-cell or AGM batteries, what am I getting for my extra battery dollars? Are the AGM and gel-cell batteries worth the extra money? The answer is that there is no answer—at least not one that fits all circumstances. The type of battery that's best for you depends on your needs and the use to which you put your boat. Here are some cost comparisons.

Comparing charging cycles to typical cost per battery gives you a feel for the true cost of these batteries over the long haul. Using a group 27 battery (a common size) for comparison gives a cost-per-cycle based on the average number of cycles in each type used above.

The table below compares typical group 27 deep-cycle battery prices taken from the 2006 West Marine catalog, and the average true cost per cycle.

Using a cost-per-amp-hour calculation, we can use the advertised total amp-hour capacities for the three group 27 deep-cycle batteries West Marine lists in the same 2006 catalog to arrive at cost over life of the battery (see table on the next page).

## Deep-Cycle Batteries Cost Per Cycle

| Battery Type | Cost |
| --- | --- |
| Wet-cell | $100, 3.8¢ per cycle |
| Gel-cell | $213, 15¢ per cycle |
| AGM | $200, 7¢ per cycle |

## Deep-Cycle Batteries Cost Over Life of the Battery

| Battery Type | Cost Formula |
|---|---|
| Wet-cell | .90 amp-hours ÷ 2 (50 percent discharge) |
| | = 45 amp-hours x 2,650 cycles |
| | = 0.0017¢ per amp-hour |
| Gel-cell | .86 amp-hours ÷ 2 (50 percent discharge) |
| | = 43 amp-hours x 1,400 cycles |
| | = 0.0027¢ per amp-hour |
| AGM | .92 amp-hours ÷ 2 (50 percent discharge) |
| | = 46 amp-hours x 3,000 cycles |
| | = 0.0014¢ per amp-hour |

Please keep in mind that these costs are based on charge-cycle numbers that are quite high. In actual use, your cost per amp-hour will probably be much higher. However, on average the findings here are as good for comparison of battery types as any other method.

Although they will require more maintenance than other types, conventional wet-cell batteries are still the least expensive of the three types to buy and own over the long haul. AGM batteries offer all the advantages of the gel-cells plus a less-finicky charge cycle. Therefore, in almost all applications, AGMs are a better choice than gel-cells, but as of this printing you'll still pay a substantial premium for AGMs over wet-cell batteries. AGMs are a particularly good choice for installations where acid spills are a consideration, as with personal watercraft (Jet Skis) and other sport boats, and they are excellent for use on boats that will be left unattended for months at a time.

## Which Battery Is Right for You?

All but the smallest open boats should have at least two batteries. The *starting battery* is for starting the engine and needs a lot of cranking capacity to spin a heavy-duty starter motor. The *house battery* is used to run equipment such as cabin lights, stereos, refrigerators, and electronic equipment that isn't connected to the engine. The starting battery should be a heavy-duty marine cranking battery, and the house battery should be a deep-cycle marine battery. One of my boats, a 15-foot dory I use for bay fishing, has a single deep-cycle battery that I use to operate my fish-finder and running lights at night. The engine is a pull-start outboard, so I don't need a cranking battery. If I had an electric-start engine on this boat, I would consider an additional cranking battery, even for a boat this small. I hate paddling; it just takes too long against a 2-knot tide.

My other powerboat, a 25-foot V8-powered walk-around, is set up with a group 27 cranking battery and a group 27 deep-cycle marine battery.

### Deep-Cycle versus Cranking Batteries

The difference between cranking and deep-cycle batteries is simple. Cranking batteries are designed to provide a burst of cranking power for a short period of time. Once the engine is running, the engine's alternator will kick in and quickly recharge the battery, replacing the power used to start the engine. Cranking batteries are not designed to be discharged deeply over and over again. You would be lucky to get one season of boating out of a cranking battery used as a deep-cycle house battery.

Deep-cycle batteries, on the other hand, are built with heavy and comparatively thick plates and have much more lead in them than cranking batteries. You can actually tell the difference between the two by lifting them. They are designed to be discharged up to 50 percent of capacity and recharged over and over again without sustaining any permanent damage. Because of the heavier and thicker plates used in deep-cycle batteries, they take much longer to reach full charge than cranking batteries. Therefore, they aren't a good choice for a starting battery, particularly where an engine will be started frequently and run for short periods of time.

Deep-cycle batteries are perfect for use as the house battery in cruisers that will be anchored away from shore power for overnight trips or for fishing boats that will be anchored for long periods with the fish-finder, radio, and beer cooler running.

Deep-cycle batteries are designed to take abuse, but even these can't be completely discharged and recharged continually without failing. Thirty percent of full capacity is generally considered a maximum level to which these batteries can be safely discharged. Fifty percent maximum discharge, however, provides a major increase in the life of the battery.

## Combination Batteries

Within the last few years I have seen what could be the answer to the battery prayers of many owners whose boats are not clear candidates for either pure cranking batteries or pure deep-cycle batteries. Previously owners of these borderline boats were forced to choose between two imperfect options. We now have batteries advertised as combination cranking/ deep-cycle units that are a perfect solution for the weekend powerboater who occasionally spends the night camping or fishing at anchor and spends the rest of the time at the dock plugged into shore power.

Combination batteries offer a compromise in performance. They won't be as capable of sustaining repeated deep discharging and recharging as a true deep-cycle battery, but they will be fine for occasional deep-cycle use and more than adequate for starting your engine. As with any battery, a combination unit must be sized to fit your specific needs and the needs of your boat.

## Some Specific Recommendations

Let's sum up all this various information and make a few specific recommendations for the right battery to put into your boat.

▶ Small, open boats with manual-start engines, minimal electrical gear, and possibly an electric trolling motor need one or two deep-cycle batteries matched to amperage needs.

▶ Personal watercraft need a single AGM or gel-cell battery large enough to meet engine-cranking requirements.

▶ Outboard center-console boats need dual combination batteries, with one for starting and one to run the electronic systems.

▶ Water-ski boats need a cranking battery or a combination unit of a size dependent upon the size of the engine and amperage requirements.

▶ Weekend cruisers need either one cranking battery for the engine and a separate deep-cycle battery for the systems, or two combination units, depending on amperage requirements and amp-hour loads.

▶ Long-range cruisers need cranking batteries large enough to meet engine requirements and enough deep-cycle capacity to meet total daily amperage requirements.

When you're choosing a battery for your boat and you find that you can't decide between units of two power ratings, always go with the larger of the two. There is seldom any trouble with a battery that's slightly too big, provided that it fits into your battery box, but one that's too small can open up a world of problems. When you really need your battery, you won't need a dead one, so always err on the side of too big rather than too small.

## Batteries for Cruisers

If you're a cruiser and spend days away from the dock, you need to get serious about batteries. Your needs are completely different from the day-tripping water-skier or fisherman. First, you should do an electrical-load survey on your boat and calculate the extent of your electricity needs while unplugged from shore power. This survey will help determine how big a battery you need and establish how many amp-hours you'll need in it. You need a dedicated starting battery and a separate house battery to run the equipment you'll be using while the engine is not running.

To do the survey, make a list of all the electrical equipment you have on your boat. List everything from the fish-finder to the light in the refrigerator. Now refer to the average power ratings found in figure 3-15 on page 37 and honestly estimate your average daily use of each item on your list. Multiply the amp-hours by the number of hours (or fraction of hours) for each item to get the amp-hours used each day by each piece of equipment. Next, add up the amp-hour-per-day figures, and the total will give you a pretty good idea of your total daily amp-hour consumption. Now double your daily amp-hour figure, remembering that you don't want to discharge the batteries to below a 50 percent charge, and you have an accurate amperage rating for your house battery. Purchase your batteries accordingly, and remember, when it comes to deep-cycle batteries, cold-cranking amps is an irrelevant number. You need to be concerned only with the amp-hour capacity, sometimes known as the 20-hour rating.

### The 20-Hour Rating

The 20-hour rating of a battery specifies the amount of amperage it can supply for 20 hours at 80°F (27.7°C). Figure 5-2 shows the correlation between typical battery size by group number, amp-hour rating, and cold-cranking amps. Never assume amperage capacity based on size or group category of a battery. Always check the actual battery specifications with the seller. You might just find that a bargain battery might not be such a bargain after all.

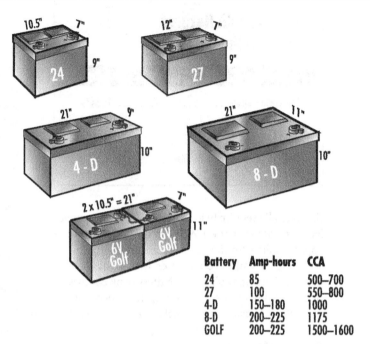

| Battery | Amp-hours | CCA |
|---|---|---|
| 24 | 85 | 500–700 |
| 27 | 100 | 550–800 |
| 4-D | 150–180 | 1000 |
| 8-D | 200–225 | 1175 |
| GOLF | 200–225 | 1500–1600 |

Fig. 5-2. Common battery group sizes, amp-hour ratings, and dimensions.

### Marine-Cranking Amps versus Cold-Cranking Amps

Most medium-sized boats need a cranking battery with enough cold-cranking amperage (CCA) to get the engine going, but it isn't that simple any more. A new classification has been added to the mix, and some vendors are now rating the batteries they sell in marine-cranking amps (MCA) in place of cold-cranking amps.

As defined by the ABYC, the two definitions are

"*Battery cold-cranking performance rating*—The discharged load, in amperes, that a battery at 0°F (–18°C) can deliver for 30 seconds and maintain a voltage of 1.2 volts per cell or higher.

"*Cranking performance* (also referred to as marine-cranking amps at 32°F or MCA at 32°F)—The discharge load, in amperes, that a new, fully charged battery at 32°F (0°C) can continuously deliver for 30 seconds and maintain a terminal voltage equal to or higher than 1.20 volts per cell."

Notice the 32° variation in the two ratings. This means that if two batteries with the same amperage—one using the MCA rating and the other using the CCA rating—are being considered, the one using the CCA rating will be the more powerful battery. Battery potential decreases with temperature. So, a battery that can put out an equal amount of amperage cranking at temperatures 32° colder than the competition is theoretically a more powerful battery.

What does all this mean? Simple: Be careful! Do your homework and know what you're buying before you pay your money. Manufacturers constantly play games with these numbers. If you're getting your batteries at the local Sears or KMart, don't expect the floor people to know any more than you do about battery ratings.

Typical CCA ratings for starting gasoline engines are shown in the following table.

Diesel engines, depending upon the type of starter motor and actual engine displacement, can

## Battery CCA Ratings for Gasoline Engines

| Engine Size | CCA Rating |
| --- | --- |
| Four-cylinder engine | 450 CCA |
| Six-cylinder engine | 550 CCA |
| Small V8 (350-cubic-inch, 5.7-liter) | 650 CCA |
| Large V8 (454-cubic-inch, 7.4-liter) | 700 CCA |

theoretically require twice as much amperage capacity as the figures above! When in doubt, consult the engine builder for the exact specification.

Again, if you have a cruiser with a lot of auxiliary equipment, you'll need a battery bank comprised of deep-cycle batteries. Use the amp-hour-per-day formula above to calculate the total amp-hour capacity.

## Battery Safety

Safety considerations around lead-acid batteries are often not taken seriously. During my career, I've seen two batteries explode, covering workers with acid. In one instance we were able to flush away the acid so that the worker escaped injury. What was his mistake? He left a ½-inch wrench on top of a battery, and it had come in contact with both the positive and negative terminals.

In the other instance, the victim was permanently scarred. His error? He disconnected a battery charger from a battery without first turning off the charger. The resulting spark ignited the hydrogen gas that had built up around the battery.

In a third, less-dangerous instance, a battery simply exploded and coated the main saloon of a friend's liveaboard cruiser with battery acid—curtains, carpets, furniture, everything. I'm not sure what caused that one, but I think he was attempting to charge a battery with low electrolyte. Fortunately, no one was on board at the time of the explosion so there were no injuries.

Battery acid is dangerous. Battery safety rules are simple but must be followed.

▶ Thoroughly ventilate the area around batteries. Highly explosive hydrogen gas, which can be ignited with the smallest spark or cigarette ash, is being produced when charging a battery.

▶ Don't put tools on top of a battery when working in the area. Metal tools can cause a short between the two terminals and will literally weld themselves to the battery. The least you can expect is a spectacular spark that could easily cause an explosion or serious burns. Also, wearing jewelry when working around batteries is risky, for the same obvious reasons.

▶ When connecting or disconnecting battery terminals, always disconnect the negative terminal first and hook it up last. This sequence minimizes the chance that a spark can jump the gap between the battery post and the cable-end terminal as you hook it up.

▶ Don't smoke. If you must smoke, don't do it around batteries.

▶ Batteries are heavy. Use the carrying handles provided on good marine batteries and get help if you need it. If your battery doesn't have carrying handles, borrow a special battery-carrying strap, as shown in figure 5-3, and use it.

▶ Don't overfill wet-cell batteries. The excess electrolyte will boil out as the battery charges, leaving an acid film all over the battery and everything in the surrounding area. Figure 5-4 shows the proper level to which each cell should be filled. When the level is correct and you look down into the cell, you should see a fish-eye staring back at you.

▶ Never attempt to recharge a frozen battery; it will probably explode. A frozen battery must be completely thawed before any attempt is made to restore it. Odds are that it's dead anyway.

▶ Never attempt to charge a battery that has electrolyte levels that are below the top of the battery plates. On sealed batteries with a charge-indicating "eye," various colors are used to indicate the state of charge. Depending on the manufacturer, one of the colors will indicate electrolyte loss. This battery should not be charged, but replaced. Sealed batteries should have a sticker on the top explaining the color codes.

► Keep batteries in a properly designed box secured to prevent battery movement in rough seas. Make sure that all cable connections are tight and permanent. No alligator clips or twisted-on connections are allowed.

► Keep batteries clean and free from corrosion and any moisture or oily film on the battery top. This is not only a safety consideration but also a great way to increase the life of your batteries.

► Know which battery terminal is positive and which is negative. This is important for the connect-and-disconnect procedures described above. It will also prevent damage to polarity-sensitive equipment like GPS and radar.

► Battery terminals should be marked with a plus (+) or minus (–) sign, or the positive terminal may be marked with red paint. With a post-type battery, the positive terminal is always slightly larger in diameter than the negative. Don't believe the cable colors. Lots of people replace cables with whatever color cable is available at the time they needed a new one. Be absolutely certain you know which is the positive and which is the ground (negative) cable.

Remember, battery electrolyte is sulfuric acid. It will burn through shirts, pants, shoes, wood, most metals, and your skin. Anything exposed to battery electrolyte should be thoroughly flushed and immediately rinsed in fresh water. Even then, your favorite jeans or T-shirt will probably end up with a souvenir set of holes after the first wash.

## Battery Location

A major part of battery safety is directly related to the way batteries are installed in your boat. Our friends at the ABYC have addressed this issue in section E-10 of the *Recommended Standards*. They list three acceptable possibilities for battery installation.

*Fig. 5-3. Battery carrying strap in use. This type of strap assembly will only work for smaller group 24 and 27 batteries. Larger batteries all have carrying handles attached, and should be handled by two people.*

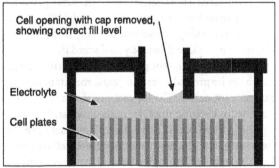

*Fig. 5-4. Correct battery cell fill level.*

1. Covering the positive battery terminal with a boot or nonconductive shield

2. Installing the battery in a covered battery box

3. Installing the battery in a compartment specially designed only for the battery or batteries

In addition, there are a few other rules in the standards with which you should be familiar.

► The battery should not be located near fuel-system components such as lines, filter canisters, or tanks.

► Battery-box covers must be ventilated, and the area around the box must be vented to outside air.

► All battery boxes and cases must be constructed of nonconductive, noncorroding materials.

► Batteries must be secured so that the fasteners cannot come in contact with battery electrolyte.

► Everything within 12 inches of the battery must be covered or in some way protected so that it's completely nonconductive. This is to prevent any accidental short circuit between the item and the battery terminal.

An easy way to satisfy these standards is to install all batteries in a commercially made plastic battery box such as the one shown in figure 5-5. Pre-made battery boxes in a variety of sizes are available at any marine supply store. Just remember to secure the box with the straps provided, and make sure that the battery is well ventilated to outside air.

## Battery Maintenance and Testing

There are several situations that can cause premature battery failure, but the most common by far is owner neglect. The second most common cause of a battery cashing in its chips before its time is the malfunction of the charging system. However, I classify even this as owner neglect, because the conscientious skipper should monitor this charging system closely enough to catch a malfunction long before it can permanently damage the battery. Other common causes

*Fig. 5-5. Typical plastic battery box.*

of premature battery burial are using the wrong type of battery for a given application, such as a deep-cycle battery where a cranking battery is needed and vice versa; and using batteries that are too small for the task at hand. (The information on selecting batteries at the beginning of this chapter should have corrected any problems you may have had in those areas.) And then there are the boatowners who chuck out perfectly good batteries they have convinced themselves are bad.

I've seen more batteries unnecessarily replaced than any other systems component I can think of. It seems that many otherwise sane people blame the battery for everything from an autopilot that doesn't work properly to warm beer. They will throw away a healthy battery without a thought to the more probable causes of their troubles. Just because your engine is cranking over slowly or your cabin lights are getting dim doesn't mean you need a new battery. With the retail price of a small marine battery bouncing around $100, I think it's worth checking the old one to make sure if you really need to replace it before you discard it.

As battery technology and construction methods have improved over the years, maintenance has gotten a lot easier. The biggest problems we used to have were keeping the terminals clean and topping up the cells with distilled water. These tasks are still necessary with the new versions of wet-cell batteries, but the new technologies have greatly reduced the constant need to add water.

Battery case construction has reached new highs also. Posts and case tops seem to remain sealed much longer than before, so electrolyte leakage and the resultant corrosion are not as important as they were. I'm still going to insist that you regularly check electrolyte levels and terminal integrity, though. A faulty charging system can literally boil the electrolyte out of the cells, damaging the battery and creating dangerous hydrogen gas, and it can do this in a very short period of time!

As you'll remember from the basics covered earlier in this book, loose or corroded connections cause excessive resistance, and that causes heat. When a high current is drawn from a battery, such as when you start your engine, a loose corroded connection can generate enough heat to actually melt the plastic casing of the battery around the terminal stud. This opens the door for an electrolyte leak at the terminal that further compounds your problems.

The following maintenance checklist will go a long way toward keeping battery problems at bay, and I recommend doing at least the visual part of these checks once every week, especially if you're hooked up to a shore-power charger.

▶ Keep the tops of your batteries clean and dry. Use a little warm water on a rag to wipe away any ac-

cumulated dirt and grime. A mixture of baking soda and warm water is excellent for cleaning dirty or corroded batteries. Don't overdo the baking soda, though. If it leaks through the caps or vent holes into a cell, it will neutralize the acid in the cell and destroy it.

▶ Check cables and connections for integrity and tightness. At any sign of corrosion, remove the cables and use a wire brush or dedicated terminal-cleaner brush to clean the post and the cable connector. Terminal cleaning is shown in figures 5-6 and 5-7. Don't cheat and think that you have done anything constructive by cleaning the exterior of the cable-end terminal and post. The electrical contact is made on the inside of the terminal—that's what counts. If your battery has stud-type terminals, as many marine batteries do, the cleaning tool will have to be helped a little with coarse sandpaper or with a wire brush or pocketknife. The socket on the terminal tool just isn't deep enough to clean the entire length of a studded terminal.

▶ Top up the battery with distilled water. If you can't get distilled water, at least use low-mineral tap water. There is a considerable variation in the mineral content of tap water from one municipality to the next. Some tap water with low mineral

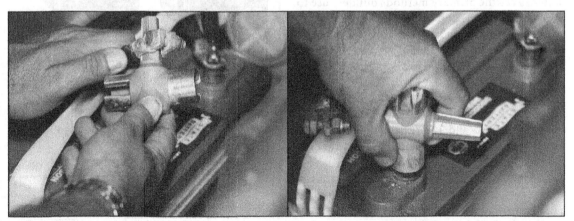

*Figs. 5-6, 5-7. Steps to cleaning the battery post and clamp, using a battery service brush. Use these tools until you see shiny surfaces on both the post and inside the clamp. Figure 5-6 shows the terminal being cleaned; figure 5-7 shows the battery post being cleaned.*

content (soft water) is fine for batteries; some is terrible. The best bet is to check with a local battery shop and ask about their experience with the local water.

▶ Keep tabs on both your engine's alternator and your boat's 110-volt battery charger, if you have one. Overcharging or undercharging is damaging to any battery. Overcharging will boil the electrolyte and rattle the lead off the plates. Undercharging will allow the lead sulfate to permanently harden, reducing the surface area of the plates. A sulfated battery will not develop full power and will eventually have to be replaced.

## Battery Installations

There are a number of ways to hook up and combine batteries. For the small, open boat, the choices are fairly simple and easy to understand. But, if your boat is a medium-sized cruiser with twin engines and both a bank of starting batteries (for starting the engines) and a bank of house batteries (for supplying your needs while away from the dock), the battery systems can get fairly complex. I will only attempt to present the most common systems here.

First, refresh your memory on series and parallel wiring hookups as we discussed back in chapter 1. These two methods of connecting battery cells and batteries are the primary methods builders use to alter system voltage and amp-hour capacity. Also, you need to know a little more about battery characteristics. To create a 12-volt lead-acid battery, manufacturers connect a series of six cells, which each produce a little more than 2 volts, to attain the 12 volts in batteries used by most boats. Larger boats might use 24-volt systems, and some boats even use a combination 12- and 24-volt system, but these are just 12-volt batteries connected in series to get the higher voltage.

When battery cells are connected in series, the voltage is multiplied. Thus, multiplying the number of cells in a lead-acid battery by two gives the final system voltage. If we hook these cells or batteries up in parallel, the voltage stays the same, but the amperage of the system is multiplied. Thus, if you have

two 6-volt batteries with 25 amps each, wired in series, you'll end up with a 12-volt bank having 25 amps of current available. If you wire these same two batteries in parallel, you'll have a 6-volt system with 50 amps of current available.

The majority of recreational boats today operate on 12-volt battery systems, so we'll stick with those. Figure 5-8 shows two pairs of 12-volt batteries. One pair is connected in series, the other in parallel, and the resulting amperage and voltage of each arrangement is shown. This is very important. I've seen more than one boater trying to connect batteries in the spring, and they just can't remember how they were attached when they took them out.

Here's a quick tip to prevent this confusion: Simply mark the cables when you remove your batteries in the fall so you'll remember how they go when you're ready for your spring launch. Remember that connecting 24 volts to a 12-volt system can be a very interesting but very expensive mistake. The parallel hookup is not what you'll find on your boat, as a bat-

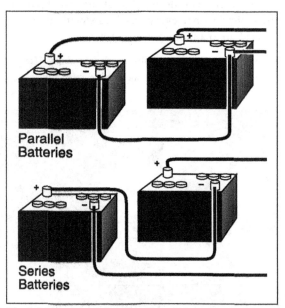

Fig. 5-8. Two 12-volt battery pairs, one in series, one in parallel. Remember that series connections combine the voltages of the batteries connected; parallel connections combine the available amperage but do not change the voltage.

tery switch will usually separate the batteries (unless, of course, you're building a large battery bank from multiple batteries). I am just trying to illustrate what happens to amperage and voltage in these circuits.

## Battery-System Components

Besides the batteries, other components found in any battery system are as follows: Every system will have *cabling* connecting the batteries to each other and to the distribution panel and starter. There will be a *master control switch* of some type to separate and isolate the individual batteries. In some cases a diode-type *battery isolator* is used to prevent batteries discharging into each other. And in some of the newer installations, a device called a *battery combiner* will be used to do the same thing. Naturally, all of these circuit components must be rated for the amperage they are expected to carry. Let's go through this list and take a look at each component.

## Battery Cables

In the latest version of the ABYC battery standard, E-10, a major wording change has altered the requirements for cabling attached to battery terminals. It now states: "**10.8.3.** Battery cables and other conductors size 6 AWG (13.3 mm²) and larger shall not be connected to the battery with wing nuts. **10.8.4.** Multiple conductors connected to a battery shall be installed with the highest ampacity conductor terminal closest to the battery, followed by successively smaller ampacity conductor terminals. **10.8.4.1.** A maximum of four conductor terminals shall be permitted to be installed on a single battery stud. **10.8.5.** Flat washers, if used, shall only be installed immediately under the split lock washer and nut of the attachment stud." This whole matter of the wing-nut attachment has been a bit contentious for years. These wing nuts do have a tendency to loosen and this will cause the terminal connector to heat up excessively due to the inherent resistance that is created. This represents a fire hazard on board!

Battery cables are the extremely heavy wires that connect your batteries to each other and to your distribution panel and starter motor. They might also be used to connect other high-amperage equipment

such as generators, anchor winches, and large inverters. The battery cables are by far the largest wires you'll find in your boat. They are also among the most important and the most neglected. Most medium-sized and larger boats will use a variety of sizes of cables in the battery system. A medium cruiser, for example, might have AWG 00 cables the diameter of your thumb between the individual batteries and AWG 2 cables connecting the batteries to the boat's systems. (In general, conductors larger than AWG 8 are called *cables* instead of *wires*, and the wire-end fittings are called *lugs* instead of *terminals*.)

Battery cables, as with any other wiring on board your boat, must be large enough to carry the current that the equipment connected to them will need. The size of battery cables is based on the maximum amperage that the starter motor and other high-demand equipment needs. Manufacturers generally do a good job of providing information on cable sizes in their workshop manuals.

The table below shows minimum AWG cable sizes required for various installations. When using this chart to select cable sizes, the positive and negative cables must be the same size. Typically, the gauge of the wire will be embossed on the insulation for easy identification.

## Battery Selector Switches

We have already established the need of larger boats, those much bigger than an open runabout, for a

### Battery Cable Recommendations

| Cable Length | AWG Gauge and Metric Equivalent |
|---|---|
| Up to 3½ feet (1.1 m) | 4 (25 mm²) |
| 3½–6 feet (1.1–1.8 m) | 2 (35 mm²) |
| 6–7½ feet (1.8–2.3 m) | 1 (50 mm²) |
| 7½–9½ feet (2.3–2.9 m) | 0 (50 mm²) |
| 9½–12 feet (2.9–3.7 m) | 00 (70 mm²) |
| 12–15 feet (3.7–4.6 m) | 000 (95 mm²) |
| 15–19 feet (4.6–5.8 m) | 0000 (120 mm²) |

combination of cranking batteries to start the engine and deep-cycle batteries to run the boat's systems. The longevity of these batteries will be greatly decreased if they are used for the wrong application, so you need a means to select which battery is in use at the appropriate time. The very best way to do this is with a battery selector switch with the familiar "off," "No. 1," "No. 2," and "both" switch positions.

These switches should be installed on any boat with an electric system, even if you have only a single battery. Of course, a single-battery installation doesn't need the four-position switch. A simple two-position on-off switch will do fine. The ABYC recommendations exclude boats using batteries smaller than 800 CCA from the requirement for a battery isolation switch, so if you buy one of these smaller boats, you'll probably have to install the switch yourself. Fortunately, it's an easy and straightforward job.

A recent experience I had brought home the importance of being able to quickly shut down any boat's electrical system in case of emergency. I was motoring across the bay when I noticed a small boat with smoke billowing out from under the port-side deck into the cockpit. I immediately altered course to investigate and found a fellow who was, along with his entire family, in a complete panic. The fire had been started by a severe short circuit, and the boat had no means of shutting off the electrical system. Current from the battery was feeding the fire, making it impossible to extinguish as long as the battery remained connected. There was no master switch of any kind. It was an all-too-typical situation of a single battery installed on a small outboard-powered boat. I jumped aboard the runabout and cut the positive battery cable with a cable cutter I keep on board for working with heavy shark leaders. The boat did have a working fire extinguisher aboard, and once the battery was disconnected we were able to extinguish the blaze in time to save the boat. Even so, I'm not sure if this fellow's family will ever again go boating with him on any kind of boat.

This little melodrama points out how important it is to be able to disconnect the battery power when there is an electrical fire. It's imperative to disconnect the power before you attempt to put out the fire. As long as there is battery current available, your attempts to stop the fire will be futile. A $40 switch could have saved this fellow hundreds of dollars in damage and made his family feel a whole lot better.

## Some Typical Selector Switches

Let's look at some typical battery selector switches and learn how to deal with them. My purpose here is not to attempt to show you every possible arrangement of batteries and selector switches, but to give you a good understanding of the key elements in some of the most popular circuits. Modification of these basic systems into more complex designs should not be too difficult once you understand the basic circuits.

The Guest Co., a major supplier of battery switches and components (now part of Marino), has some excellent diagrams available that could be quite helpful if you do decide to undertake a major system upgrade on your boat. Some examples of these diagrams follow in this chapter.

Battery selector switches have a continuous and an intermittent (sometimes called *momentary*) rating for amperage. The *continuous rating* is the amperage the switch can sustain while the switch is in normal use. The *intermittent rating* is the much higher amperage that a switch can sustain over a short period of time, usually measured in seconds. It's important to know what these ratings are when you purchase switches for replacement of existing switches or for additions to your system. You can't tell much by simply looking at the switch.

The battery switch you select must be capable of handling the extreme intermittent current associated with engine cranking and the maximum continuous current of the electrical loads in your system. Rating numbers look something like 230 amps continuous and 345 amps intermittent. Heavy-duty switches often have ratings of 360 amps continuous and 600 amps intermittent. Be certain that the switch you purchase is intended specifically for battery switching.

Battery switches available today have an important feature known as *make before break*. When switching from one battery to another, the contact inside the switch connects the battery you're selecting before it disconnects the battery you're deselecting. Without this feature your alternator could be destroyed in an instant. An alternator cannot stand even a momentary disconnect from the battery it is charging without damage. Therefore, never shut your battery switch off with your engine running. An alternator is essentially a dumb device. Without the load of a battery on it while it's running, it will automatically surge to its full output, burning out the diodes inside it.

Maintaining battery switches is not something many people think of, but the most common cause for failure of these switches is loose connections on the back of the switch. These loose connections cause resistance, which in turn causes heat. With starter-motor current trying to get through the loose connection, that heat is often enough to actually melt the plastic housing around the cable studs. This effectively loosens the stud in the case and destroys the switch. The answer here is to occasionally check the tightness of the connections at the back of the switch. In fact, some switch manufacturers even recommend using a specialized torque wrench to ensure proper tightness!

## Battery Isolators

The next commonly found component in multiple battery systems is the *battery isolator*. By using these isolators correctly, we can eliminate the problem of batteries discharging into each other. Isolators use heavy-duty diodes, which only allow electrical flow in one direction, to separate batteries, preventing one from discharging into the other.

It's important to separate batteries for several reasons. First, one of the characteristics of batteries is that a fully charged battery will try to recharge its weaker brother in a system. So, if you have a two-battery system and one battery is discharged with the battery switch left on "both," the first battery will discharge into the second one until they reach the same voltage. The ideal system will prevent this, but it involves installing a battery isolator.

Battery isolators use a group of *diodes*, which are electrical check valves that allow electricity to flow in only one direction. Isolators are installed between the batteries on a system to prevent a charged battery from trying to recharge a discharged battery to which it's connected. Isolators are an excellent addi-

tion to any low-end multiple battery installation. Figure 5-9 shows a typical 70-amp, two-battery isolator.

Isolators need a little care, just like the other parts of your battery system. Isolators are rated to carry a maximum amount of amperage, so you need to select the correct unit for your boat's system. Standard

*Fig. 5-9. Typical battery isolator.*

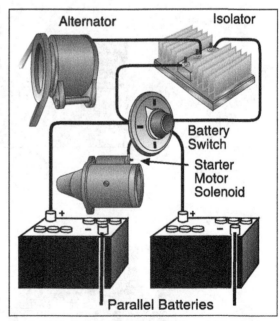

*Fig. 5-10. Typical two-battery installation with isolator installed.*

ratings are 70, 130, and 160 amps. The rating you use should be, at a minimum, equal to your engine alternator's maximum output capacity. Check the manual for your boat's engine to get this specification. Isolators are also configured to be used with either two- or three-battery systems, so make sure you have the correct one for your system before you install it.

Figure 5-10 shows a typical two-battery system with an isolator installed. The current flowing through the circuit shows the isolator effectively separating the two batteries so that one cannot discharge into the other.

Isolators have several faults that you need to be aware of before you buy one. First, the diodes used in them are electrically expensive. The big diodes have an inherent voltage drop of around 0.7 volt or almost 6 percent of the system voltage; this means that charging times will be just that much longer. The second

problem with isolators is heat. All diodes produce heat—it's where that 0.7 volt goes—and isolators are mounted on a substantial heat sink to dissipate that heat. This means that the isolator needs to be well ventilated, or heat buildup in the heat sink will destroy the diodes. The third problem is that on some isolators the heat sink is a part of the circuit and the entire thing is hot when the battery is being charged. This type of isolator must be mounted where there is no chance of any conductive material coming in contact with it, because otherwise an unfused direct short circuit can result. In spite of these faults, an isolator may be your best bet as an inexpensive way to keep your batteries from discharging into each other.

### Testing Battery Isolators

Testing battery isolators to determine if they are functional is a straightforward matter. First mark and disconnect the cables connected to the isolator.

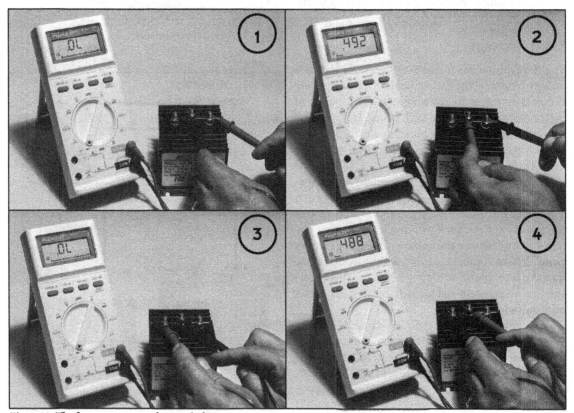

*Fig. 5-11. The four steps to test a battery isolator.*

Set your multimeter to the diode-check function and test for continuity in one direction through each diode and no continuity in the opposite direction. Figure 5-11 shows the four steps required to test a typical isolator connected to one alternator and two batteries.

If you discover that you have continuity in both directions for any of the diodes in the isolator, or no continuity in either direction on any of the diodes, the isolator must be replaced. Repairs are not practical in the field. Also, alternators described as one-wire alternators won't work with battery isolators without internal modifications to the alternator that must be done in a professional shop. One-wire alternators have been widely used by both MerCruiser and OMC.

Figures 5-12, 5-13, and 5-14 show three typical multiple battery installations using the components described above. Figure 5-12 shows a typical single-engine, two-battery setup with a master switch and

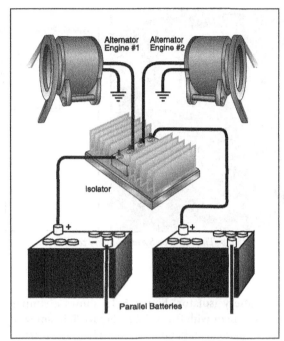

*Fig. 5-13. Similar arrangement, with the addition of an isolator.*

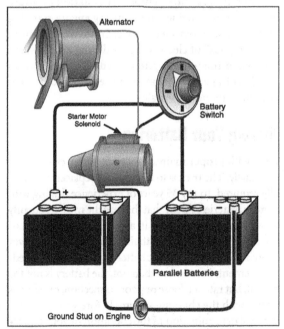

*Fig. 5-12. Single-engine, two-battery circuit with battery switch installed. Remember that battery switches must be matched to the maximum expected amperage they need to handle.*

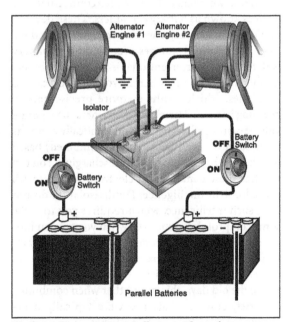

*Fig. 5-14. Twin-engine installation with two battery switches and an isolator.*

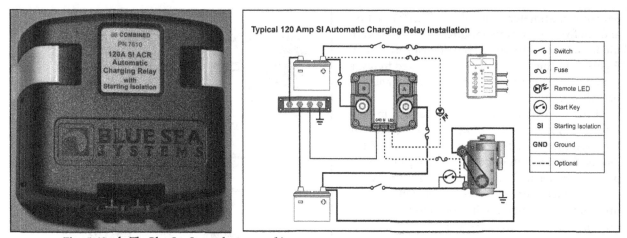

*Figs. 5-15a, b. The Blue Sea System battery combiner.*

no battery isolator. Figure 5-13 shows a similar arrangement with the isolator. Figure 5-14 shows a twin-engine installation with dual battery switches and an isolator.

### Battery Combiners

Relative newcomers to battery interconnectivity are devices known as *battery combiners*. These devices, available from all major marine equipment vendors, offer significant advantages over diode-type battery isolators. Unlike conventional isolators, combiners don't suffer from the inherent voltage drop caused by diodes, which results in more precise battery charging control. These new combiners incorporate voltage-sensing circuitry that automatically connects or disconnects multiple batteries (combined) based on whether they are charging or discharging. You can think of these combiners as electronic devices with some built-in intelligence. Diode isolators do not have such intelligence, which requires you to make some compromises, especially when you are combining different kinds of batteries, such as a cranking battery and a deep-cycle battery. Cranking batteries recharge much more quickly than deep-cycle batteries. In the old days, this meant that when combining batteries, cranking batteries were typically overcharged while deep-cycle batteries continued to charge. The Blue Sea unit shown in figure 5-15a over-

comes that problem by just turning off the charge to the cranking battery in the circuit once the battery reaches a prescribed voltage level. Additionally, the new combiners allow temporary isolation of house loads from the engine circuit during engine cranking to protect sensitive electronics. So there is no more "blinking out" of electronic gear during engine starting, when the whole system used to experience so much voltage drop that many electronic devices couldn't function normally.

## Testing Your Batteries

Even with proper maintenance, all batteries wear out eventually. The trick is to know when replacement is really required. In my 35 years of experience dealing with storage batteries, I'd say that they are the most frequently misdiagnosed component in any electrical system. People assume that because their engine is turning over more slowly than usual, the battery is at fault and it needs replacement. More often than not, the battery is not the culprit, but rather a loose or poor connection, or perhaps a fault with the charging system. Before you can make any real determination of the condition of your battery or begin any other serious testing, you must first test your battery. You need to recharge your battery first, then check the battery's load-handling capability.

# Hydrometer Test

So, what are these tests and what do they mean? Let's start with the hydrometer test. Hydrometers are used to measure the *specific gravity*, the ratio of one liquid density against another. You're likely to encounter two and possibly three types of hydrometers used to check battery electrolyte condition, antifreeze strength, and diesel-fuel quality. These hydrometers are all different and cannot be interchanged, and they are designed and calibrated against a standard for the liquid you're checking.

A battery hydrometer is used to check the state of charge for each cell of a wet-cell battery. This test can only be performed on batteries that have removable cell caps—not gel-cells, AGMs, or sealed no-maintenance batteries.

Do you remember when I explained how a battery works? I described a chemical reaction where the acid is absorbed into the battery plates, leaving only water. The hydrometer measures the change of the electrolyte from acid to water and tells us the percent of charge of each cell in the battery. Knowing the percent of charge does not tell you whether or not you need a new battery. If all the cells are equally low, something is either discharging the battery or you have a charging-system problem. The only other possibility is that there are one or two bad cells, and the battery has discharged the good cells into the bad cells, equalizing the hydrometer readings.

You're looking for a different reading between cells. If all the cells are equally low, recharge the battery and recheck the specific gravity for any variation between cells. One low cell after recharging indicates a battery on its way out.

Three very important points must be made regarding specific-gravity testing:

1. Don't attempt the test immediately after adding water to a cell.

2. Don't test immediately after charging.

3. Do test only after the electrolyte mixes and the battery stabilizes.

This stabilization may take an hour or so, or you can bring down what is known as the *static charge* by putting a load on the battery for about 15 seconds after the recharge to stabilize the battery. It's still bet-

ter to wait a while, but loading the battery will give a quick stabilization. Remember that the variation between cells is more important than the actual maximum specific gravity reading.

Most quality hydrometers have a built-in thermometer, and it's not there to tell you it's time to go to the beach. Specific gravity is calibrated at 80°F. To compensate for readings above or below this temperature, add or subtract 4 points for each 10° your reading is below or above 80°. This compensation can make the difference between condemning your battery or hanging onto it for another season. Maximum specific gravity readings for electrolyte from a charged battery will range from 1.260 to 1.280, as compared to pure water with a specific gravity of 1.000.

At a hydrometer reading of 1.260, the electrolyte

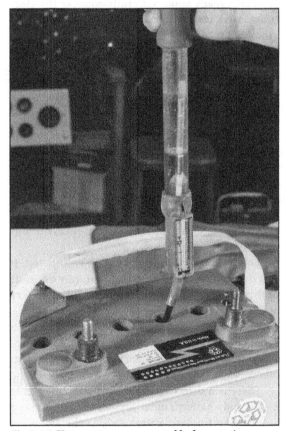

*Fig. 5-16. Temperature-compensated hydrometer in use.*

is 0.260 times as heavy as water because of the sulfuric acid in the solution. As the battery discharges, the acid leaves the water and goes into the plates in the cell, and the specific gravity moves closer to 1.000. A specific gravity reading that shows a 50-point difference between any two cells after recharge and stabilization indicates that your battery needs replacement.

Figure 5-16 shows a hydrometer in use. Experiment a little if you're going to use this method of checking your batteries.

Always wear safety goggles when working around batteries. Hold the hydrometer in an upright position and draw in just enough electrolyte to float the bulb—no more or less. Too much electrolyte in the hydrometer tops out the bulb and gives you a false high reading. When not enough electrolyte is drawn into the hydrometer, the bulb float indicates a bad cell that's really good. Carefully squeeze the electrolyte back into each cell as you check and record each cell's reading. When you have taken a reading from each cell, wipe away any electrolyte drips from the battery top and throw out the rag.

## Open-Circuit Voltage Test

The newer sealed batteries cannot be checked with a hydrometer, but you can still test the specific gravity on these batteries. You can't compare individual cells within a sealed battery, because you don't have a way to get into them. However, this test is still a good way to evaluate the overall state of charge of a sealed battery. If you have a digital voltmeter built into your boat's instrumentation, you can continually monitor the state of charge.

This test is called the open-circuit voltage test. If you don't have a built-in meter, you can use your multimeter and take a reading right at the battery terminals.

Figure 5-17 shows the voltmeter connected to a battery for an open-circuit voltage test. Be sure all accessories are turned off when performing this test; otherwise you'll get a low reading.

There is a direct relationship between specific gravity and a battery's open-circuit voltage. You need a digital voltmeter for this test, as the accuracy

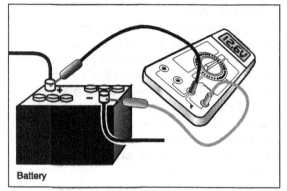

Battery

*Fig. 5-17. Voltmeter connected for an open-circuit voltage test. This test will give you an indication of the battery's state of charge, but can't tell you which cell within the battery is the culprit.*

required is difficult to read on an analog unit. As with the hydrometer test, the battery must be stable. A heavy load or a recharge just before doing this test will give you a totally inaccurate reading. Let the battery sit for an hour or so before the test, and your multimeter will give you a meaningful reading. Use a digital voltmeter hooked up as shown in figure 5-17, and compare the reading to the table at right; this will give you a good indication of your battery's state of charge.

## Load Test

The load test tells you whether the battery has enough amperage to back up the open-circuit voltage

## Open-Circuit Voltage versus State of Charge/Specific Gravity

| Open-Circuit Voltage | State of Charge (%) | Specific Gravity |
|---|---|---|
| 11.7 | 0 | 1.120 |
| 12.0 | 25 | 1.155 |
| 12.2 | 50 | 1.190 |
| 12.3 | 75 | 1.225 |
| 12.6 or more | 100 | 1.260–1.280 |

reading you took above. Open-circuit voltage readings can be misleading and give you a false sense of security due to a phenomenon known as the *surface charge*. A battery in poor condition may give you a reading as high as 12.5 volts or more if it has been sitting idle for a few hours. However, as soon as you try to crank your engine with this battery, you'll hear that disheartening "click-click-click" sound that tells you there's a battery problem. Load testing will give you some real answers about how your battery will perform when the chips are down.

An easy way to load-test your battery requires no special tools and is quite conclusive. Make sure all battery-cable connections are clean and tight. Next, disable your engine's ignition system, or, if you have a diesel engine, activate the fuel shutoff so the engine won't start during the test. To disable the ignition system on a gasoline engine, follow the workshop manual for the engine. On engines built from about 1992, you should be able to disconnect either a plug at the coil or distributor to disable the ignition system. Do not try to disable the ignition by removing the center high-tension lead on the coil; not only is this dangerous, but it could damage the ignition system. (More on this in chapter 7.) Once the ignition or diesel engine shutoff has been dealt with, hook up your voltmeter across the battery you're testing, just as you did with the open-circuit voltage test. With the meter set to the DC volts scale, crank the engine over for no more than about 15 seconds. Carefully observe the meter's lowest reading in volts during the cranking. If it drops below 9.6 volts, perform a three-minute charge test to determine if the battery is worth saving. With electronically fuel-injected engines, the minimum cranking voltage allowed is 10.5 volts.

## Three-Minute Charge Test

Begin the three-minute charge test by disconnecting the battery's ground cable to take the battery out of the boat's circuitry. This will prevent any voltage spiking of precious electronic equipment you have on board. Next, connect your multimeter set to measure voltage across the battery terminals. Connect a battery charger with a quick-charge capability to the battery. The charger should have 40 to 50 amps of output, so it's not your typical trickle-charger. Turn the charger on to about 40 amps and maintain this charge rate for three minutes while you observe your voltmeter. The battery is serviceable if the voltage reads less than 15.5 volts during the three minutes. Recharge the battery and redo the load test to be sure everything is OK. If the battery reaches more than 15.5 volts during this three-minute period, it's time to replace the battery.

After going through this series of tests, you'll know for sure whether you need a new battery or not. It may sound like a lot of effort, but really, these tests can be performed in less than half an hour. I don't know about you, but I'd rather spend half an hour than $75 to $400 for a new battery.

# Chapter 6

# Battery-Charging Systems

In the last chapter we went into some detail on the various types of marine batteries and how to maintain and install them. However, the most crucial concern of battery performance isn't installation or maintenance, although these two procedures are certainly important enough, but in the method and extent to which they are recharged once they have been depleted to acceptable levels. A battery that's regularly overcharged is going to shed material from its plates and boil away its electrolyte, dooming it to a tragically short and ineffective life. A battery that's regularly undercharged is going to have its plates choked with impenetrable and indestructible lead sulfate and is likewise doomed to a premature trip to the local recycling station.

The three types of batteries we have discussed so far—wet-cells, gel-cells, and AGMs—respond to charging in different ways, but they are all very particular about how they get their electrons reenergized. Batteries must be recharged just so, and if you don't do it right, you as a boatowner are going to be making a lot more trips to the battery store than you need to make. There are better things than new batteries on which to spend your boating dollars, so this chapter is dedicated to seeing that you get the maximum life and performance out of your batteries by recharging them properly.

There are many acceptable ways to recharge boat batteries. Auxiliary generators, wind-driven generators, solar panels, and water-driven generators are all used on boats in varying circumstances. However, the vast majority of us weekend powerboaters with small to medium-sized powerboats rely almost entirely on the engine-driven alternator and shore-powered battery chargers to keep our boat's batteries up to snuff. Thus, I am going to concentrate on these two methods of recharging and leave the others alone. I will, however, close this chapter by touching on solar-powered means of keeping batteries topped up and ready to go boating.

## Alternator Basics

Many books that cover the subject of alternators go into all types of alternator internal testing procedures and into details of how alternators actually work. I'm not going to do that in this book for just the same reasons I didn't go into great detail on battery chemistry. It's way too complicated to be covered quickly, and it frankly isn't very practical information for the average boatowner. You want to know how to tell if your alternator is working, and if it isn't, you need to know how to fix it. Everything else is excess baggage, so we are going to avoid it.

You should, however, be familiar with the basic underlying principles of alternator operation—just enough to understand what is going on as your precious batteries are being recharged. Before I go much further, here are some terms you need to know that define components common to all alternator systems.

► *Stator windings.* These are the windings that produce current inside the alternator. The stator is the stationary part of the alternator inside which the rotor rotates, which makes these two terms easy to remember.

► *Rotor.* The rotor is the magnetized coil that spins inside the stator windings. The coil on the rotor is known as the *field windings.* (This is easy to remember because *field* is just a shortened form of *magnetic field.*) The rotor provides the magnetism that induces alternating current in the stator.

► *Diode.* A diode is an electronic check valve that allows electrical current to flow in one direction and blocks it from flowing in the other. Diodes are mounted inside the alternator as part of a bridge rectifier circuit.

► *Bridge rectifier.* This is the internal circuitry that uses silicon diodes to convert alternating current created in the stator windings to direct current usable for recharging your batteries.

▶ *Voltage regulator.* This critical device adjusts the current in the field windings to match your alternator's output and the needs of your batteries. The voltage regulator also controls the output of the alternator so that it doesn't overcharge your batteries.

Alternators work on the principle of *induction* (discussed in the Word about Inductive Pickups sidebar in chapter 3) whereby a magnet placed adjacent to a wire will induce electrical current in the wire. Each stator winding in your alternator has a very long wire wound in a coil, and the rotor is a powerful electromagnet. By spinning the rotor inside the stator, electrical current is induced in the stator, and by varying the amount of magnetism in the rotor (the primary function of the voltage regulator) the amount of electrical current produced by the stator can be precisely controlled. Remember, all conductors with electrical current flowing through them are surrounded by a magnetic field. We can induce electron flow in nearby conductors by rapid movement of this field in proximity to the conductors (this works in reverse as well, by moving a conductor rapidly in close proximity to a stationary magnet).

If the stator windings in your alternator (there are usually three) all had the same polarity (the positive and negative terminals arranged the same way), you wouldn't have an alternator, you would have a generator producing direct current. However, alternators have their stator windings arranged in fingers so that as the rotor rotates past the stator windings, the positive and negative poles are constantly and rapidly reversing, thus inducing alternating current. Because your battery needs to be charged with direct current, this alternating current is passed through a bridge rectifier where it's converted to usable direct current.

Why, you may well ask, do we go to all this trouble to generate alternating current, and then convert it back to direct current, when an old-fashioned generator would develop direct current without all the complicated circuitry of the bridge rectifier? The answer is efficiency. An alternator can be built much

lighter than a generator, and it will produce much higher currents than a generator of the same size. It's ironic, but true: it's easier and better to produce alternating current and convert it to direct current than it is to produce direct current straight from a generator.

## Engine-Driven Marine Alternators

There are four broad categories of engine-driven charging systems commonly found on boats today. The chances are better than good that your boat's charging system will fall into one of the following groups.

1. Outboard engine with remote rectifier and no voltage regulator
2. Outboard engine with remote rectifier and voltage regulator
3. Inboard or stern drive with remote voltage regulator
4. Inboard or stern drive with integral voltage regulator

## Alternator Problems

Most problems with alternators are best corrected by removing the alternator from the boat and taking it to an alternator shop, which has the special equipment needed to make delicate repairs. Some manufacturers have factory exchange programs that allow you to exchange your unit for an identical factory-rebuilt replacement—for a fee, of course. It's a simple matter to pop the old alternator out, exchange it at the dealer's, then pop the new one back in. This exchange is sometimes available no matter what condition your old alternator is in—a real blessing when you experience an engine fire or after your alternator gets doused with salt water. Many offshore boats carry a spare rebuilt alternator that can be substituted for a defective unit if it should give up the fight while fishing the Gulf Stream or on a long weekend in the Bahamas.

This swap-and-replace procedure presupposes that you're able to diagnose when and why the alternator in your system is acting up.

## Marine versus Automotive Alternators

Before one of your dockmate electrical "experts" (there's one in every marina) tells you otherwise, remember that there is a big difference between marine and automotive alternators. The brushes are sealed on ignition-protected marine alternators used on gasoline engines; this prevents dangerous sparks that could cause an explosion. (If you want to see the difference, just open the hood of the family car in the dark while it's running. You're likely to see sparks arcing inside the ventilation ports of the alternator.) Other differences between alternators for cars and those for boats are that marine alternators are of heavier construction, may have a higher output, and have fewer corrosive parts than those for cars do. Don't let anyone talk you into substituting. This is an area mandated by the USCG on gasoline-powered vessels.

Those ventilation ports mentioned above also testify to an alternator's need for cooling air. That thing on the pulley that looks like a fan is, in fact, a fan. Often these fans have blades that are set to work in one direction only, and the direction of engine rotation must be considered. If you have a twin-engine boat, the engines may rotate in opposite directions to compensate for torque. The alternators on twin-engine boats may not be interchangeable without switching the pulleys and fans. Straight fan blades on an alternator usually indicate that the unit will cool rotating in either direction. If the blades

are offset, look for an arrow stamped on one of the blades that will show the direction of rotation, and always check the manufacturer's literature for exact installation instructions.

## Alternator Electrical Connections

The best bet for identifying the wires connected to your alternator is to use your engine's workshop manual and wiring diagram. If, after testing your alternator, you discover that it must be removed for overhaul or replacement, carefully mark all the wires with tape. Also mark the terminal identification on

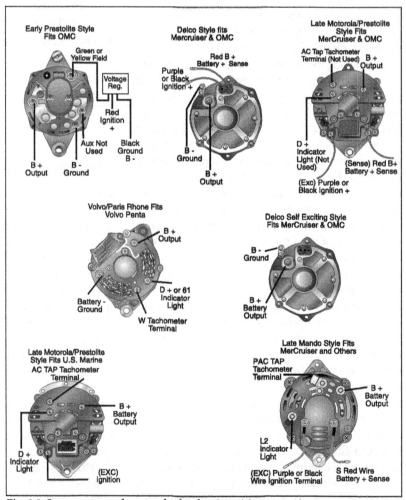

*Fig. 6-1. Seven common alternator backs, showing wiring connections.*

the back of the alternator to ensure that the wires go back where they should. Incorrectly reconnecting these wires will render the new alternator inoperative or burn it out. In the seven diagrams on page 88 in figure 6-1, alternators used by MerCruiser, OMC, Volvo Penta, and US Marine are shown with the terminals identified. You'll need your engine's service manual to match the wiring harness to these diagrams.

## Charging-System Symptoms

Regardless of the charging system used on your boat, the following symptoms usually indicate a problem:

1. Constant undercharging of the battery, indicated by poor battery performance.

2. Constant overcharging of the battery, indicated by having to add water, electrolyte accumulation on the top of the battery, or a rotten-egg odor in the area of the battery.

3. Abnormally high or low voltage or amperage readings from any meters installed in your system when the engine is running.

4. A noisy alternator.

5. A constant whirring noise from radios or a sudden reduction in signal strength with Loran-C receivers.

## Simple Checks

When you experience one of the above symptoms or when you otherwise suspect you have a charging-system problem, several preliminary checks should be made before you assume the worst and replace your alternator.

### Belt Tension and Replacement

First, check the belt that drives the alternator to see if it's too loose. Alternator drive belts, as shown in figure 6-2, should have no more than about ½ inch of deflection for each foot of span between pulleys. If the belt is loose, inspect it for excessive wear. Any fraying of the belt's edge, or cracks or grooving in the belt, indicates that it's time for a replacement.

When replacing an alternator belt, exactly match the new belt to the old one. Belt profile is just as important as the length of the belt. There are differ-

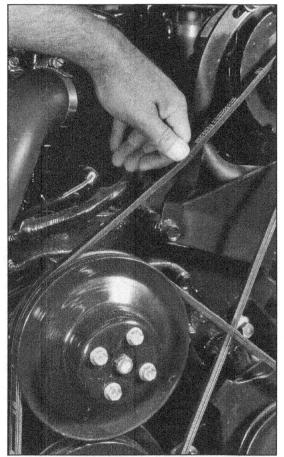

*Fig. 6-2. Checking belt deflection. This belt is adjusted just about right!*

ences in the V on various belts, as well as the actual belt width at the outer edge. These dimensions must be correct so that the belt makes a tight fit into the pulley V to minimize slipping and to ensure long belt life. Figure 6-3 on page 90 shows the correct pattern for a properly sized belt.

Make sure all the pulleys used by the alternator belt are aligned in the same plane. Any misalignment will rapidly wear away the belt and scatter black residue from the deteriorating belt all over the engine. Misalignment must be corrected to ensure long belt life. Align the pulleys by shimming the alternator mounts until all are in perfect alignment.

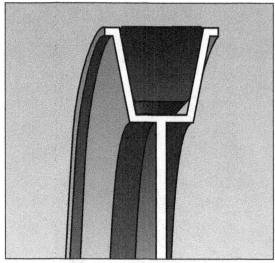

*Fig. 6-3. Proper belt profile in the pulley.*

To replace an alternator belt, loosen the bolts indicated by the arrows in figure 6-4. Pivot the alternator toward the engine, remove the old belt, and slide the new one in place. Adjust to the correct tension—not tighter. Belts that are overtightened will wear out the bearings that support the pulleys, such as those on the alternator and water pump. Adjust the belt to the correct tension as determined by measuring the deflection of the belt, then retighten the bolts. Recheck the belt tension after about 10 hours of engine operation, as the belt will have a tendency to wear and loosen. This is normal, but must be attended to. Newer boats are now coming through with "serpentine" belts (figure 6-5), familiar to the automotive world for several years now, and these promise to last much longer than the conventional V-belt. In addition, all of the systems using these belts have a self-adjusting mechanism built into the pulley system.

With these belt-drive systems, it is extremely important that all the belt-driven pulleys are in perfect fore-and-aft alignment. Any spacer shims used to adjust the fore-and-aft position (such as an alternator mount pivot bolt) must be reinstalled after any component in the system is removed and replaced. Misaligned pulleys will cause the belt to "walk" off them once the engine is running.

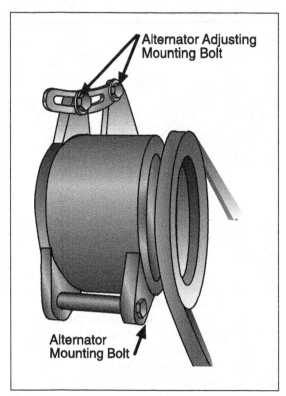

Alternator Adjusting
Mounting Bolt

Alternator
Mounting Bolt

*Fig. 6-4. Alternator mounting and adjustment bolts, typical locations.*

*Fig. 6-5. Serpentine belt.*

"GND" on the back of the alternator. Other times the alternator is grounded by an internal connection, so make sure all the mounting bolts are free from corrosion and tight. Also make sure that the engine's ground strap is secure.

The alternator is only grounded as well as the engine to which it's bolted. Clean and tighten the ground strap and mounting bolts as required, but disconnect the battery first. If you short out any of the terminals with your wrench, you may create more damage.

## Testing the Charging System

If, after making all the preliminary checks listed above, your problem still exists, it's time for some in-depth investigation. Start at the heart of your charging system, the battery. If the battery has failed, the best charging system in the world isn't going to fix it. So, the first step in checking out your charging system is to test the battery, as described in the last chapter. If the battery is up to snuff, you can test further to make sure your charging system is OK.

For any of the tests described here, the batteries should not be fully charged, because any charging system with a voltage regulator senses the battery charge and adjusts the charge rate to the charge needed. Since a charged battery doesn't need any more charge, the voltage regulator will tell the alternator not to put out any current; it's just not needed. All these tests require current from the alternator, and by discharging the battery a bit you ensure that there will be some.

To discharge the batteries, disable the ignition system or diesel-injection system and crank the engine for 10 or 15 seconds several times. Allow several minutes between intervals for the starter to cool off so you don't damage the starter motor.

Never disconnect or reverse any battery cables or alternator leads with the engine running; damage to the alternator diodes will occur instantly. When the battery is disconnected, the voltage regulator sees that the battery voltage has disappeared and tells the alternator to get to work. The alternator responds with full output that can instantly shoot up to several hundred amps, and those internal diodes will

*Fig. 6-6. Engine-mounted circuit breaker.*

## *Engine-Mounted Circuit Breakers*

While you're at it, check all the circuit breakers located on your engine. Each of these will have a little red button with a number like 10, 25, 30, 40, 50, etc. stamped on the end. Figure 6-6 shows a typical circuit-breaker installation. One or more of these circuit breakers might be associated with your charging system and might have to be reset. Just remember that when a circuit breaker of any type is tripped, there is always a reason for it, and further testing will determine the cause. Check the entire system for corroded battery terminals, loose connections on the alternator, and perhaps a corroded plug on the harness that connects the engine wiring to the rest of the boat's systems.

## *Engine Ground*

Make certain that the alternator is well grounded to the engine. The alternator is sometimes grounded with a short jumper lead from the alternator body to the engine. It will be connected to a terminal marked explode just like so many kernels of popcorn in a hot pan. Exactly the same thing happens when the battery cables are accidentally reversed. If you aren't planning on serving fried diodes for lunch, be very careful when connecting or disconnecting your battery cables.

### Three Step Voltage Test

Now you're ready to hook up your multimeter and do the three-step voltage test. This simple test is effective on systems that have built-in voltage regulators not serviceable by the owner.

Turn off all the accessories on your boat, set your multimeter to read voltage, and connect the probes across the battery terminals—red to positive (first) and black to negative. Make sure the battery master switch is turned to the battery on which you're working. Read and record the battery voltage. It should be around 12.5 volts if you adequately discharged the battery from full charge. This reading is called the *reference voltage*—write it down somewhere handy.

Next, start your engine and run it up to a normal mid-range operating rpm with all accessories turned off. Take and record your voltage at the battery. This is the *no-load voltage*—and it should be no more than 2 to 2.5 volts higher than the reference voltage. Write down the no-load voltage next to the reference voltage.

With the engine running at the same rpm you used to check the no-load voltage, turn on all your DC electrical accessories. Read your voltage at the battery. This is the *loaded voltage*, and it should be at least 0.5 volt above the reference voltage. Write it down with the others.

If the no-load voltage is no more than 2.5 volts higher than the reference voltage and the loaded voltage is at least 0.5 volt more than the reference voltage, your alternator and regulator are operating correctly.

If the no-load voltage is above the 2- to 2.5-volt limit, the battery is being overcharged and the voltage regulator is either defective or has a poor ground. On alternators with internal regulators, remove the alternator and get it overhauled. If your engine has an external regulator, use your ohmmeter to check for continuity between the regulator's ground terminal (marked GND) and a good ground on your engine.

If the voltage readings are below the limits de-

scribed here, you'll need to make one more check to ensure that the alternator is getting field current when the boat's ignition key is turned on. Use the diagrams in figure 6-1 on page 88 to identify the terminal on the back of the alternator marked by either an F, EXC, or IGN. This terminal, which is supplied ignition voltage (hence the possible "IGN" marking) is where the excitation (supply of voltage) is sent through to the field (F) windings wound around the alternator's rotor.

With your boat's ignition key turned on, there should be a voltage reading very close to the reference voltage at this terminal. If not, use your workshop manual to determine if the wire has a fuse in it, as it should. Replace the fuse if it's blown and recheck for voltage.

If you still have no voltage reading, you could have a faulty ignition switch or bad wiring. Further investigation will be needed, but the charging system problem you were originally checking out is in

*Fig. 6-7. Checking for field-excitation voltage at the alternator. Remember, the ignition key must be switched on when making this test. You should get a reading of approximately 12 volts. The meter red lead is connected to the F terminal and the black lead to a good ground, in this case, the GND terminal on this particular alternator. The key switch isn't on yet, but a reading of about 12 volts will show on the meter if all is well.*

all probability not with the alternator but with this wire. If you read battery voltage at the alternator, there is an internal problem with either the alternator or possibly the regulator. Either way, these units must be removed and sent to the specialty shop mentioned earlier.

Figure 6-7 shows the field excitation voltage being checked. Remember, the boat's ignition key must be in the "on" position when checking for field voltage.

## Charging Amperage Test

Voltage is not your only concern when you're checking alternator output. It's possible that your alternator amperage has diminished from its rating. Reduced amperage can be caused by a fault in the stator windings inside the alternator (a rare occurrence) or by a fault in one or more of the alternator's rectifier diodes. Unless your boat is equipped with an ammeter (and most are not), you'll need to test the charging amperage with your multimeter. The inductive multimeter, such as the one I discussed in chapter 3, is the easiest to use for this test.

Clamp the inductive pickup of the meter over the largest wire coming from the back of your alternator (the one on the terminal marked "B+") and take an amperage reading with the engine running at about 50 percent of normal rpm and with all your DC accessories turned on. As the alternator tries to keep up with this load, the ammeter should read very nearly the full output. If it doesn't read full alternator output, don't be alarmed, as the reading will vary depending upon the number and extent of the loads you turned on. If you're checking this system because your battery has gone dead, and the reading you get is much below about 35 to 40 percent of the alternator's rated output, there may be a problem, and further testing is called for. Figure 6-8 shows the amperage test.

Two additional tests, the ripple-voltage test and the draw test, are needed to confirm if an alternator problem exists or not. You can do one with your multimeter; the other will require a special LED test tool.

## Ripple-Voltage Test

Think of ripple voltage as a tiny amount of alternating current that has escaped past the bridge rectifier and has imposed itself on the direct current charging your battery. A small amount of ripple current is normal, but if you find a significant amount it indicates a problem with one or more or the alternator diodes.

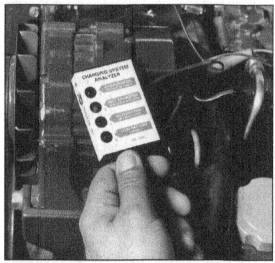

*Fig. 6-8. Using an inductive ammeter to check alternator output. When checking amperage output in this fashion, turn on all your DC accessories and see if the alternator can keep up to the demand.*

*Fig. 6-9. LED charging system tester, connected. Simple, two-wire connection; simply follow the instructions on the tester. Actron makes a similar tool for about $25.*

*Fig. 6-10. AC ripple-voltage test. Your black meter lead should be connected to a known good ground and the red lead to the B+ (output) lead on the back of your alternator. Remember to make sure that your meter is set to the AC volt scale.*

If you have one of the LED testers shown in figure 6-9, alternator testing is a one-step procedure. The tester has red and black leads and probes just like your multimeter. Attach the red probe to the B+ terminal at the back of the alternator and the black probe to a nearby ground (one of the alternator mounting bolts will do), and start the engine. Observe the LEDs on the meter. Any lights flashing or constantly lit indicate a problem with either the alternator or the voltage regulator (assuming the alternator is getting excitation voltage as described earlier). Follow the instructions printed on the tester to determine what course of action is required. Figure 6-9 shows the LED tester connected and ready to check a charging system. If you're not sure which terminal is B+ on your alternator, refer to figure 6-1.

If you don't have the tester, you can do an alternating-current ripple test using your multimeter, as shown in figure 6-10. Connect your meter leads to the battery with the red probe to the positive post and the black probe to the negative post, and set it to the AC volt scale. Run the engine up to a fast idle, switch the meter to the alternating-current volt scale, and check the reading. You should have no more than 0.250 volt AC at the battery. If the reading you get is greater than that, the diodes in your alternator are defective and the alternator must be serviced.

### Draw Test

The last test I will mention is the draw test. Particularly in the marine environment, it's possible to get electrical crossovers from a hot wire to a nearby ground, causing a voltage leak that can drain your battery. Testing for crossover current is fairly simple, but a few precautions need to be mentioned.

You're looking for a constant electrical draw on your battery. Make sure all the electrical accessories on your boat are turned off and the engine is not running. Make sure you have disconnected everything including any radios and stereos with memories and clocks that bypass the switches. Next, disconnect the positive terminal at the battery. Set your multimeter to read amps and connect it in series with the terminal end of the battery cable and the positive post on the battery. A reading of any significant amperage (over 0.01 amp) indicates something on board is draining your battery.

Now you must locate which circuit is the culprit. If your boat has fuses, isolate each circuit by removing the circuit fuses one at a time and checking to see if the amperage reading is eliminated or reduced. If you have circuit breakers, carefully turn off the breaker switches one at a time until the amperage reading disappears or decreases to practically nothing. Once you have located the circuit that's causing the battery to be discharged, you should be able to troubleshoot the circuit just as I described above.

## Outboard-Engine Charging Systems

Outboard-engine charging systems come in two varieties: with or without voltage regulators. The unregulated systems have an alternator built into the top of the engine that puts out constant amperage of 5 or 6 amps (or more on newer, bigger engines) any time the engine is running. Regulated systems use a voltage regulator that's similar to the one we discussed above. However, there are enough important differences to warrant a closer look.

## Unregulated Systems

Smaller outboards from 6 to 10 horsepower usually do not have a voltage regulator. The charging systems on these small engines generally produce between 4 and 6 amps of current at maximum output. The problem is that even this small amount of current can be too much if the battery is charged and you aren't using any electrical equipment. This constant charge creates a built-in overcharge that will boil away battery electrolyte. If you have one of these small motors, it's critical for normal battery life that you check and top up the electrolyte frequently. You should never use anything but a wet-cell battery on these motors.

This nonregulated system consists of four major components plus the wiring that connects them all. On the top of the engine there are permanent magnets attached to the inside of the flywheel and a series of stator windings. When the engine is running, the permanent magnets spin very close to the stator windings and produce alternating current via magnetic inductance, just as it's produced in the inboard alternator discussed above. This alternating current is converted into direct current that can be used to charge the battery by passing it through a diode rectifier that's slightly different than a bridge rectifier.

This rectifier is not contained in the same housing as the alternator, as are the ones found on inboard alternators. It's really nothing more than a group of diodes mounted in a heat sink that's bolted to the engine block. The heat sink provides a ground and helps conduct the heat away from the diodes. Some makers of outboards also install a fuse in the circuit, so check your owner's manual.

The last component in this basic system is the battery.

A common question regarding unregulated systems is whether they can be run without connecting the motor to a battery, without damaging the stator-rectifier. The answer is that it depends. Some motors can be run without batteries, and some can't. Follow the recommendations in your owner's manual. Some manufacturers provide caps to cover the

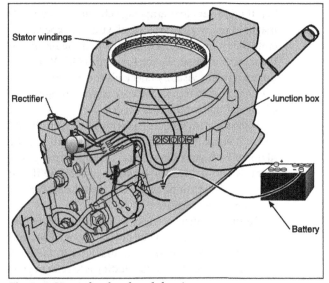

Fig. 6-11. Unregulated outboard charging system.

battery-cable terminals to prevent them from touching while the engine is running without a battery. However, some companies, Mercury for example, also recommend disconnecting the stator wires from the rectifier and insulating them from each other if you're going to use their motors without a battery.

Figure 6-11 illustrates a typical unregulated outboard charging system.

### Testing the Unregulated System

From years of experience, I can tell you that the boatowner causes 99 percent of the problems that occur with these unregulated charging systems. Rarely is there any trouble with the permanent magnets or the stator windings under the flywheel. Problems are almost always due to corroded or loose connections or to a failed rectifier. As I've mentioned before, diodes are very sensitive; they hate it when battery wires are crossed or grounded unexpectedly.

So, how do we verify the system is producing charging voltage? It's easy if you have one of the inductive ammeters described earlier: Simply clamp the meter over the positive battery cable with the engine running and rev the engine (don't over-rev it). Most inductive meters work on a 100-amp scale, so don't expect to see much needle movement. Remem-

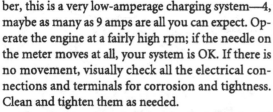

ber, this is a very low-amperage charging system—4, maybe as many as 9 amps are all you can expect. Operate the engine at a fairly high rpm; if the needle on the meter moves at all, your system is OK. If there is no movement, visually check all the electrical connections and terminals for corrosion and tightness. Clean and tighten them as needed.

If your system is equipped with a fuse, you should check it visually or test for continuity through the filament with your ohmmeter. Check your engine's owner's manual for the location of the fuse if you have one. If everything seems OK then the problem is probably in the rectifier.

Testing rectifiers is tricky without the wiring diagram for your engine. They don't all look alike, and the wiring varies from one manufacturer to the next. The best approach for rectifier testing is to refer to your engine's service manual. All you'll need for equipment is your multimeter set to the diode-test scale.

If you test the rectifier and determine that it's OK, you must next test the stator. These are all different, so work from your engine's manual, and if you're uncertain of the procedure, consult your local dealer.

## Regulated Outboard Systems

Larger outboard engines (and, on the newest units, even the smaller ones) have voltage regulators installed into the circuitry. Sometimes these are combination regulator-rectifiers like you might find on an inboard system. If a component is going to fail in the system, it will most likely be this regulator-rectifier. The three-step voltage test described on pages 92–93 will work on these systems just like on inboard systems. It's best to use your engine manual for the tests necessary to isolate charging system problems in the regulator.

# Shore-Power Battery Charging Systems and Installations

Permanently installed battery chargers connected to your boat's shore-power system fall into one of two general categories. The most common is the *ferro-resonant constant-output charger*. The other is known generically as a *smart charger* or *three-step charger*.

Many of the smart chargers available today also have a fourth stage known as an *equalization stage* and are thus *four-step chargers*. (More on that later.) A third popular type of battery charger is really a combined device known as an *inverter-charger* that not only converts 12-volt direct current into 120-volt alternating current, but also incorporates a quality multistage battery charger into one handy and compact unit.

As you'll see in the following descriptions, the differences between the basic types of battery chargers are significant.

## Ferro-Resonant Battery Chargers

Ferro-resonant battery chargers are deceptively simple devices, nothing more than a simple transformer (a ferro-resonant transformer) that converts 120-volt alternating current into 12-volt alternating current and a rectifier that converts the alternating current into direct current. The basic units, the simple household battery chargers sold at the auto parts store, work just fine for getting the car started on a cold morning or for a quick charge on a dead battery, but they have no place on your boat.

Ferro-resonant chargers designed for use on boats are a little more complex than the basic units. They incorporate some elaborate circuitry that will gradually taper the charging current to roughly match the demands of your battery. The better ferro-resonant chargers work fine on wet-cell batteries, but even the best don't do a very good job with the new gel-cell and AGM batteries. In fact, many of the problems associated with premature battery failure, such as a rotten-egg odor and boiling of battery electrolyte (the result of constant overcharging), are often caused by the use of the ferro-resonant chargers. Unfortunately, some of the largest producers of powerboats, such as Bayliner and Sea Ray, still install ferro-resonant chargers in their boats because they are considerably less expensive than newer smart chargers.

To determine which type of battery charger you have, you'll need to find the charger itself. It will be mounted somewhere near the batteries. If you don't see things like a battery-type selector switch or a temperature-compensation calibration switch somewhere on the charger, you probably have the ferro-resonant type and should seriously consider an upgrade to a smart charger.

If you do have a ferro-resonant charger on your boat, make sure that none of your batteries are gel-cells or AGMs. You must be able to check your battery electrolyte level regularly if you have a constant-rate charger. The tendency, particularly for people who plug into shore power and use their boats infrequently, is to overcharge the batteries and boil out the electrolyte. One trick used by many boatowners who have this type of charger is to leave on a DC-powered cabin light or two, even when they are away from the boat. This light puts a small drain on the batteries, minimizing the overcharging effect.

If you have a constant-rate charger, you should check all the cells in your batteries every two weeks or so and top them up with distilled water as needed. Batteries that run low on electrolyte will burn up in short order. Figure 6-12 shows a typical constant-rate charger.

## Smart Chargers

The newest wave of electronic battery chargers, generically called smart chargers, is a by-product of power-supply technology for computers. Smart chargers are small, reliable, and highly efficient. They are also extremely complex as compared to the simple ferro-resonant chargers, and I won't even begin to describe their circuitry. Suffice it to say that they charge your batteries in precise *steps*, or phases, that are highly beneficial to the longevity of your batteries. More important, these steps are adjustable to accommodate the type of battery you have, making them the only choice if you have gel-cell or AGM batteries.

These new smart chargers are produced by a number of manufacturers and have really gone a long way toward maximizing the potential for the newest battery technologies, both gelled and AGMs. However, don't for a minute assume that a smart charger will be a waste of money if you have standard wet-cell batteries. All batteries will benefit from using a smart charger. These chargers are available in a variety of configurations for single-, dual-, and three-battery-bank installations and have amperage ranges from

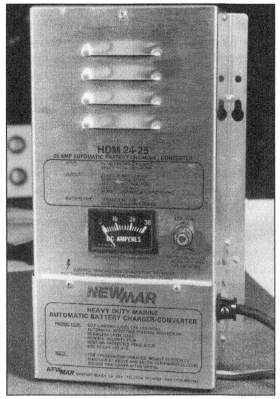

Fig. 6-12. A ferro-resonant charger. These constant-rate chargers have destroyed many a battery!

as few as 8 amps to as many as 130 amps for the largest inverter-charger combinations.

### Phases of Battery Charging

Unlike the ferro-resonant chargers that gradually reduce the charge rate along a rather steadily sloping curve as a battery comes up to charge, smart chargers use three and sometimes four distinct phases for revitalizing your batteries.

1. **The bulk phase.** The first phase of the battery-charging cycle is known as the *bulk phase*. This is where most of the charging occurs. A discharged battery can accept a higher rate of charge, up to about 70 to 75 percent of the total charge, in the initial stages of charging than it can in the final stages. Typical charge rates during the bulk phase are 20 to 40

percent of the battery's capacity in amperes with a voltage of about 14.4 volts. Gel-cells will charge at about 14.1 volts. When the battery is 75 percent charged, the smart charger automatically switches to the acceptance phase of the charge cycle.

2. **The acceptance phase.** The second phase of the battery-charging cycle is known as the *acceptance* or *absorption phase*. During this phase the voltage is maintained at 14.4 volts for wet-cell and AGM batteries and at 14.1 volts for a gel-cell. The charging amperage is gradually reduced until a rate of 4 percent of the battery's capacity is achieved. Thus the acceptance phase for a 100-amp-hour battery ends when the charging amperage the battery will accept reduces to 4 amps. The smart charger automatically switches to the float phase.

3. **The float phase.** The final phase of a normal charging cycle is known as the *float* or *finish phase*, during which the smart charger reduces the voltage to 13.3 volts for wet-cells and AGMs and 13.7 volts for gel-cells. Gelled electrolyte batteries typically have a slightly higher fully charged open-circuit voltage than their wet-cell brothers do.

The float phase is more maintenance than an actual charge because it keeps the battery at a full charge without overcharging. This is the big difference between the smart chargers and the ferro-resonant units described earlier.

4. **The equalization phase.** The fourth phase of battery charging I want to discuss is really another maintenance phase and is only used on wet-cell batteries. In fact, use of the equalization phase is quite damaging to gel-cells and a waste of time on AGM batteries.

The equalization phase takes care of minor irregularities in specific gravity between cells that develop as a battery ages. As your battery gets older, the chemical reactions inside the individual cells can vary slightly with variations in the chemicals in the water you've added to the cells and with minor variations in the manufacturing tolerances of the battery. Lead-sulfate particles will

eventually begin to cling to and build up on your battery's cell plates. As this buildup continues, less and less of the battery's cell-plate area is exposed to the electrolyte and the cell's capacity is effectively reduced.

The equalization phase minimizes this premature buildup of lead sulfate by charging the battery at amperage equal to 4 percent of capacity until the voltage reaches somewhere between 15.5 and 16.2 volts. This controlled overcharge literally rattles the sulfate particles out of the battery plate, forcing them back into the electrolyte where they belong.

The danger with using the equalization phase is that you can do it too often. In some industrial applications, equalization is used as a part of every charge cycle because maximum battery "punch" is required. This is simply not the case on a powerboat, and you should equalize your batteries no more than three or four times per boating season.

Not all smart chargers offer an equalization phase. On those that do, it's not automatic and must be selected manually.

## Temperature Compensation

All of the smart chargers I have worked with have some form of temperature compensation built in to help the brain of the charger determine the proper charge rates. Three common arrangements are available. One method requires the installer to select a temperature setting from a selector switch mounted on the charger housing. Another uses automatic temperature compensation with a built-in temperature sensor on the charger. I feel that these two methods, although certainly offering a technological quantum leap from the ferro-resonant chargers, are still a bit lacking. The best sensing for temperature compensation can only be made at the battery itself. The temperature of the battery will change dramatically as it charges, whereas the temperature surrounding the charger itself may not if it's mounted as it should be in a well-ventilated location.

The best chargers today use the third type of temperature compensation: a temperature sensor that's mounted to either the side of the battery or inside the battery box. Always look for this feature when you upgrade your battery charger.

## Testing Battery Chargers

Testing your shore-powered battery charger to determine if it's functioning is easy. With the charger turned off, do an open-circuit voltage test (as described in chapter 5) at the battery the charger is connected to. Turn the charger on and observe your voltage reading at the battery. If the charger is functioning, you'll get a reading of at least 0.5 volt greater than the open-circuit voltage. If it's not working properly, the charger may have a blown fuse. The fuse is usually accessible on the outside case of the charger and is easily changed.

One charger I've worked with, however (made by Statpower), locates the fuse inside the charger housing, necessitating partial disassembly of the unit to check the fuse. Check the manual for the charger on your boat to determine the exact location of the fuse.

If the fuse checks out, you may have a problem with the shore-power side of the circuit supplying the charger. Remember: Alternating current can kill you! Before starting to troubleshoot the battery-charger circuit, be sure to read chapter 11 of this book, and if you have any doubts about your ability, call in a professional marine electrician to help.

Figure 6-13 shows a state-of-the-art Xantrex multiphase smart charger. It also has a manual gel-cell,

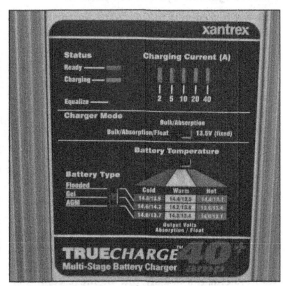

*Fig. 6-13. Xantrex 40 amp charger.*

wet-cell, or AGM selection switch, a battery-mounted temperature sensor, and switching parameters for different phases.

## Solar Cells

Solar panels are increasingly being used on some cruising powerboats to supplement other onboard charging systems. The silent energy that solar panel arrays provide is quite appealing to many boaters, and once installed, solar panels are virtually maintenance free. For boats that spend a lot of time at anchor away from the dock, and not much time underway, the 50 to 80 watts that medium-sized panels provide can be the difference between keeping the batteries charged up or running them down over time.

There are several important points to remember about solar panels. First, they do get hot sitting in the sun. If they get too hot, their output will actually decrease. Several years ago, when I was testing solar panels for *Cruising World,* I discovered that at noon on a July day at 42° latitude, the panels were being heated to 120°F, at which point their output began to diminish. So when mounting panels on flat surfaces, you must raise them above the surface to allow air to circulate on both sides of the panels.

Since a solar panel will allow a battery to discharge through the panel when the panel is not exposed to the sun, all panels must have a blocking diode in the positive feed from the charger to the battery. The diode lets current flow from the panel to the battery but blocks current flow from the battery back through the panel. On most panels, the diode is in a small box mounted at the output terminals on the back of the panel.

Finally, no panel should be installed without a charge controller—a fancy term for a voltage regulator—since the 15 to 20 volts a solar panel can produce is too much for sealed, gel-cell, or AGM batteries. Some charge controllers have internal blocking diodes, however, and you don't want redundant blocking diodes since in marginal light situations the panel output could be reduced to a useless value (remember, diodes have an inherent 0.7 voltage drop through them). You can bypass or eliminate the blocking diode on the panel if the charge controller has an internal blocking diode.

# Chapter 7

# Maintaining Marine Ignition Systems

## Ignition-System Components

When people think of their boat's electrical system and its parts, they generally don't think of the engine ignition system as being a part of it. Well, if your engine suddenly quits one day and you find that the fuel system is OK, then the most probable cause for the shutdown will be a faulty ignition system, and you'll definitely be working with electrical components to correct the problem.

If your boat has a diesel engine, it neither has nor needs an ignition system, and you can skip this chapter, reveling in the luxury of never being troubled by overgapped spark plugs, out-of-control control modules, or miswired ignition wires. However, if you own a small to medium-sized powerboat, the chances are very good that it's powered by a gasoline engine replete with a complex assortment of ignition-system parts. All gasoline engines need an ignition system to light the sparks that fire the cylinders that turn the crank that spins the prop that gets us over the water to where we want to go.

Inboard gasoline-engine ignition systems all work on the same simple principles. When you turn your starter switch, the ignition-control module or CDI unit senses your desire to start the engine. Electrical energy is drawn from a battery (usually) and sent to a coil where it's transformed from a low voltage to a very high voltage. From the coil, this high voltage is sent via heavy ignition wires to the distributor where it's directed through the distributor cap and additional ignition wires to the individual spark plugs. Inside the spark plug the voltage comes to a dead end where in a fit of intense frustration it leaps across a precisely calibrated air space, creating the spark that ignites the fuel vapors in a cylinder of the engine. If several hundred other engine parts are all doing their thing at precisely the right time, you're on your way. If not, it's time to break out the oars or look for a

tow. Fortunately, such malfunctions are unusual because the modern ignition system is about as dependable as electromechanical contrivances can get. But they do, on occasion, fail, and when they do, you'll want to be able to identify and deal with the problem. That's what this chapter is about.

To maintain and troubleshoot your ignition system, you need a basic understanding of how it works. Most people I talk with about marine electrical systems begin with the feeling that they really know what's going on with their ignition system. Then I probe a little and find that in most cases they know just enough to be dangerous. Quite often when there is an ignition-system failure, all the "experts" on the dock come up with some interesting suggestions for this or that. All of this free advice, in my experience, adds up to the boatowner replacing perfectly good parts. Knowing how your system works will go a long way toward eliminating this problem.

## Inboard Ignition-System Components

The key ingredients in the recipe for this witch's brew of electronic and electrical apparatus that makes up your ignition system are as follows: one battery, one control module, one distributor (with cap), several yards of ignition wire, and one spark plug for each engine cylinder. Let's take a brief but close look at these ingredients one at a time. I will have a lot more to say about all of these items later in the chapter. Right now I just want you to know what they do.

### Ignition-Control Module

The ignition-control module (called the *capacitive-discharge ignition,* or *CDI unit,* on PWCs and outboard engines; we'll look at this in more detail later in the chapter) is the little black box that coordinates and controls all the various functions of the ignition system. It's usually one or more computer chips, and when it malfunctions there is nothing to do but replace it with a new one. There are many different designs of these modules, and no two engine builders use just the same one.

To be useful in an ignition system, the high voltage produced in the secondary coil windings needs to be continuously turned on and off as the engine runs. This ensures that each cylinder gets spark at exactly the right time. With early ignition systems, before ignition-control modules, breaker points acted as the switch for the primary voltage. On today's engines the ignition-control module does the switching, and it may have several other functions as well, depending on the manufacturer.

## Ignition Coil

The ignition coil uses the principle of magnetic induction to transform 12-volt battery voltage to the 25,000 to 50,000 volts needed at the spark plugs. The ignition coil is nothing more than an electrical transformer, a miniaturized version of the transformers you see hanging from utility poles all over the world. Transformers use two coils wound around opposite sides of a doughnut-shaped iron core. Running 12-volt battery power through the first coil, called the *primary*, or *low-voltage side*, induces up to 50,000 volts of power in the second coil, called the *secondary*, or *high-voltage side*. As you already know from your previous reading, all wires that have electrical current flowing through them are surrounded by a magnetic field.

The higher the current, the stronger the magnetism. If a very long, thin wire is coiled around a metallic core, the strength of the magnetism is increased. If a magnet is moved close to a coil of wire, electrical current is induced in that coil of wire, just as with the alternator field windings discussed in chapter 6. By increasing the number of windings in the coil, we increase the amount of voltage. Conversely, if we reduce the number of windings, we reduce the voltage. This induced voltage is how step-up and step-down transformers work. An ignition coil is really a step-up transformer.

The primary side of the coil has a series of windings that conduct battery voltage. The magnetic field

that's created around the primary coil engulfs secondary windings inside your coil. Because there are a great many more windings in the secondary side of the coil than there are in the primary side, the voltage that's induced by the magnetic field is stepped up to the high level needed by the spark plugs. By altering the number and ratio of windings in the primary and secondary sides of the coil, engineers determine the exact voltage we will get from the secondary side of the coil.

## Distributor

When the very high secondary voltage leaves the coil, it goes to the distributor where it's directed by the rotor inside to the correct cylinder at exactly the right moment to fire each spark plug. The rotor rotates inside the distributor cap and directs secondary voltage into the correct ignition wire and ultimately to

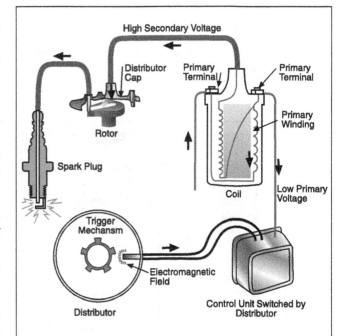

*Fig. 7-1a. Current flow through a typical electronic ignition system. In this diagram the thicker lines indicate secondary high-voltage conductors. Primary voltage is equivalent to battery voltage and is indicated by the arrows, which also show the direction of flow at the point indicated.*

the spark plug for the cylinder that needs to be "lit off" at that time.

Figure 7-1a on page 101 illustrates the flow of current through a typical electronic ignition system, showing both the primary and secondary sides of the circuit.

### Distributorless Ignition

Ignition systems on gas inboard engines have evolved to a system that eliminates the distributor entirely. These systems, which are widely used in automotive applications, have been adopted by MerCruiser, Crusader, and others and are becoming the norm. Distributorless ignition systems (DIS) offer some distinct advantages, particularly the elimination of the distributor, cap, and rotor, parts that require periodic maintenance and inspection. A short list of the advantages of a DIS is:

► No timing adjustments are needed; it's done automatically via the engine computer.

► No moving parts to wear.

► No distributor to accumulate moisture and cause starting problems.

DIS also allow more precise timing and spark control over the full spectrum of engine rpm, all controlled by a mini-computer. The primary components of this system are:

► Engine control module (computer).

► The ignition module, which is interfaced with the engine module.

► A magnetic sensor, or triggering device, that is keyed to either the engine flywheel or the engine camshaft to sense piston position in the cylinders.

► High-tension coils to supply secondary level high voltage to the spark plugs.

A DIS may have one coil per cylinder, or one coil for a pair of cylinders. On paired systems, each end of the secondary windings of the ignition coil will be connected to a spark plug as shown in Figure 7-1b. These ends are connected to cylinders that are opposite in the engine's firing order, but both at top dead center (TDC) simultaneously. One plug will fire on the compression stroke and the other will fire simultaneously on the opposing cylinder's exhaust stroke, referred to

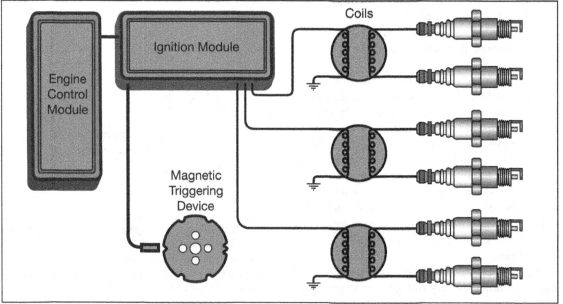

*Fig. 7-1b. A paired cylinder DIS.*

as "wasted" spark. It doesn't really hurt anything, but it reduces the number of components required.

Employ the basic maintenance considerations as for any ignition system. Keep coil towers and plug wires clean and free from any oily film that can attract dust and then moisture droplets (which will ultimately cause high-voltage arcing and insulation damage on the wiring and coil cases). If a problem does occur with one of the electronic components, specialized scan tools are required to properly diagnose computer and ignition modules.

To date, I've only had to replace the spark plug wires about every 750 to 1,000 hours of engine run time. Spark plugs last almost indefinitely with these systems but it's best to remove the plugs seasonally for inspection and to apply a light coat of antiseizing compound to the threads. If you wait until the plugs actually wear out, you may find that they've rusted themselves in place, making removal almost impossible.

### Ignition Wires
While the voltage coming from the secondary side of the coil is very high (up to 50,000 volts), the amperage is comparatively low. This means that the wires that transmit this current from the center tower of the coil through the distributor and on to the spark plugs must be of a very high quality and contain a very low resistance. Cheap or deteriorated ignition wires are one of the primary causes of ignition-system failure. They can also cause maddening radio interference and a host of problems with other sensitive electrical equipment, not only on your boat but on the boat in the next slip as well. It really pays to keep a sharp eye on your ignition wires. When they start to look deteriorated, they are deteriorated. Replace them.

### Spark Plugs
The last and one of the most important parts of the ignition system is the spark plug. It's the spark plugs that deliver the sparks to the cylinders, and those sparks are the focus of the entire system. Spark plugs come in a bewildering variety of types and sizes.

Fortunately, your job as a boatowner is fairly simple. The engine manufacturer will have precise specifications on spark plugs, so all you have to do is keep the plugs clean and properly gapped and replace

them when (or before) it becomes necessary. I'll discuss changing plugs later on.

## Regulations Regarding Ignition Systems

I need to make several important points before continuing much farther into this chapter. Most of the ignition systems in use today employ solid-state devices for control. In some cases the best approach to troubleshooting will be to consult this book along with the workshop manual for your engine. You may find that the only way to be certain of a diagnosis is to try a new component. At that point it's time to call in a pro, unless you're quite experienced and have full confidence in your mechanical ability. When that's the best bet, I'll point it out in the text.

At the very least, after reading this chapter, you'll be able to perform all routine maintenance on your boat's ignition system. When you do need to call a mechanic, you'll be able to intelligently talk about your problem. Ignition-system components used on boats fall under the jurisdiction of the U.S. Coast Guard and must be manufactured in accordance with their regulations. Use of ignition parts that do not comply with these rules and regulations could result in a fire or explosion. Don't even think about cheating on this by buying less-expensive automotive replacement parts. These may look the same as the marine-grade parts; they are not.

The USCG mandates that ignition-protection requirements be met in the Code of Federal Regulations (CFR), so this is not a mere recommendation but law. The bottom line on ignition service is that no shortcuts are allowed. Follow the advice in this chapter, and you'll be way ahead of the game.

## Outboard and PWC Ignition Systems

Unlike those on inboard engines, most outboard and PWC ignition systems don't use battery power to feed the primary side of the ignition circuit. With these systems, voltage required for the primary side of the circuit is generated under the engine's flywheel, using the same principle of magnetic induction already discussed in chapters 3 and 6. The essential difference is that these systems use a series of permanent magnets located around the inside perimeter of the underside of the flywheel.

As the engine rotates, these magnets move past carefully placed coils of wire mounted on a timing plate, which is also located under the flywheel. You guessed it: voltage is produced by induction in these coils. One coil acts to produce the primary voltage, which initially is much greater than with inboard systems. Typical primary voltage is around 175 to 300 volts alternating current. The coil producing this voltage is generally known as the *charge coil*, and it sends its current directly to the system's ignition module where it is converted to direct current via a rectifier circuit built into the ignition module. Once converted, the current is stored in a capacitor (an electrical device designed to temporarily store an electrical charge), which is also built into the ignition module, for later delivery to the ignition coil feeding a given cylinder. Unlike most inboard systems, outboard engines use an individual coil for each cylinder.

The second coil, also found under the engine's flywheel, is known as the *sensor, trigger,* or *pulsar coil,* depending upon the engine manufacturer (we will use trigger coil). This coil sends a much smaller voltage, typically from 1 to 9 volts, to the same ignition module as the charge coil where it triggers a transistor (a silicon-controlled rectifier, or SCR) matched to a cylinder. Once the SCR gets its cue, it triggers the capacitor to release its stored charge and sends it to the primary side of the ignition coil for the cylinder that needs to be fired. A much higher voltage is sent to the primary side in outboards and PWCs than is sent in the inboard-engine systems. The output of the secondary side of any ignition coil is proportional to the input on the primary side. By sending a much higher voltage into the primary side of the coil, we get the same high output from a physically smaller package than on inboard motors; this saves valuable space under the outboard-engine cowl. These systems are generally referred to as *capacitive-discharge ignition (CDI) systems,* and we will take a closer look at them later in this chapter.

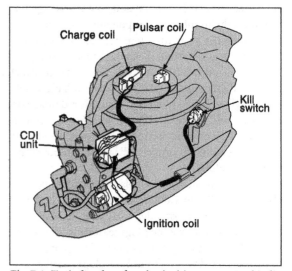

*Fig. 7-2. Typical outboard engine ignition system. In this diagram, the key components of a typical outboard-engine capacitive-discharge ignition (CDI) system are noted, with their typical location shown.*

Figure 7-2 shows the layout of a typical outboard engine CD ignition system. Figure 7-3 on page 104 illustrates a typical PWC installation of this same type.

## Maintaining Ignition Systems

Maintaining your boat's ignition system is an easy task requiring just a little care and tidiness. The biggest enemies to your ignition system are the same as those for any other part of your boat's electrical system. It's just that the consequence of improper maintenance is more obvious in the ignition system because of the extremely high voltage found on the secondary side of the system.

### Corrosion Protection

All wiring connections and terminals need to be protected against corrosion. On modern systems, sealed *Deutsch plugs* are the norm today, and they work exceptionally well, requiring no maintenance. Their three-ribbed silicone-rubber sealing rings effectively keep all moisture away from the electrical contacts inside the assembly. Other systems using

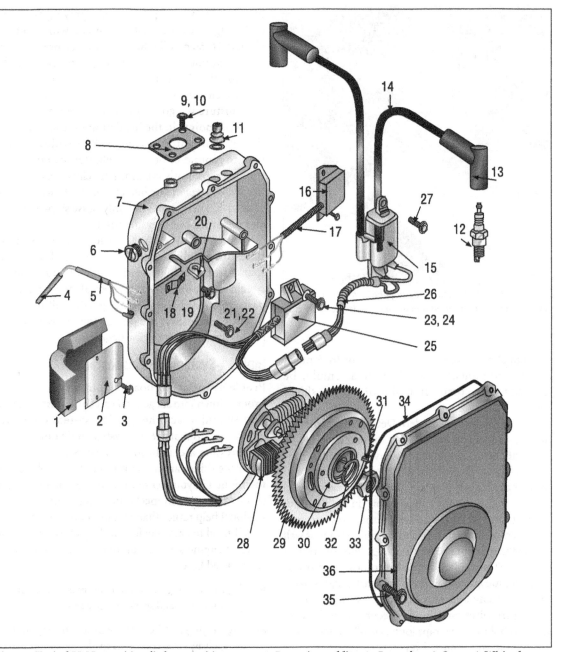

*Fig. 7-3. Typical PWC capacitive-discharge ignition system: 1. Protective padding. 2. Cover plate. 3. Screw. 4. Wiring harness. 5. Hose guard. 6. Access plug. 7. Ignition system housing. 8. Bracket. 9. Lock washer. 10. Bolt. 11. Cap. 12. Spark plug. 13. Cap. 14. Cables. 15. Ignition coil. 16. RPM Limiter. 17. Screw. 18. Wiring hold-down. 19. Screw. 20. Grommet. 21. Lock washer. 22. Bolt. 23. Washer. 24. Screw. 25. CDI unit. 26. Harness sheathing. 27. Screw. 28. Stator plate. 29. Flywheel ring-gear. 30. Flywheel. 31. Woodruff key. 32. Lock washer. 33. Nut. 34. O-ring cover seal. 35. Screw. 36. Outer cover.*

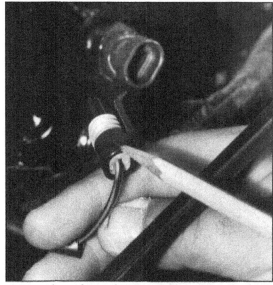

Fig. 7-4. Photo of Deutsch-type gang plug. These offer the best waterproof connections and are now widely used by engine makers.

traditional ring-eye terminals and studs to connect circuit components should, after assembly, be sprayed with a corrosion inhibitor like Boeshield T-9.

Figure 7-4 shows a modern Deutsch plug with the silicone-rubber sealing rings that make these plugs an excellent choice for the marine environment.

Apply a coating of dielectric grease to the metal surfaces of all spark-plug wires before they are plugged in. Also, make sure the rubber boots on both ends of the plug wires are supple and are pushed down around the towers on ignition coils and distributor caps as well as over the spark plugs. Any heat-hardened or cracked boots must be replaced. The biggest cause of problems with the ignition wires to the spark plugs is damage from chafe and exposure to exhaust-manifold heat. These wires must be kept secure in the factory-supplied hold-down straps found on all engines. Failure to do so will almost always result in problems like engine misfiring and skipping.

## System Cleanliness

Probably the biggest cause of ignition-system failure on any engine is the accumulation of dirt and oil

film. Contrary to popular belief, spraying down the coil, plug wires, and distributor cap with products like CRC 6-56 or WD-40 to seal them from moisture is, in fact, one of the worst things you can do. The oily film they leave behind is a magnet for dust and dirt, which attract moisture and condensation.

Moisture is a good conductor of electricity, and any weak points in the insulation on the secondary side of your ignition system will provide a natural path to ground or between cylinder towers on distributor caps. Both situations are classic examples of the *short-to-ground* or *intercircuit shorts* described in chapter 1. These shorts not only cause skips, sputters, and misfiring, but they are unsafe.

Remember! We want ignition protection at all times on gasoline-powered boats, and any stray sparks from the high-tension side of your ignition system clearly preclude that. Keep all of your ignition parts clean and free from any oily buildup at all times. If necessary, use one of the many products readily available for engine degreasing.

## Ignition-System Troubleshooting

Problems with your boat's ignition system can be broken down into six general categories, listed below. You should attack the ignition system only after you're certain that the fuel system and your engine's compression are up to snuff; the procedures for doing those things are not covered in this book but are mentioned in your service manual. If you don't have some experience in mechanics, you should get professional help rather than troubleshoot on your own. You'll need to carefully follow the procedures found in your engine's workshop manual for some of the items listed here.

► *Engine runs sluggishly and overheats.* Check the ignition timing and spark-advance system.

► *Engine pings.* Check the ignition timing and spark advance. Make sure the spark plugs are of the recommended type.

► *Engine is hard to start.* Check for spark at the plugs and the spark plugs themselves. Check the ignition-bypass circuit, the battery and associated wiring, and the distributor cap. Figures 7-12 and

7-13 on page 113 show my favorite spark tester in use, but more on that later.

▶ *Engine misfires.* Check the spark plugs and leads, rotor and distributor cap, and ignition coil for loose connections at the coil and ignition switch. Also check the engine firing order, plug wire routing, and the engine timing.

▶ *Engine fires when cranked but stops when key is released.* Check the ignition switch and related wiring.

▶ *Engine cranks but doesn't start.* Check for spark at the plugs; check the coil and bypass circuit to the coil positive terminal; and check the wiring. Also check the engine timing and plug wire routing, and the tachometer and related wiring.

Some of the items mentioned here, such as engine timing and tachometer wiring, have not yet been discussed, but I will cover them in the following sections. This list is a guide for inboard and inboard/outboard (IO) engines only. Use it for sorting out your thoughts as you approach a problem. You must work with the specific information for your ignition system if you expect to be successful as an ignition-system diagnostician.

I will discuss two of the most common inboard engine electronic ignition systems, the MerCruiser Thunderbolt IV and Thunderbolt V. Other widely used systems with similar design and features are made by Prestolite and Delco. Use this chapter as a primer on electronic systems in general, and refer to the workshop manuals for the specific information you need to troubleshoot these other systems.

# MerCruiser Thunderbolt IV and Thunderbolt V Systems

With about 75 to 80 percent of the market at this writing, MerCruiser is the largest producer of gasoline-fueled inboard engines in the world. The Thunderbolt series of ignition systems has been quite popular over the years, and for the last 15 years the Series IV and Series V systems have been the mainstay of the MerCruiser line. The Thunderbolt IV system

comes in two variations, one with a remotely mounted ignition module (located on the port side exhaust elbow) and the other with the ignition module mounted on the side of the distributor body.

Repair procedures for both variations are the same. Ignition-module replacement will be slightly different.

Service procedures for this system are not too difficult. Besides the generic procedures already mentioned for ignition systems, some specific system information follows.

## Distributor-Cap Service

The distributor cap needs to be kept clean and dry. MerCruiser recommends periodically removing the cap (annually will be fine) and giving it a thorough inspection. Be sure to mark the high-tension wires with tape and a marker before removing them from the cap so you can be certain they go back in the same order.

Loosen the four screws that hold the cap in place and carefully lift the cap off its seat on the distributor. There should be a gasket between the cap and the edge of the distributor housing; be careful not to damage it. If it's damaged in any way, it will have to be replaced. This gasket is an integral part of the ignition protection for the distributor. Look closely and observe the alignment tab molded into the cap and the corresponding indent on the body of the distributor housing. Upon reassembly, make sure this tab and groove are aligned; otherwise, damage to the distributor cap and rotor can occur the first time the engine turns over, regardless of whether it starts or not. Figure 7-5 on page 108 shows the cap orientation with the position of the tab indicated.

Once you have the cap off, clean it thoroughly with warm soap and water and dry it (use compressed air if you have a supply). Next, carefully inspect the cap looking for excessive burning or corrosion. Check the center contact for deterioration. Minor corrosion, which is not unusual, can be removed with the tip of a straight-bladed screwdriver. Look for any signs of *carbon tracking* on both the inside and outside of the distributor cap. Carbon tracks will show up as random, fine lines etched into

*Fig. 7-5. Distributor cap showing positioning tab. Make sure this tab is lined up with its corresponding groove in the distributor housing when reinstalling the cap.*

*Fig. 7-6. Carbon tracking inside a distributor cap. These tracks provide a highly conductive path for your ignition voltage to short-circuit between cylinders.*

the surface of the plastic. These tracks, often mistaken for cracks, are actually secondary voltage leaks short-circuiting the intended path. The spark actually etches a carbon groove into the surface of the cap. Carbon tracks are most often caused by dirt and oil accumulation on the cap. If there are any signs of carbon tracking, the cap will have to be replaced. Figure 7-6 shows a carbon track on the inside of a four-cylinder distributor cap.

Next inspect the rotor-sensor wheel, located under the distributor cap. Again, you'll be looking for corrosion and any signs of carbon tracking.

One problem with the Thunderbolt system is that this rotor is attached to the distributor's center shaft with a product known as Loctite. As the name implies, Loctite is a kind of glue that secures the rotor to the shaft. Unlike most rotors that simply lift off the shaft against the pressure of a small spring clip, these rotors are on tight. Don't expect to simply lift it off for inspection.

To remove the rotor, place two flat-bladed screwdrivers under the rotor at its base and push them snugly up against the distributor shaft. The screwdrivers should be at 180 degrees from one another. Push both screwdrivers down against the distributor housing, and hope the rotor pops off. If this doesn't work, use an electric hair dryer on high heat and fan the rotor and sensor wheel until they begin to feel warm to the touch. Try prying again, but don't bend the sensor wheel blades. The slightest distortion of the wheel will render it useless, so alignment of the blades with the sensor inside the distributor is critical. With diligence, the rotor will eventually lift off.

Once the rotor is removed, carefully inspect it for carbon tracks and any damage to the key inside the center section. Replace the rotor if there is any damage here. If all looks well, ensure that the tang that's attached to the rotor and follows the center contact inside the distributor cap is bent to allow for ¼ inch (6 mm) clearance, as shown in figure 7-7.

## Ignition Sensor

Next, take a close look at the ignition sensor. It's best to use a magnifying glass for this, because you'll be

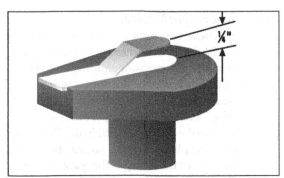

*Fig. 7-7. Rotor contact bent to allow ¼ inch clearance.*

looking for hairline cracks, called *jumpers*, in the metal connecting links on the sensor. If you find any cracks, replace the sensor. Figure 7-8 shows the sensor and points out the jumpers in question.

If the sensor does require replacement, it's easily removed at this point by backing out the two retaining screws indicated in figure 7-9.

When you reassemble the distributor, you'll need some Loctite (#271), which is available at any good auto-parts store. Apply several drops to the inside of the rotor at the positioning key and put several drops in the keyway on the distributor shaft where the key fits into the rotor. Immediately reinstall the rotor. Do

not, under any circumstances, use a silicone-based sealer on the inside of the distributor (to repair the cap gasket, for example). As they cure, most silicone sealers give off acidic vapor that can cause corrosion on the ignition contact points and conductors inside the distributor.

## MerCruiser Thunderbolt V System

The Thunderbolt V system offers some significant technological advantages over the Thunderbolt IV system, the most significant of which is known as the *knock-retard spark control*. This feature is a giant step forward in avoiding internal engine damage due to pinging. Engine cylinders are designed so that the compressed gas-air mixture burns very rapidly but progressively. When the mixture explodes instead of burns, a loud rapping or "pinging" noise is heard. Thus, *pinging* is sometimes called *detonation*.

Whatever it's called, pinging is bad for your engine. Incorrect timing, low-quality fuel, or excessive carbon buildup inside the combustion chamber are the primary causes. If it's allowed to continue, pinging will eventually cause valves and piston tops to literally melt away.

By adding two electronic devices to the ignition system, engineers have devised a way to minimize

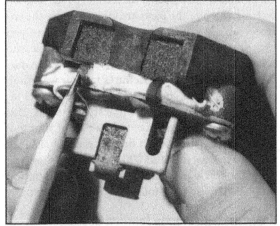

*Fig. 7-8. MerCruiser ignition sensor, pointing out metal jumpers. These jumpers are famous for corroding through, effectively shutting down your ignition system.*

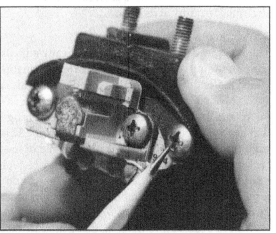

*Fig. 7-9. Retaining screws holding an ignition sensor in place.*

pinging as a cause of engine damage. The knock-retard spark control is operated by one of these two additional devices.

The knock-control module receives an electrical signal from a sensor, called a *knock sensor*, which is screwed into the engine block. This sensor "hears" any pinging inside the combustion chambers and sends an electrical pulse to the knock-control module. The module then sends a signal to the ignition module, ordering it to retard the ignition timing in small (3-degree) increments until the pinging stops.

In addition to controlling ignition timing to eliminate pinging, the Thunderbolt V also controls engine over-revving, acceleration, spark advance, and idle speed. It also has a feature called mean best timing, although this feature is not available on all engines.

## Mean Best Timing

MerCruiser's Thunderbolt V system uses a sophisticated feature called *mean best timing (MBT)* that fine-tunes the ignition timing during light-load cruising. The ignition-control module searches for the perfect setting for ignition timing by automatically adding a few degrees of advance and waiting to see if the engine rpm increases. If so, the module will add a little more advance until engine speed stops increasing. If the rpm drops for any reason, such as a change in sea conditions, the module will automatically retard ignition timing as needed. This is true electronic wizardry at its finest.

## Idle-Speed Spark Control

The idle-speed spark control automatically adjusts ignition timing so that a specific idle speed is maintained under different operating conditions. This is accomplished by making small spark-advance adjustments and is only used within a speed range that generally falls between 400 and 700 rpm. This variation in exact speed specifications is one of several reasons that if module replacement is ever needed, the exact module for your engine (as determined by the serial number of the engine) must be used.

Don't be fooled into thinking that a module that looks just like yours is the correct one for your engine; the internal calibration of the look-alike could be very different from yours.

## Acceleration Spark Advance

All ignition systems need some sort of acceleration spark advance mechanism. Older systems with breaker points used a mechanical advance with centrifugal weights attached to the plate inside the distributor to which the points were attached. As engine rpm increased, it generated centrifugal force and the weights moved the ignition points relative to the center shaft within the distributor. This changed the place where the points opened and closed, and adjusted the timing of the spark. On newer engines with electronic ignition, timing is controlled by the ignition-control module or, on the latest computerized engines, by the onboard microprocessor.

This change in timing allows more time for the fuel-air mixture to completely burn as engine speed increases. The faster the engine turns, the more time is required for combustion, and the more the timing must be advanced. When the engine is accelerating, the ignition-control module may add more spark advance to the "base timing" (the starting point for timing on all engines). The amount of spark advance added depends on how fast engine rpm increases. Rapid throttle changes induce rapid timing changes.

# Beyond the Basics: Outboard and PWC Ignition Systems

On outboard and personal watercraft (PWC) ignition systems, some of the parts are located under the engine flywheel. So if your diagnosis leads you here, you may need the services of a professional mechanic who has the tools needed to get at these parts. All manufacturers include test procedures in their workshop manuals that use special test equipment, such as Stevens or Merc-o-tronic ignition system testers. This equipment is too expensive to be a part of your tool kit. Unless you do this sort of work daily, it just isn't practical to have this stuff. This section will show you how to narrow down the most common ignition problems using simple tools and your multimeter.

## Capacitive-Discharge Ignition System

If your engine was built after 1975, it most likely has some variation of a *capacitive-discharge ignition*

*(CDI) system*, which works by charging a capacitor and releasing this charge to the appropriate igni-tion coil at just the right time. We have already taken a brief look at this in the overview of how out-board and PWC ignition systems work earlier in this chapter.

Different engine makers use different names to describe the parts they use in their CDI systems, but they all are similar.

Magnets carefully positioned on the engine's flywheel induce an electric current as they rotate past specially designed coils located very close to the magnets. One of the coils under the flywheel is called a *charge coil*. As the flywheel magnets spin by, this coil sends a fairly high alternating current voltage to the *ignition-control module*, which is sometimes called the *power pack*, or *CDI unit*. This will be around 200 volts AC, depending upon which system you have.

As already mentioned, the other ignition coils found under the flywheel are called *sensor* (OMC), *pulsar* (Yamaha), or *trigger coils* (Mercury). I will call them trigger coils here to avoid confusion. The trigger coils send electrical signals to the CDI unit to tell it which cylinder to work with at the correct time.

Next you'll find the CDI unit itself. This device is the brain of the system and serves several functions. First, it converts the alternating current from the charge coil into usable direct current. Next it stores this current in the built-in capacitor mentioned earlier. The CDI unit also adjusts timing by changing the interval at which the trigger coil sends a signal to the module. The timing changes with any change in engine rpm and is adjusted by a change in the relative position of the trigger coil to the flywheel magnets.

A timing plate to which both the charge and trigger coils are mounted controls this adjustment. Mechanical linkage connected directly to the engine throttle linkage constantly adjusts the timing relative to the position of the carburetor throttle. In addition, the CDI unit electronically controls the discharge of the built-in capacitor and sends this voltage to the appropriate primary side of the ignition coil for the correct cylinder.

The CDI unit may also have electronic circuits within it to limit engine speed to prevent over-revving, and some even have a circuit that reduces engine rpm if for any reason the engine begins to run too hot. Some of the larger engines may automatically advance ignition timing during initial start-up and when the engine is running at temperatures of less than approximately 100 degrees.

Manufacturers often use one CDI unit for each bank on V-type power heads. One module will control the odd-numbered cylinders and the other will service the even-numbered cylinders. Once the voltage leaves the CDI unit, it's sent to the high-tension coil, which is similar in design to the inboard-system type already discussed. Here, the voltage is stepped up to anywhere between 15,000 and 40,000 volts, the voltage that's required to jump the air gap in the spark plugs. The high-tension ignition coil has two sides, primary and secondary, just as it does on an inboard system. It's really two coils combined into one neat, compact case. Figure 7-10 shows the internal construction of a typical ignition coil with primary and secondary windings.

The coil works by using magnetic induction, just like one on an inboard engine. The voltage generated by the primary winding creates a magnetic field around the secondary winding, which has many more windings than the primary coil. The CDI unit controls the rapid turning on and off of electrical flow in the primary winding, thereby turning this magnetic field on and off. The effect of this is the same as described earlier. The rapid movement of this magnetic field past the secondary windings in-

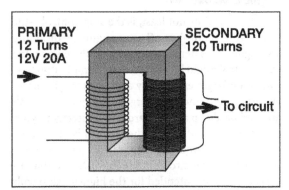

*Fig. 7-10. Typical internal construction of an ignition coil, showing the primary side windings (with fewer coils) and the secondary side (with more windings).*

Fig. 7-11a. Surface gap and traditional spark plugs.　　Fig. 7-11b. A spark-plug gapping tool.

duces electrical current. The more windings, the more current is produced.

As the secondary voltage leaves the center tower of the ignition coil, it travels through the spark-plug wire (the high-tension lead), which is heavily insulated and designed to carry high voltage. If all is well, the high voltage will jump the gap between the center electrode of the spark plug and the ground electrode, completing a circuit to ground. On larger engines with surface-gap plugs, the side of the spark plug is the ground electrode. Figure 7-11a shows both plug types. Figure 7-11b shows a spark-gapping tool being used to adjust the electrode gap.

## Engine Stop Control

Last, but certainly not least, is the stop control—the device you use to shut off your engine by disabling your ignition system. Depending on the engine, the stop control might be activated by a simple stop button or, on larger engines, by a key switch. On newer engines, you'll find an emergency-stop button with an overboard clip and lanyard wired directly to your system's CDI unit. When the lanyard is pulled, the clip is yanked out of the stop button. This creates a momentary short circuit inside the CDI unit that diverts the voltage intended for the high-tension coils directly to ground and shuts off the ignition long enough to stop the engine. These stop circuits can cause a lot of problems, and procedures for testing

them will follow a little later in this chapter.

## Outboard and PWC Ignition Tests

The first step with all electrical-circuit testing is to carefully use your eyes. Look for the obvious! Whenever a problem develops with any engine or system that has been regularly maintained, troubles are almost always due to some minor oversight and are easily solved. Check all the wiring for any loose connections on your engine. Look for signs of corrosion on terminals and connectors. Check for any broken or frayed wires. Make certain the problem is not something as silly as a blown fuse. Any of these things can be the cause of ignition problems, and they can be quickly fixed with basic tools.

## Testing for Spark

As with the inboard systems, the first step in troubleshooting your ignition system is to verify that you're getting spark. However, with outboard and PWC systems you need to check each cylinder because each cylinder has its own high-tension coil, and partial system failures of one cylinder are not uncommon. When checking the coils, it's extremely important that you check for any fuel leaks and make certain that all fuel line fittings and connections are secure.

It is a good idea to create some shade near the

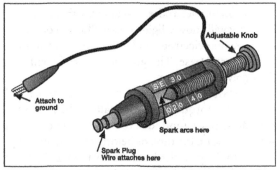

*Fig. 7-12. Snap-On spark tester. I prefer this type over all others because it's adjustable, which gives you the ability to determine the strength of the available spark.*

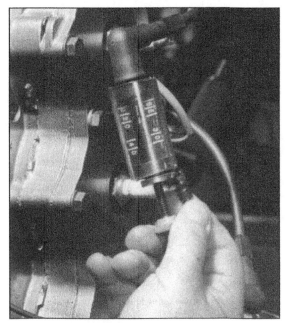

*Fig. 7-13. Spark tester in use.*

spark-plug wire you're checking. It's very difficult to see a spark jump a gap in bright sunlight. Use the spark tester shown in figure 7-12. Adjust the knurled knob on the tester to give an air gap of about ⅜ to ⁷⁄₁₆ inch between the two pointed contacts inside the cylinder. Figure 7-13 shows the spark tester properly connected and ready to go. Hold the tester so you can see inside the cylinder as shown, and crank the engine. You should see a bright blue spark (not yellow) jumping between the two contacts. If you do, then ignition output is satisfactory. If not, further investigation will be needed.

If your engine is skipping or misfiring, check all of the spark-plug wires this way to be sure that each secondary coil is sending a spark through its respective plug wire to the spark plug. The beauty of this spark tester over similar tools is that the air gap between the two contacts is adjustable. This is important because some manufacturers will give an air gap specification in their manuals. The wider the air gap a spark will jump, the higher the total ignition-system output. So, by comparing the maximum gap that a spark will jump for each ignition coil, you can find a weak or faulty coil.

Be careful not to get the spark plug wires mixed up when you do this test. Each wire is timed to a specific cylinder and must be replaced on the same spark plug from which you removed it. If you don't see a spark, check the fuse for the ignition system and replace it if it is blown. Also, if you have one, make sure

the emergency-stop button and clip are set correctly. It's amazing how easy it is to forget this simple device. Check for spark again; if it's still not evident, further investigation will be needed.

## Checking the Spark Plugs

Just because you're getting adequate spark to the spark plugs doesn't mean the spark plugs are firing. They could simply be worn out, but there are many other things that can cause a spark plug not to fire. An oil blend that's too rich (too much oil in the gas), a weak spark to a given cylinder, incorrect heat-range spark plugs, and fuel system problems are just a few. If you have regularly serviced your engine, worn-out plugs should not be a consideration.

So, what's left? Look at the plugs and verify that they can actually fire. Remove the plug using a ratchet and spark-plug socket, or use the plug wrench supplied in the tool kit for your engine, and look it over. The plug should not be soaked with black fuel-oil mixture. Are the center and ground electrodes intact? If not, throw away the plugs and put in a new set.

Fig. 7-14. Testing a spark plug to see if it fires.

oration on the electrodes. A spark plug that's burning correctly will show a light brown "fluffy" coloration on the center electrode and a fluffy black coloration on the metal base. The ground electrode will be a light gray-brown color.

One last thing regarding spark plugs: be careful not to over-torque when reinstalling them into the cylinders. It's a good idea to put a light coating of white grease on the threads before screwing the plugs back into the cylinder head. Screw them in by hand until the sealing washer seats; then use your spark-plug wrench or a socket and ratchet to tighten them an additional half to three-quarter turn. Any more torque than that could damage the plug threads in the cylinder head. You should never replace just one plug. Replace them in sets and don't bother saving the old ones for use as spares. (They actually make good sinkers for offshore fishing.) You should always have a fresh set of gapped and ready-to-go plugs on board your boat—just in case.

If the plug's center and ground electrode are OK and the plug is gapped correctly, check the number on the plug and match it to the manufacturer's recommendations. It may be the wrong heat range for the engine. If all of these things check out OK, insert the plug into the correct plug-wire boot, wedge the plug into a spot on the side of your engine, as shown in figure 7-14, being sure that the metal case of the plug is grounded, and crank the engine. If you see a blue spark jumping from the center electrode to the edge of the plug on a surface-gap plug or to the ground electrode on a standard plug, the spark plug is OK and should fire in the cylinder.

If you don't see a spark, or if you see a weak yellow one and you're sure that adequate current was getting to the plug, the plug must be replaced. If it's a standard plug, check the gap before installing the new plug as shown in figure 7-11b on page 112. Surface-gap plugs require no adjustment.

Spark plugs are among your most valuable diagnostic tools. Whenever you remove your plugs, keep them in order for the cylinders they came from. Check each plug; carefully look for cracks in the ceramic insulator body, black oily buildup, or discol-

## Ignition Problem Quick-Check List

If you have checked the spark plugs, as described above, and determined that you don't have a spark at any of the cylinders, or you have a spark at some cylinders and not at others, further investigation is needed. The following list will help organize your search through the ignition system, and the accompanying tests will help you to pinpoint the source of a problem. These tests should only be completed using this book and the manual for your particular engine. Each manufacturer uses different color coding for wires and slightly different test procedures for their respective systems. However, by following this guide you should be able to trace your way through your system and isolate any problems in the CDI unit in the rare instances when you have a problem.

These tests assume that you have eliminated any possibility of a problem with fuel or compression. The sequence for testing your outboard or PWC ignition system is as follows.

1. Check to see if your engine has a fuse for the ignition system. If it does, check the fuse and replace it if it's blown or corroded.

2. Check the spark-plug wires.

3. Test all the ignition coils.

4. Do a water-spray test of the engine.

5. Test the charge and trigger coils and output to the CDI unit using your multimeter and Mercury DVA tester (part number 91-89045).

6. Test all engine stop circuits.

7. Test the tilt switch, if your engine is equipped with one.

Let's discuss the details for each of these procedures in a little more detail.

## Testing Spark-Plug Wires

Testing spark-plug wires is easy. If you have already used the spark tester and seen a spark at the end of the spark-plug wire, you know the wire is conducting

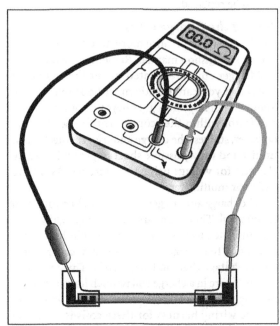

*Fig. 7-15. An ohmmeter test of a spark-plug wire. Depending on your engine type, you may or may not measure resistance of any value when performing this test. With "resistor-type" wires used on some of the newest engines, readings of 5,000–10,000 ohms for each foot of wire length are not uncommon.*

electricity to the plug. But that's not all the wire has to do. It also has to insulate this electricity under all engine-operating conditions and conduct electricity when your boat is underway and the engine is vibrating. Look at the wire and the wire ends inside the protective boots. Look for any sign of cracking, worn insulation, and any sign of green corrosion on the metal clips that lock the ends of the wire to the coil and spark plug. If you find corrosion, slide the boot back onto the wire and carefully clean the connector with a wire brush until the metal is bright and shiny. If the wire is chafed or cracked, replace it.

To check the wire electrically, set your multimeter on the low-ohms scale and insert the meter probes into the wire as shown in figure 7-15. The meter should read near zero ohms, except on some of the newest engines, where "resistor-type" wiring is used, in which case some resistance will be indicated on your meter. Next, hold the probes in place and bend and flex the wire while carefully observing the meter. If the reading fluctuates, there is a break in the wire inside the insulation. Replace the wire.

When reinstalling ignition wires, make sure to use the hold-downs found on many engines. These hold-downs keep the wire from coming in contact with moving engine parts that may chafe the wire and ultimately cause it to fail. Apply a light coating of waterproof grease to the ribbed ceramic insulator and metal connector of the spark plug and coil connector before reinstalling the spark-plug wire. The grease will help the boot to seal out moisture that would eventually corrode the metal connector on the end of the wire.

## Testing High-Tension Coils

In the repair shop, a technician normally uses one of the testers specially designed to work with CDI systems. These testers are quite expensive and should not be a part of your tool collection, even though not having one will limit your ability to do advanced ignition-system tests. You can, however, do many tests with your spark tester, your multimeter, and a spray bottle filled with fresh water. These simple tests will enable you to narrow down possible causes of an ignition fault and in most cases find the culprit behind it. At the very least, you'll be able to point the professional mechanic in the right direction and save on expensive labor charges.

As already stated, each of your ignition coils is really two coils combined into one unit consisting of a primary winding and a secondary winding. The trick is to identify which external coil wires and connections go to which coil inside the insulated case. To do this you need the wiring diagram and workshop manual for your engine. Using the diagram in the manual as a guide, check the resistance of each of the coil windings with your multimeter's ohmmeter. If you find electrical continuity and normal resistance, you can be reasonably certain your coil is OK. If you find excessive resistance, or if the meter indicates an open circuit within the coil, then the coil must be replaced.

Figure 7-16 shows these tests on a typical outboard engine high-tension coil. Remember, though, that you must identify the correct wire connections and resistance values for these tests to work on your specific make and model of engine.

Whenever removing an ignition coil from your engine, carefully note the location of any insulating washers that you find under the coil or the hold-down bolts. Misplacement of these washers can cause a no-spark condition with a perfectly good coil.

## Water-Spray Test

Another simple test for determining the integrity of your secondary ignition system is to run the engine and use a spray bottle with fresh water to wet the area of the ignition coils, spark-plug wires, and spark plugs. Do this in the shade or at dusk. Any weakness in the insulation of connecting boots, high-tension coil cases, or spark-plug wires will immediately show up as sparks jumping from the poorly insulated wire or connection. Any component that shows spark should be replaced.

## Testing the Charge Coils

For these tests you'll once more need to consult your engine's workshop manual. Remember, your charge and trigger coils are located under the engine flywheel and you can't see them without removing it. Removing the flywheel goes beyond routine testing, and is not within the scope of this book. You can, however, still test the charge and trigger coils for continuity and for a possible short to ground. You can also test for voltage using the Mercury DVA tester and your multimeter.

The charge and trigger coils are just like your high-tension coil. They are made with a long, tightly coiled wire insulated from ground. Charge coils have higher resistance than trigger coils, so they can generate higher voltage than do trigger coils. This means the length of wire in a charge coil is much longer than that in a trigger coil and therefore has a higher resistance.

The wiring harness for these coils is always secured to the movable timing plate under your engine's flywheel and usually exits from under this assembly on the starboard (right side looking toward the bow of the boat) of the engine power head.

Once you have located the harness and found all the wires that come through it, match the color coding on the wires to your wiring diagram and deter-

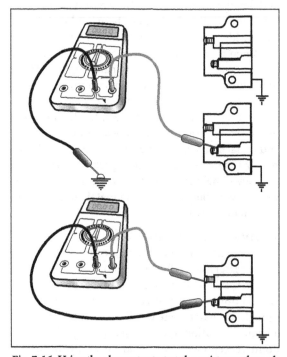

Fig. 7-16. Using the ohmmeter to test the resistance through an outboard-engine ignition coil: testing for a short circuit to ground (top) and testing resistance through the coil windings (bottom). Make sure to get the proper specifications for your engine from the workshop manual.

mine which wires go to and return from the charge and trigger coils. These wires often terminate in a gang plug that connects to the CDI unit. Disconnect this plug to continue testing.

To test the charge coil, set your ohmmeter to the scale for the expected resistance as specified in your engine manual. Insert the red and black test probes into the plug socket that matches the correct color wire and take a reading. Charge coils generally have resistance between 400 and 900 ohms. If the reading is more than that or if a reading of infinity indicates a break in the wiring, the charge coil is defective and must be replaced.

Next, check for a short to ground by removing one of the meter probes from the plug assembly. Now switch your meter to the high-ohms scale (if it's not self-scaling) and touch the free probe to the metal timing plate to which the lead harness is secured. Any reading on the meter other than "OL" indicates a short to ground. The flywheel must be removed to correct the problem, which is either frayed or melted insulation or a bad charge coil.

To test the continuity of the trigger coil follow the above procedure for the charge-coil tests, only adjust your meter to a much lower resistance—between 15 and 50 ohms is usually about right. To test for a short to ground in the coil lead, set the meter on the same high scale as for the charge-coil short test. If your engine is equipped with more than one trigger coil, test them all.

Figure 7-17 shows these tests and the point at which the wiring harness emerges from under the flywheel. It also shows the timing-plate assembly.

To test for voltage from these coils you need the DVA adapter shown in figure 7-18 and available through outboard engine dealers. This adapter can be used with any system of this type and converts the AC voltage from your charge and trigger coils to a DC voltage your multimeter can easily read. Sufficient readings from 1 to 9 volts will not only attest to the performance of the coils but also verify that the

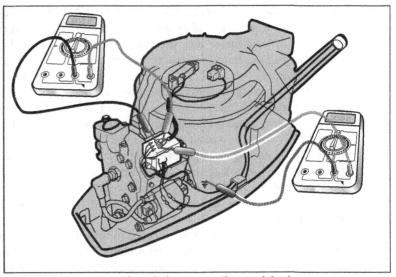

*Fig. 7-17. Continuity tests through the trigger-coil test and the short-to-ground test. Again, you'll need your workshop manual to get the proper specifications for these tests.*

magnets under the flywheel have enough magnetism. As you know, voltage increases in direct proportion to the speed of the engine and the strength of these magnets.

To test voltage, plug the red lead from the tester into the DC volt socket on your multimeter and

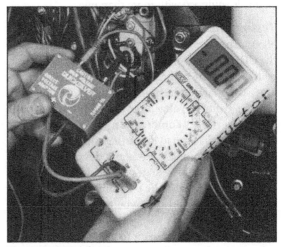

*Fig. 7-18. DVA adapter.*

connect the black lead from the tester to the ground or negative socket. Next, plug the red and black probes from your meter into the corresponding sockets on the DVA tester, and you're ready to take a voltage reading.

To test the charge coil, set your voltmeter to a scale that will read about 400 volts. Typical readings at cranking speed for charge coils are between 150 and 275 volts. You must check the workshop manual for your engine to get the exact specifications. Plug the meter leads into the socket or connect them to the leads coming from the charge coil. Again, your manual will help you identify these two wires.

Crank the engine or use the pull cord to turn it over while you take a reading from your meter. You may need a second set of hands here. Some of the newest meters have a "peak-reading" button that will hold the reading until you can look at the meter. If your reading is within specifications, the charge coil has tested OK and is not causing any ignition problems.

### Testing the Trigger Coils

Next, test the trigger coil the same way you tested the charge coil, only switch your multimeter to a voltage scale of 20 volts or less. Typical trigger-coil voltage readings will be between 1.2 and 9 volts at cranking speed. Again, verify the specification in your engine manual. Make sure to check all the trigger coils if your engine is equipped with more than one.

### Testing the CDI Unit

Next, using the multimeter and DVA adapter, test the CDI unit for voltage to each of the high-tension coils. Be sure the ground wire for your CDI unit is secure, as damage to the module could occur if it's not. Use this ground to attach the black probe from your multimeter-DVA combination. It's a good idea to use a wiring diagram to locate the stop circuit ground lead for your ignition module and disconnect it from the stop circuit; this isolates the CDI unit from that circuit and eliminates the possibility that a defect in the stop circuit could cause you to misdiagnose your CDI unit as faulty.

Next, switch your meter to a scale that will read about 400 volts (or allow it to self-scale). Locate the high-tension coil primary-feed wire, which is the wire that runs from the ignition module to the coil. Attach the multimeter's red probe to the terminal on the high-tension coil, and crank the engine.

Your reading here, which should be somewhere between 150 and 350 volts, is the discharge from the capacitor inside the ignition module. Match your reading to factory specifications for your engine. Do this test on each lead coming from the CDI unit. Your readings should be approximately the same for each one. If you discover a lead with no output or a considerably lower output (check it against the specs in the workshop manual), the ignition module is defective and must be replaced.

Some of the latest CDI systems use a module with an integral trigger coil, and the module is located under the flywheel. In this case, you won't be able to get at the charge coil to service it, and you won't find any reference to trigger-coil testing in your workshop manual. The flywheel must be removed to service these parts; you'll need the services of a dealer or another pro if your tests on the plugs, secondary wiring, and high-tension coil lead you this far.

Problems with charge coils, trigger coils, and the permanent magnets under the flywheel are extremely rare and something that you may never have to deal with on your engine. The only thing that usually causes early failure of these parts is accidentally submerging the engine in salt water and not properly cleaning it. A saltwater dunking will cause excessive corrosion in all the parts under the flywheel and, in most cases, ruin the engine if it isn't tended to right away. If you should dunk your engine in salt water, flush it with fresh water and get it to your dealer without delay.

So, you have checked for spark to your spark plugs. You now know how to check your system's spark with a simple spark tester. You can remove your plugs, check them, and replace them when it's necessary. You can check your spark-plug wires and high-tension coils, and with the help of your workshop manual you can check your charge and trigger coils. Permanent magnets rarely lose their magnetism and don't need to be checked. So what's next? Your engine stop circuits and a few thoughts on some of the other functions your CDI unit may have.

# Testing Your Stop Switch

Your engine, depending its size and the way it's installed, might have a remote key switch to turn the ignition on and off, or it might have a simple stop button mounted on the engine or steering tiller. In either case, the tool of choice for testing the stop-switch circuit is your multimeter, set to read resistance. You also need the wiring diagram for your engine.

If you don't have a remote-control starter switch, look under the engine cowl where the wiring and cable controls come out of the steering tiller. You should find two wires, one going to ground and the other going to the CDI unit. Verify you have the correct wires by checking your engine-wiring diagram. Next, find a good ground on your engine. Install the emergency-stop clip if your engine has one, and make sure your engine is ready to run.

Connect your multimeter's black probe to ground and the red probe to the plug or to the wire coming from the stop button. If all is well, you'll get a high (infinity) reading, indicating an open circuit. Any reading showing continuity indicates a defective switch or a short to ground in the wire coming from the switch somewhere inside the tiller handle. In either case you'll have to replace the assembly.

If all appears to be OK to this point, push in the stop button and check your meter. It should indicate continuity with a low reading. Finally, if you have a stop clip, pull it out and observe your meter reading. It should again show a low reading. If pushing the stop button or pulling the emergency clip does not give the desired low ohmmeter reading, the assembly must be replaced.

Figure 7-19 shows a typical meter hooked up for these tests.

On larger engines with a remote-starter switch, you still check the switch for short circuits to ground; you'll just have to cover the distance between your engine power head and the key switch. Use your ohmmeter and your engine's wiring diagram just as before. Identify all the terminals and connections on your key switch by removing the back cover of the control unit to get at the back of the switch. Some manuals show a detailed picture of the plug assembly coming from the back of the switch and identify all

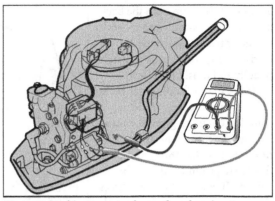

*Fig. 7-19. Multimeter tests of an outboard-engine stop circuit.*

the terminals and connections. If you can get at the plug in this case, you won't have to remove the remote-control assembly.

If removal and partial disassembly of the remote-control assembly are necessary, carefully follow the instructions for opening the control unit. In some cases removal of the central pivoting screw can create quite a mess, and it can be difficult to reassemble. If the remote-control assembly has a key switch separate from the shift control, this central-pivot screw will not be a problem. You can usually access the back of the switch without removing the switch from the panel.

Now use your wiring diagram to identify the wire coming from the back of the ignition switch to the ground shut-off at the power pack. As with the smaller engines, this wire will usually terminate at a gang plug under the engine cowl in the harness going to the power pack. Once you find it, disconnect the plug or connection to the remote-control assembly. Now you're ready for your ohmmeter tests. Check at the engine end first, and, for your multimeter's safety, be sure your battery is disconnected before doing this test.

First, connect the red probe on your ohmmeter to the wire that runs from the ignition switch to the remote-control assembly. Connect the black probe to a good ground. With the ignition key on, you should get a high reading or infinity. If your meter indicates a complete circuit with a resistance reading near zero,

# POWERBOATER'S GUIDE TO ELECTRICAL SYSTEMS

disconnect this wire from the back of the ignition switch and recheck the meter reading. If the meter now reads infinity, the ignition switch is faulty and must be replaced.

If the meter reading has little or no resistance, it indicates a complete circuit to ground, meaning the wire that connects the ignition switch to the engine is shorted to ground and must be repaired. If all of these readings check out, turn off the key switch and check your meter. You should have a low resistance reading near zero ohms. If your meter still gives a reading of infinity, check that the ground for the key switch is connected and in good condition. If it is, you may have a break (open circuit) in the wire leading from the switch to the terminal on the engine. Check the entire length of this wire for a break and either install a new wire or splice the break.

Figure 7-20 shows a typical wiring diagram for a remote-key installation with the typical test points shown and the possibly faulty wires indicated.

If after testing the stop circuit you still have a problem with your engine not shutting down with either the key switch or the stop button, the fault is in the CDI unit itself. Unfortunately, it's a solid-state sealed device and is not repairable; it will have to be replaced.

## Mercury Tilt-Stop Switch Testing

Some mid-sized and larger outboards have a switch designed to cut out the ignition if the engine is trimmed up too much. It's located in the trim-mounting bracket assembly. The tilt-stop switch prevents the lower-unit water-pickup port from raising out of the water enough to cause inadequate water flow. Figure 7-21 shows this switch on a 70-horsepower Mercury outboard.

To test the tilt-stop switch, remove the mounting screw that secures it to the engine. Disconnect the

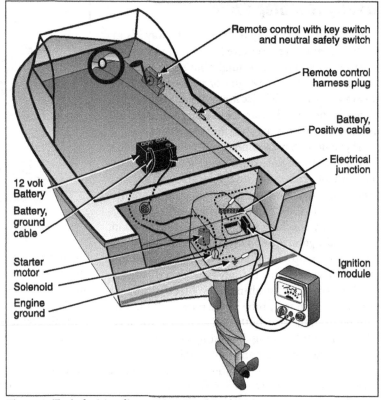

*Fig. 7-20. Typical wiring diagram for an outboard-engine remote-key installation.*

remaining lead coming from the switch. Now with your multimeter set to the low-ohms (R × 1) scale, connect the meter probes to the two switch leads (it really doesn't matter which probe goes where) and position the switch in your hand as it would normally rest on the engine with the trim down. The switch should be open, and the meter should read no continuity or infinity.

Next, tilt the switch in your hand and tap the high end of the switch with your finger. The switch should close, and the meter should now indicate continuity through the switch. If your test readings are not as described here, replace the switch.

## Final Checks and Ignition Timing

It is possible to thoroughly test all of the ignition parts, have everything check out, and still not have

120

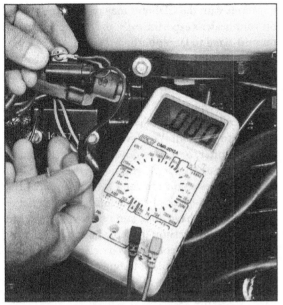

Fig. 7-21. Mercury tilt switch. This switch is designed to prevent engine starting with the prop out of the water. If it malfunctions (open-circuits), your engine won't start with the prop in the water, either! In this picture I've removed the switch and am testing its function with a multimeter set to check continuity when the switch is tilted manually. I'm verifying with the meter that the switch turns off and on.

any spark. Or you might have a strong spark and an engine that backfires when you try to start it or one that misfires at high speed. Your ignition system could still be the culprit. Before blaming the CDI unit or ignition-control module for a no-spark condition or bad timing (the backfiring), there are several additional things to check.

First, be absolutely certain that all wires are hooked up correctly. It's all too easy to cross plug wires, or switch primary-feed wires going to the high-tension coils so that the CDI unit sends its signal to the wrong coil. Double-check everything against your engine-wiring diagram. Gang-plug connections are always keyed so they only go together one way, but it's easy to make a mistake on engines with individual terminals. To avoid the possibility of crossfire between cylinders, make sure that all high-tension leads go into the proper hold-down clamp on the engine.

## Loose-Flywheel Check

Next, consider the flywheel. Remember that it has carefully positioned magnets attached inside. The flywheel is keyed to the crankshaft so that these magnets pass the appropriate charge or trigger coil at a specific point in the engine's rotation. On rare occasions, usually after the flywheel has been removed and improperly reinstalled, the flywheel becomes loose on the end of the crankshaft and shears off the key. The flywheel may spin independent of the crankshaft and change position of the magnets relative to the crankshaft, ruining the ignition timing.

To check for a loose flywheel, disconnect the master plug to the ignition module to disable the ignition system; you don't want the engine starting with your hands on the flywheel. Next, grasp the flywheel firmly with both hands and feel for any side-to-side or up-and-down movement, as shown in figure 7-22. Any movement indicates a loose flywheel. An experienced mechanic must remove the flywheel, and the crankshaft and flywheel must be inspected and repaired or replaced as needed. With luck, you'll just need to install a new key and to re-torque the flywheel.

Fig. 7-22. Checking for a loose flywheel.

## Timing Check

If all wiring is properly connected and your flywheel is secure, a timing check is in order. This is not a procedure for the inexperienced outboard-engine mechanic. The procedure varies somewhat for every outboard made, and verifying the position of the ignition-timing pointer is a precise and difficult job requiring special tools that the average boatowner won't have. The timing should be checked at idle and for maximum advance at high speed. This is best done in a special test tank or with the aid of a dynamometer specially designed for outboard engines. The average boatowner doesn't have these tools.

If you're well equipped and have a reasonable amount of engine experience, you can set the timing by following the procedure outlined in the Engine Synchronization and Timing section of your workshop manual. On smaller, single-carburetor engines, the procedure is not especially complicated, and by following the instructions carefully someone with limited experience can do it. On the larger engines of over 25 horsepower, do-it-yourself is not recommended. The variables here are many and go beyond the scope of this book.

To sum up timing and its importance in ignition-system diagnosis, remember these important facts: Timing will rarely change unless someone alters the carburetor linkage or adjustments. Or the flywheel comes loose from the crankshaft. Or the flywheel magnets become unattached from the underside of the flywheel (a fairly common problem on some engines). Or the engine has many hours on it, and the timing plate under the flywheel is worn and has excessive play.

So if no one has tried to adjust your carburetors, and your flywheel isn't loose, it's highly unlikely that your ignition timing has changed. But if you have any doubts based on all the information presented here, get your timing professionally checked.

## More on the CDI Unit

If your engine has been intermittently quitting or intermittently losing rpm, there is still a remote possibility that your CDI unit is acting up. Unfortunately, questions with the CDI unit may require you to rely on your dealer's expertise for some tests, particularly on mid-sized to larger outboard engines. However, if you have a no-spark condition, and you have carefully performed all of the tests outlined above, you can feel quite comfortable purchasing a new CDI unit and installing it. That was your problem.

Other problems with the CDI unit are a little more difficult to pinpoint. Your system may have a built-in rpm limiter, or a slow-down circuit designed to reduce engine rpm if the engine overheats. If all of your other tests point to the CDI unit in anything other than a no-spark situation, inform your dealer of everything you have done and rely on the dealer to make the final decision on replacing the CDI unit. Dealers will not accept returns on electrical parts, so trial-and-error methods of testing can be expensive.

## Optical-Timing Systems

If you own a medium-to-large outboard made within the last several years, you may have a subsystem integrated into your CDI unit called *optical timing*. This is a very sophisticated system that electronically controls the timing advance and retards the spark for easier starting. Unfortunately, troubleshooting this system requires an arsenal of specialized test equipment and adapters. If your engine has an optical timing system, consult your dealer for diagnosis once your problem goes past checking the fuse, spark plugs and wires, coils, and looking for corroded or loose connections, all of which I described earlier in this chapter.

To sum this section up, remember these important facts. Most problems with ignition systems will be visible—a broken wire, a corroded connection, or bad spark plugs that should have been replaced. Also, because of the variety of engines and ignition systems, you must use this book together with the service manual for your engine.

If you follow the guidelines and the simplified test procedures in this chapter, you'll be able to pinpoint and repair the most common (and some not-so-common) ignition-system problems. If your tests lead you to a difficulty that must be handled by the dealer, you'll have saved the labor dollars you would have spent for the tests.

# Chapter 8

# Tracing and Repairing Starter-Motor Circuits

Here is an all-too-familiar scenario: You wake before dawn, get the old Donzi hooked to the back of the station wagon, and are at the launch ramp a good hour before the weekend rush. Half an hour later she is in the water, tied to the dock, loaded with your entire family, a few friends, a picnic lunch, beer, soda pop, fishing gear, water skis, two gallons of SPF 30 sunblock, and the family rottweiler. The rising sun is shining, the birds are singing, the sea is flat calm. In short, it's the start of a glorious day—a perfect day to spend on the water.

Finally, you're ready to go. You run the bilge blowers for a while, then with a captain-like flourish you turn the ignition switch—and nothing happens. Suddenly everyone is staring at you and the rottweiler is making rumbling noises deep in his throat. In desperation you try the switch again—still nothing. Then you check the battery switch, the batteries, and all the terminals. They are all OK, but the rottweiler's lip is starting to curl and your passengers are picking up blunt objects as they form a circle around you. What are you going to do? Well, it's a good thing you bought this book.

Sooner or later it's bound to happen. You turn your ignition key to start the engine, and it welcomes you with a disheartening click-click sound, or perhaps no sound at all. These classic symptoms could well indicate a starter-motor or starter-circuit problem. Let's take a look at these symptoms, try to understand what they mean, and then look at a few ways to fix the problem before the rottweiler makes an early brunch of your leg.

Like all problems with electrical circuits discussed in this book, you need to systematically attack difficulties with your starter motor and not skip any steps in your diagnosis. Mistakes here can be expensive not only in the cost of replacement parts, but in time spent getting to the starter motor. Boatbuilders have an uncanny knack for burying these important parts in obscure places where you'll swear you need arms 10 inches longer than normal to reach them.

Follow the steps I have outlined in this chapter, and you'll make the correct starting-system diagnosis every time without fear of unnecessarily replacing expensive parts, or of your spouse asking for a divorce.

## Coast Guard Regulations for Starter Motors

The U.S. Coast Guard mandates that, like alternators and distributors, starter motors used on gasoline-powered boats be the ignition-protected type discussed in chapters 4 and 7. This is serious business, and an area where I have personally seen more than one act of foolishness end in catastrophe. A former student of mine owned a small marina that, like most marinas, did routine service on customers' boats. In a well-intentioned attempt to save a few dollars for a customer, my student (this happened long before he was my student, of course) made the fatal error of installing an automotive starter motor in the customer's boat. All went well until one day at the fuel dock, the customer started his boat after a fill-up. A large explosion blew the boat to pieces, killing the man.

The insurance investigator for this tragic accident traced the installation of the inappropriate starter motor to my student. The customer's wife sued and ended up with a handsome settlement that included my student's boatyard. He lost everything as a result of this one act of negligence. The lesson here is obvious: Do not even consider for a moment the idea of installing a low-cost automotive starter motor in place of a proper marine one—it could be deadly.

# Starter-Motor Problems and Solutions

Because engine makers all use similar engine blocks and parts, starter-motor circuits have many similarities from one brand of engine to another. Therefore, I have been able to develop a generic procedure for troubleshooting and repairing them. However, the specifics for your boat's engine can only be found in your workshop manual. Use the procedures in this chapter as a detailed guide to get you started in the right direction for locating and correcting specific problems. I will try to direct you to sections of your workshop manual when they are needed. The illustrations that follow show the major parts of the most common starter-motor circuits.

Figure 8-1 shows a typical OMC/Volvo Penta starter circuit with all the important parts mentioned in the list that follows. Figure 8-2 on page 125 shows a typical MerCruiser starter circuit.

## Basic Diagnostics

There are five basic symptoms of starter-motor and starter-circuit problems, and basic diagnostics. Let's look at the symptoms first, and we'll explore each in detail in the next sections.

▶ *The starter motor is lethargic and turns the engine slowly.* First check the condition of the battery and cable connections; then check the engine and reverse gear assembly to be certain they are not bound up. If these check out OK, make sure the cable connections at the starter motor are tight and clean. Finally, if all the wiring and the engine itself seem to be in good order, the starter motor itself is the likely culprit.

▶ *The starter motor turns intermittently.* Check the terminals at the ignition switch, the ignition switch itself, the neutral safety switch, the engine-mounted slave solenoid or relay, and finally the starter motor itself.

▶ *The starter motor doesn't turn, but the solenoid makes a clicking sound.* Check the battery and connections, the solenoid, the engine and drive for seizure, and finally the starter motor itself.

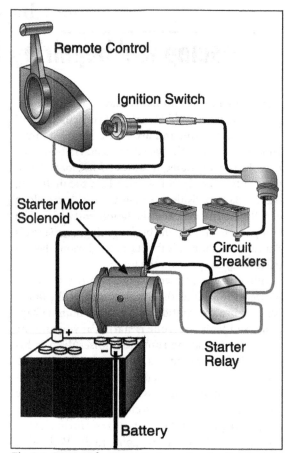

Fig. 8-1. OMC/Volvo Penta starter-motor circuit.

▶ *The starter motor doesn't turn and the solenoid makes no clicking sound.* Make sure the remote-shift lever is in neutral; then check the battery and connections, all fuses and circuit breakers, and the starter-motor solenoid.

▶ *The starter motor remains engaged and runs with the engine.* Check for a faulty or shorted ignition switch, a faulty solenoid, or a faulty starter motor.

This list should make it clear that the most common cause of all the starter problems, except for a starter motor that remains engaged with the engine running, is found in the battery and cable connections. This cannot be emphasized enough. A battery troubleshooting. Have the workshop manual close at hand so you can identify all the circuit components for your boat.

As a first step, look at all wiring and connections to all starter-circuit parts. Tighten any loose parts and terminals, and clean any corroded terminals. Don't forget to check the fuses and circuit breakers. A blown fuse or a tripped circuit breaker on a starter-motor circuit could be caused by a partially seized starter motor or, in the worst case, a seized engine, both of which situations will be covered in more detail later on in this chapter.

If all connections and fuses or breakers appear to be in good order, a faulty part is certainly the cause for your starter-circuit grief, and a step-by-step approach will be needed to determine which part is at fault.

## Starter Solenoid

Most marine inboard engines have a remote *solenoid*, sometimes called a *slave relay*. A solenoid is used as a remote switch to control a circuit, such as your starter circuit, that carries heavy amperage. Acting as a shortcut, the solenoid is connected to the starter switch with a smaller wire to save on the amount of heavy wiring needed to operate the starter circuit. In other words, instead of having a cable as big as your thumb running from the battery to the ignition switch and then from the ignition switch to the starter motor, the heavy cable connects directly to the starter motor through a solenoid. The solenoid is operated by a much smaller (usually 10 or 12 AWG) wire that connects the solenoid to the ignition switch.

Many starter circuits use a solenoid as a remote relay that does not carry full starter-motor current. To determine if your solenoid is intended to carry starter-motor current, first locate the solenoid. It's generally cylindrical and is often found on a bracket at the top forward end of the engine. It will have two large wires and two small wires attached to it. Look at the size of the wire on the solenoid terminals. If the large wires are the same size as your battery cables (typically 4 AWG or larger), the solenoid carries starter-motor current. However, if the large wires are smaller than the battery cables—around the 12, 10, or 8 AWG range—the solenoid does not carry full

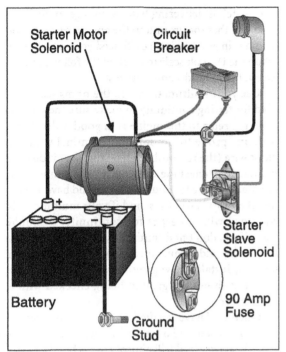

*Fig. 8-2. Typical MerCruiser starter-motor circuit diagram.*

weakened by a sticking bilge-pump float switch or a light left on while the boat was unattended for an extended period is a common cause of an engine failing to start. Always be certain your battery is charged to at least 70 percent of its capacity before you assume that you have starter-motor problems.

If your boat doesn't have a voltmeter to help you determine battery charge, use your multimeter and take a direct reading of open-circuit voltage at the battery, using the Open-Circut Voltage versus State of Charge table in the Open-Circuit Voltage Test section on page 84. If your battery is low, you will, of course, have to find out why, and the steps outlined in chapter 5 will help you to isolate the cause.

## Troubleshooting Starter-Motor Circuits

Once you confirm that the batteries are not the cause of your starter problems, you should begin starter-motor current. The small wires are usually 14 or 12 AWG in both cases.

If you have a medium-to-large boat (over about 20 feet) with an inboard engine that does not have a remote solenoid, it will have one mounted on top of the starter motor. In this case, it will have only one large wire with one end connected to the solenoid and the other terminal connected directly to the battery or to the battery selector switch.

## Solenoid Test

Testing a solenoid is really rather simple once you know what the four wires do. One of the large wires on the solenoid comes from the battery and the other goes to the starter motor. One of the small wires comes from the ignition switch, and the other, if there is one, connects to ground. Some solenoids are designed to ground through the case, and the bolt that attaches it to the engine acts as the ground. Figure 8-3a shows a heavy-duty solenoid; figure 8-3b shows a similar solenoid that does not carry full starter-motor current.

To test a solenoid, first make sure that the igni-

tion switch is delivering battery voltage to the solenoid and that the ground to the engine from the solenoid is in good order. You'll need your multimeter set on the DC volt scale to do all of the following tests except the ground-continuity test.

Use your multimeter set to the ohms scale you used for testing continuity to make sure the ground from the relay to the engine is in good order. Connect one probe to the solenoid terminal with the black wire (the red probe will be fine, but it doesn't matter when checking continuity) and connect the remaining probe to ground. You should have a reading of almost zero ohms, and if your multimeter is equipped with a beeper for continuity, it should beep. If you don't find continuity, clean the terminals at the relay and engine, then recheck. If the problem persists, install a new ground wire. Figure 8-4 on page 127 shows the ground being checked with a multimeter.

Once you have verified continuity to ground, check the power lead on the solenoid for battery voltage. The power lead will almost always be a large red wire, but verify the color on your wiring diagram.

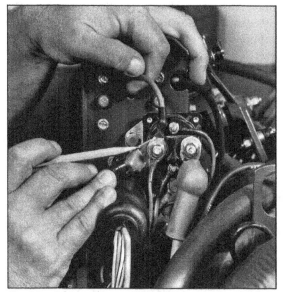

*Fig. 8-3a. A heavy-duty remote solenoid.*

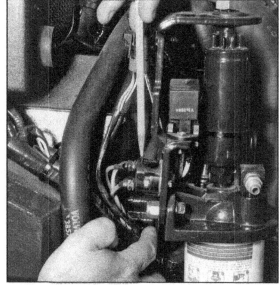

*Fig. 8-3b. A light-duty relay.*

You might need a helper to turn the ignition switch while you check the meter. Connect the meter as shown in figure 8-5 with the red probe attached to the red wire and the black probe connected to ground. Next, have your helper turn the ignition switch to start. If your boat has a starter button separate from the ignition switch, turn the key on before pushing the starter button. Make sure the transmission shifter is in neutral. You should get a reading of approximate battery voltage as the engine cranks. If you don't find battery voltage and the engine won't crank, there is an open circuit, which could be caused by a blown fuse, between the ignition switch and the relay.

A third wire on the relay will have battery voltage present with the key on. In some cases this terminal will be hot whenever the battery master switch is on. If not, trace this wire back to its source and repair the open circuit. Use your wiring diagram to determine where the wire is connected to power.

If battery voltage is present, determine if the remaining wire on the relay has battery voltage with the key in the start position. If it does, your starter-circuit problems have nothing to do with the solenoid or any of the wires going to it. If it doesn't, the solenoid is faulty and must be replaced.

### Current-Draw Test

Measuring the current drawn by the starter motor as it operates will give you some important information. However, specifications for the amperage drawn by different makes and models of engines are difficult to come by. Manufacturers usually don't provide these data even in their workshop manuals. As a means of estimating current requirements for starter motors, mechanics have for years used 1 amp for each cubic inch of engine displacement as a starting point for gasoline engines. Diesel engines operate with much higher compression ratios, so a diesel starter motor might draw as much as 2 amps per cubic inch of displacement. Both these values are only good for very rough estimates of starter-motor current. Gear reduction starter motors, which have become increasingly popular in recent years, typically draw much less current than do direct-drive motors—about half, for a two-to-one reduction ratio.

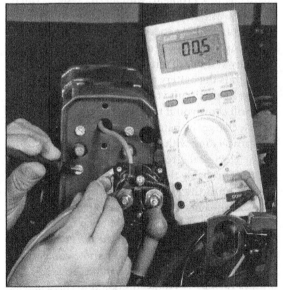

*Fig. 8-4. Using an ohmmeter to check ground continuity at the solenoid.*

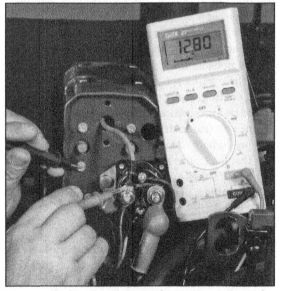

*Fig. 8-5. Checking for voltage supply to a starter-motor solenoid. You should get a reading of approximate battery voltage here.*

So, if the amperage specifications aren't available from the engine maker, how do we get them? Easy! Just do a current-draw test when you know your starter is working normally and record the amperage the starter motor uses in your manual. Then when a problem does crop up, you'll have a known value to work with as a benchmark.

To do the current-draw test, first make sure your starting battery is in good, serviceable condition. If you have an inductive-clamp multimeter capable of measuring up to about 500 amps, clamp the inductive pickup over the main battery cable going to the starter motor and take a reading while a helper cranks the engine. Now you have the normal amperage you can expect your starter motor to draw. If you don't have an inductive-pickup multimeter, one of the inexpensive Snap-On inductive meters shown in my tool collection in chapter 1 will do the job.

When you have a starting problem that you think might be caused by the starter motor, first double-check your battery to make sure it's charged and in good condition, then repeat the current-draw test. If your new reading is lower than the previously established benchmark reading, the starting problem is probably due to loose or corroded terminals in the battery cable connected to the starter motor. If the cable has been replaced since you established your benchmark and the terminals are clean and tight, the new cable is probably undersized and needs to be upgraded.

If the reading you get is higher than the benchmark reading, make sure that the problem is not caused by a mechanical fault such as a partially seized engine or a frozen drive unit. You may need to call in a pro to help out at this point. Once you're certain that the engine is not causing the problem, you can be sure that any excess current drawn by the starter motor is due to a fault within the motor. Remove it and send it out for overhaul.

### *Voltage-Drop Test*

Another useful test for your starter motor and starter circuit is to trace the circuit while checking for voltage drop at various points. This test will be outlined in the following section on outboard-engine starter circuits and will work just as well for inboard engines.

# Outboard-Engine Starter Circuits

A system overview of a typical starter-motor circuit on an outboard engine with remote control is shown in figure 8-6a on page 129. On many engines the remote-control harness plug is located under the engine cowl, so this plug is not as shown in the diagram.

If your outboard engine doesn't have a remote ignition switch, it will have a starter button located on the engine, and may have a neutral-safety switch integrated into the mechanical shift linkage under the cowl. A simplified wiring diagram of this circuit is shown in figure 8-6b on page 129. Your engine may have some of these connections in a wiring junction box. Also, starter-motor battery terminals are often used by manufacturers as handy places to attach additional circuits, so refer to your wiring diagram and narrow the number of wires down to what you see in this drawing; ignore the rest.

All outboard engines use inertia-type starter motors that engage the flywheel ring-gear when centrifugal force throws the drive gear upward. Medium-to-large outboard engines also use a remotely mounted solenoid just like those used on inboard engines. Problems with inertia systems can be as simple as a low battery, or corroded terminals causing a cranking speed that's too slow to generate enough inertia to engage the drive gear. So, as with any system, the first thing to check if trouble develops is the battery and all its connections.

The open-circuit voltage test described in chapter 5 will show you if the battery is fully charged. If it isn't, charge the battery to bring it up to snuff before proceeding with any of the following tests. Of all the electrical circuits on your boat, the starter circuit is probably the one that draws the most amperage; until the engine starts, the starter motor needs all the juice the battery can give it.

After you make sure your battery is fully charged, it's time to trace circuits. To test the integrated system found on small engines without remote control, first check for voltage at points throughout the circuit. Figure 8-6c on page 129 shows the points to check and the sequence in which you should check them. Make sure your engine ground and the ground bolt or cable (it should be the black one) are free of corrosion and tight.

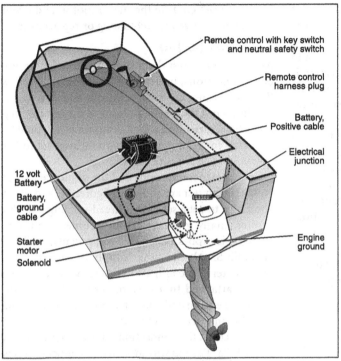

At point 1, check the power to the push-button switch. With your meter's black probe attached to an engine ground (the bolt or cable grounding the starter motor to the engine is a good point), use the red probe to check the other points along the circuit. The voltage at point 1 should be very nearly the same as your direct reading across the battery. If it isn't, there is a bad wire or broken connection between the battery and the terminal at point 1. This test illustrates how battery voltage gets to the hot side of the starter button, usually via a red wire.

If the voltage is good here, proceed to point 2. Disable the ignition to prevent the engine from starting as you do the next four tests. Press the starter button while holding the red probe to point 2, the output side of the starter button. You should find a reading of approximately 12 volts. If you don't, your starter button is defective and will need to be replaced.

*Fig. 8-6a. A typical outboard-engine starter-motor circuit with remote control.*

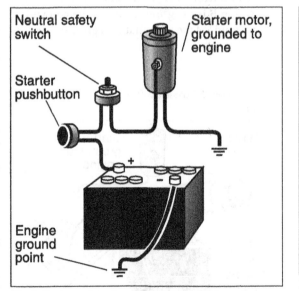

*Fig. 8-6b. An outboard engine with integrated starter-motor circuit and no remote control.*

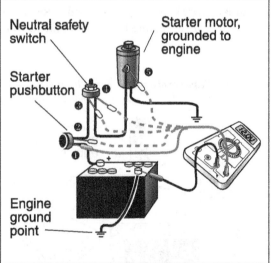

*Fig. 8-6c. Using a voltmeter to check the outboard integrated starter-motor circuit. Use the voltmeter to check voltage at each point indicated in the circuit.*

If you do find 12 volts at point 2, proceed to point 3 and connect the red probe to the hot side of the neutral-safety switch, which disconnects the starter-motor when the transmission is in gear. You should get another 12-volt reading. If not, the connection is bad or the wire between the starter button and the neutral-safety switch has a break in it. Repair or replace the wire as needed.

Next, be sure the transmission is in neutral and move your probe to point 4 (the output side of the safety switch). Push the button and take a reading; you should get 12 volts. If you don't, the neutral-safety switch is defective or out of adjustment. To check for proper adjustment, unbolt the switch from its bracket, allowing the switch button to extend fully. If you still cannot get a 12-volt reading at point 4, the switch is bad and must be replaced. If you do get a 12-volt reading, adjust the neutral-safety switch by repositioning it in its mount so that the shift linkage extends the button as far as it will go.

If you do get a 12-volt reading at point 4 and the engine still won't crank, move the red probe to point 5 at the battery terminal on the starter motor (the connection with the large red wire). With the engine in neutral, press the starter button and check for 12 volts. If you don't find it, there is a poor connection or a broken wire between points 4 and 5. Repair or replace the wire as required. If you do find 12 volts here, the problem is in the starter motor, and it will have to be removed for rebuilding or replacement.

## Voltage-Drop Test

Another simple test that can help you to locate any bad connections, undersized wires, or faulty parts that could cause excessive resistance and slow-crank condition in a starter circuit is called the *voltage-drop test*. This test requires a digital multimeter (you'll be checking for readings of 0.3 volt or less) set to the low-volts scale if it isn't self-scaling.

The meter connections and the sequence for the voltage-drop test are shown in figures 8-7a–d. It's a good idea to get a set of the thread-on alligator-clip probes (many multimeters now come with interchangeable probes as standard equipment), available at Radio Shack and other supply houses that sell multimeters. The alligator clips let you keep your probes attached to a wire or terminal while you crank the engine and take a reading, eliminating the need for an extra set of hands.

First check the connections shown as A and B in figure 8-7a. The red wire attached to connection A is from the ignition switch or starter button and provides power to the solenoid when the ignition switch or starter button is engaged. The black wire from connection B is the ground wire to the coil within the solenoid. Make sure that this ground is good.

*Figs. 8-7a–d. Sequence of a starter-motor circuit voltage-drop test being performed. Excessive voltage drop at any point in the circuit indicates a bad connection or possibly wire cabling that's too small.*

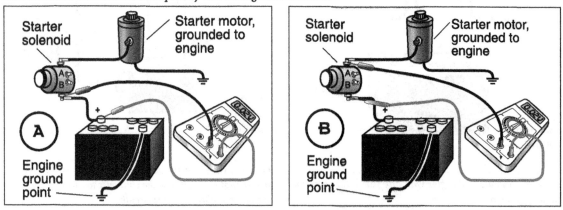

With the key off, use your multimeter set up to read resistance and check for continuity (a reading of very close to zero ohms) between the terminal at connection B and ground on the engine block. If you don't find continuity, repair the connections or replace the wire.

Next, turn the key to start and check for 12 volts at the terminal labeled connection A. If 12 volts is not present, the problem is somewhere in the wire from your starter-motor switch or neutral-safety switch. Follow the steps described later to correct this problem. If all seems well here, proceed with the voltage-drop test.

For each of the four steps to this test, the engine must be cranking but not firing. In step one, connect the meter as shown in figure 8-7a. Your voltage reading with the engine cranking should not exceed 0.3 volt. If it does, then the connection at the positive battery post is bad, the connection at the solenoid is bad, or the battery cable is too small and must be upgraded to a larger one. An easy way to check for a too-small battery cable is to feel it as you crank the engine. If it gets warm to the touch, it's too small.

Step two of the voltage-drop test, as shown in figure 8-7b, is to check the voltage drop through the solenoid. Connect the meter directly to the two largest terminals on the solenoid. A reading here in excess of 0.2 volt indicates a fault inside the solenoid, and it will have to be replaced.

Next connect the voltmeter as shown in figure 8-7c with one lead to the terminal on the output side

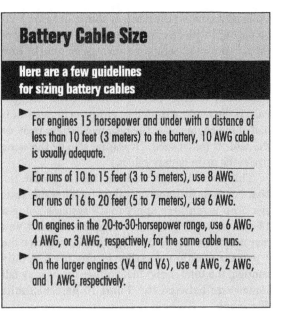

## Battery Cable Size

### Here are a few guidelines for sizing battery cables

► For engines 15 horsepower and under with a distance of less than 10 feet (3 meters) to the battery, 10 AWG cable is usually adequate.

► For runs of 10 to 15 feet (3 to 5 meters), use 8 AWG.

► For runs of 16 to 20 feet (5 to 7 meters), use 6 AWG.

► On engines in the 20-to-30-horsepower range, use 6 AWG, 4 AWG, or 3 AWG, respectively, for the same cable runs.

► On the larger engines (V4 and V6), use 4 AWG, 2 AWG, and 1 AWG, respectively.

of the solenoid and the other to the large positive terminal on the starter motor. While cranking the engine, your voltage reading should not exceed 0.2 volt. If it does, the connection at the solenoid is bad or, as with the battery cables, the wire connecting the solenoid to the starter motor is too small. (This wire should be the same size as the main battery cables.) A too-small cable would only be a problem if someone changed the cable before you. Factory wiring is carefully engineered for size and is never too small. Difficulties are caused when improper repairs are made.

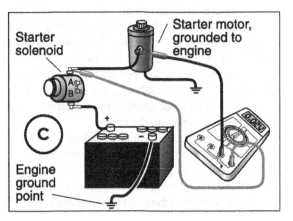

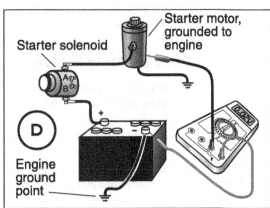

Finally, connect the meter as shown in figure 8-7d on page 131 with one probe connected to the body of the starter motor (scrape away a little paint to be sure of a good contact) and the other probe connected to the negative terminal on the battery. Turn the key to start. Your voltage reading should be less than 0.3 volt. If the reading is higher, either a connection is bad at the engine or at the negative battery post, or the cable is undersized. (It should also be the same size as the main battery cables.)

This test will work with any starter circuit, inboard or outboard, and the values for allowable voltage drop given here apply to all systems using a 12-volt power, regardless of engine size. Also, you may notice that the total voltage drop may exceed the 3 percent mentioned earlier in this book. Oddly enough, the total individual voltage drops may fall somewhere between the 3 and 10 percent limits discussed.

I have always felt that the 3 percent maximum is most important for a starter-motor circuit, meaning that the total voltage drop would be no more than 0.36 volt for the entire circuit. Having said that, I can tell you that engine-service manuals consistently use a 0.2-volt maximum drop for all the connections and parts up to the starter motor, and 0.3 volt back to the battery as the acceptable limit; this gives a maximum of 0.5 volt. The truth is, a well-done factory circuit will give voltage readings well below the 3 percent tolerance, and I prefer to use that figure for my own criterion. I mention the 0.2- and 0.3-volt specifications here only because I know you'll run into them if you follow your service manual as you should, when doing these tests.

## Testing the Neutral-Safety Switch

If your boat has remote engine controls, with the shift lever and ignition switch at the helm, the neutral-safety switch is located inside the control unit. Therefore, you should never attempt to diagnose problems with this switch without the aid of the workshop manual for your engine and control unit. There are just too many variables in wire color-coding and control-unit disassembly procedures

to cover them all here. In fact, unless you're fairly confident as a mechanic, you should never remove or attempt to disassemble the remote-control unit. It's full of spring-loaded levers, shims, and cable attachments that are critical in their placement and function. So beware!

However, it's quite easy to check all wiring and parts affected by the neutral-safety switch, enabling you to consult intelligently about the problem with your mechanic.

Your neutral-safety switch is electrically connected to both your ignition switch and the starter solenoid. When you shift into neutral, the switch should close, completing the circuit between the ignition switch and the terminal marked connection A, shown in figure 8-7a on page 130. The wire on this terminal connects the solenoid to the ignition switch and should be identified in your wiring diagram. The quick check to see if the switch is functioning is to look for a 12-volt reading at this terminal with the key on start. Simply connect your meter with the black probe to ground and the red probe to this terminal, and have someone shift into neutral and turn the key to start. If you get no reading when the key is turned to start, the problem is probably within the control unit, but not necessarily.

There could be corrosion at the remote-control master plug, or there could be a break in the wire connecting the plug assembly to the back of the boat. Using your wiring diagram as a guide, identify this solenoid feed wire. Next, disconnect the wire from the solenoid and identify which terminal it goes to in the plug assembly. With your multimeter set to the low-ohms scale, check for continuity between these two points. (Using your alligator clips, you may want to make an extended jumper lead to one of the test leads from your meter, depending on the distance between the plug assembly and the solenoid.) You should get a reading of nearly zero ohms if this wire is intact from the plug to the engine.

If you get a high reading or a reading of infinity, there is a break in the wire or a corroded connection between the plug and the engine. In some cases, this will mean replacing the extension harness as a unit. If the wire from the control unit to the solenoid is a series of individual wires wrapped in electrical tape or plastic tie-wraps, you should be able to trace the harness and find the break. Repair or replace the wire as required. If you get a resistance reading near zero, showing continuity, the problem is within the remote-control unit and must be fixed by your dealer.

Figure 8-8 shows the extension harness being tested with a multimeter.

Testing for neutral-safety switch maladjustment is quite simple. Hold the shift-control lever with one hand and the ignition key with the other. Hold the key in the start position and gently work the shift lever to its extremes in the neutral position. (Never try to shift into gear without the engine running; you could damage to your shift mechanism.) If you hear the starter motor try to engage, then the switch is out of adjustment or the remote-control mechanism is badly worn and will need to be serviced by your dealer. Don't be surprised if the control mechanism needs to be replaced due to excessive wear of the internal parts. This is not uncommon on older units.

# Engine Ignition Switch

Like the neutral-safety switch, most ignition switches are located inside the remote-control unit described above. This makes testing difficult, but some of the same procedures you used to test the neutral-safety switch also apply to the ignition switch. Essentially, you're testing for battery voltage at the switch and for continuity to the solenoid. This can be done outside the remote-control unit up to the main plug assembly on the control unit. If the wiring harness connecting the engine to the remote-control unit is in good condition, which can be checked visually by tracing it from the engine up under the coaming of the boat to the control unit, problems are probably within the remote-control unit.

All manufacturers provide good, functional descriptions of each terminal in the wiring-harness plug, and all provide a test sequence to verify continuity between the terminals on this plug with the ignition switch in different positions. However, a good quick check of these terminals can also be made using your multimeter.

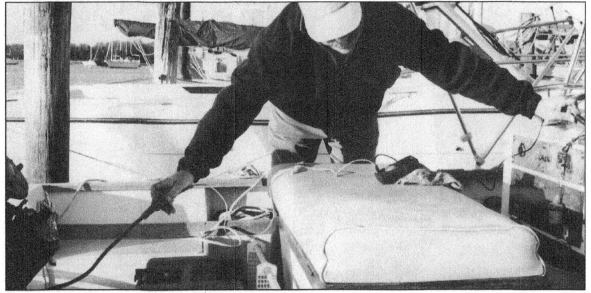

*Fig. 8-8. Checking the wiring harness for continuity between the remote control and the engine. In this picture I've disconnected the plug at the back of the ignition switch and at the engine, and am using my ohmmeter to check for breaks in the wiring harness.*

First verify that you have 12 volts at the ignition switch. Use your wiring diagram to identify the power lead from the engine to the main plug on the engine side of the circuit. (This wire is usually fed by a jumper lead that comes from the starter-motor solenoid or from a junction box bolted to the side of the engine block.) This terminal will generally be much larger than the others. If you find 12 volts at this plug and the plug terminals are in good condition, it's reasonable to assume that 12 volts is getting to the remote-control assembly and feeding the ignition switch.

In all cases there will be a wire coming from the remote-control assembly that provides 12 volts to the ignition module (CDI unit) on your engine. This wire activates the electronic circuitry within the module while the engine is running. Use your wiring diagram to identify this wire on your engine. Make sure the emergency-shutoff switch is off, and turn on the ignition key. A reading of 12 volts where this wire attaches to the ignition module tells you that this function of the ignition switch is OK. If you don't get 12 volts here, you need to trace the main harness and look for any trouble spots; correct them as needed.

If no trouble spots are found, the problem is in the remote-control unit. A possible trouble spot could be the point where you drilled a hole through the harness when you were mounting that new rod holder or downrigger.

In addition to 12 volts at the ignition module when the key is turned to start and the shift in neutral, you'll also need 12 volts at one of the small terminals on the solenoid. All manufacturers use a color-coded wire for this connection. (OMC and Mercury use a yellow-and-red one.) Remember that the black wire from the solenoid is a ground wire and not the one to check. Use the test described earlier to check for voltage at this point. If 12 volts is found while the key is in start, you know that the ig-

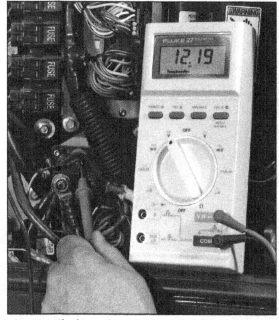

Fig. 8-9a. Checking voltage supply to an outboard-engine solenoid with the key in the start position. Remember, with the key in the start position, if the engine is cranking, the voltage reading will drop down to as little as about 9.6 volts.

Fig. 8-9b. Checking voltage at the outboard solenoid with the key in the "on" position. With this test, you should get a reading near battery voltage.

nition switch is OK. If you don't find 12 volts here, trace the harness as for the other wires. If no damage can be found, the problem is inside the control box.

Figure 8-9a on page 134 shows the solenoid terminal being checked for 12 volts with the ignition switch in start. Figure 8-9b on page 134 shows the positive wire to the starter solenoid being checked for 12 volts with the ignition switch on.

## Other Outboard-Engine Starter-Motor Problems

In addition to slow starting or no starting, some severe mechanical problems may also cause a no-start condition. The possibility of extreme engine overheating and water getting inside your engine is real. The symptom for either condition is a loud "clunk" as the starter-motor drive gear engages the flywheel, only to encounter an engine that will not turn over. In the case of a manual-start motor, the pull cord simply won't budge more than several inches as you pull with all your might. If either of these deadly symptoms is present, you have an internal engine problem that goes beyond the scope of this book.

For a solution to these and most other outboard-engine problems, I strongly recommend my book, *Outboard Engines: Maintenance, Troubleshooting, and Repair.*

This concludes the starter-motor section of this book. By following the tips and guidelines here, you should be able to trace your way through just about any starter-motor and starter-circuit problems you encounter, and keep your boat on the water instead of in the shop.

# Chapter 9

# Installing Your Own DC Accessories

Installing your own electrical equipment is not only a rewarding personal accomplishment, it can also save you a lot of hard-earned money. If you bought a new boat, it may have come with a long list of optional extras—probably a VHF radio and a fishfinder, and maybe a chart plotter and radar. If you bought a used boat, the previous owner undoubtedly added an assortment of electronic and electrical gadgetry to the list. However, no matter how well equipped your new or used boat may be, you'll eventually want to make some modifications to the electrical system. Sooner or later you'll want to add a new light fixture, an upgraded battery charger, a better VHF radio, or an extra bilge pump. By following my recommendations and advice in this chapter, even a novice electrician can easily install all these things and many more.

## Before You Begin

Before installing any new electrical accessory, there are some important things to consider. Among the most important are the voltage and amperage that will be required by the new item. However, you must also think about the capacity of your distribution panel, the fuse or circuit breaker you're going to use, and the size of the wire and how you're going to run it.

### Voltage Requirements

You must be sure that the accessory, whatever it may be, is designed to operate at the system voltage in your boat. Most small to medium-sized powerboats today operate with 12-volt electrical systems. Larger boats, however, may have 24-volt or even 32-volt systems. Some even have systems that combine voltages, with certain items running at 12 volts and others running at 24 volts. Higher voltages are used on larger boats because the higher voltage is more efficient and the builder can reduce the size of the

wiring and many parts. (A 24-volt starter motor is much smaller and lighter than an equivalent 12-volt starter motor, for example.)

With higher voltage, wiring ampacity goes up as voltage increases. This not only saves money but also considerable weight, and the smaller wire is easier to work with. If you recall from Ohm's law, as we discussed in chapter 1, there is a direct and linear trade-off between amperage and voltage. This means that an anchor winch using 80 amps with a 12-volt system only needs 40 amps to do the same amount of work with a 24-volt system. On a 40-foot boat with a 70-foot wiring run from the battery to the winch and back to the battery, this means the builder can use a 1/0 AWG cable instead of a 2/0 AWG cable. Using West Marine 2006 prices, the builder saves nearly $125 just in the cost of the cable; plus, all the components are smaller and lighter and easier to install.

When you buy a new piece of equipment to install on your boat, the manufacturer will always provide the voltage required to operate the equipment. It will be printed in the installation instructions or on the equipment itself, and sometimes in both places. Before you begin installing your new gadget, double-check to make sure you have one with the right voltage. All the following assumes you're working on a boat with a 12-volt system.

### Amperage Requirements

The next important specification is the expected amperage the appliance needs to operate efficiently. Again, the packaging should provide this important information and will often recommend the fuse or circuit-breaker rating as well. Sometimes the rated voltage, amperage, or wattage is also embossed on the equipment, but not always. Wherever you get the numbers, a consideration of the amperage and voltage should always be the first step in selecting the appropriate wire gauge to use on the new circuit.

## Length of Wire

Next, you should measure the wiring run from the distribution panel to the accessory and back to the panel. Don't just measure a straight line from the distribution panel to the location of the new accessory and back again. Make sure you measure the actual route the wire will follow. It isn't at all unusual for the actual route of the wire to be double the straight-line distance or even more.

## Voltage Drop and Wire Size

Remember that the longer the run, the higher the potential voltage drop in your new circuit will be and the larger the wire you'll need to overcome it. Before you continue, decide now the extent of the voltage drop you're willing to accept. Remember that the ABYC standards recommend no more than a 3 percent drop for any critical gear such as electronic navigation and communication equipment. However, a new cabin light could fall into the 10 percent category.

Personally, I use the 3 percent standard in all cases. Boatbuilders of high-end boats usually use the 3 percent standard throughout their new boats. However, high-volume, price-conscious builders will often use the 10 percent maximum just to save money, which is how they can offer their products at affordable prices. Many noncritical accessories will work just fine with the higher voltage drop, but others will suffer reduced performance. Interior lighting, for example, will function at the 10 percent maximum voltage drop but with a considerable loss in light intensity for a given bulb wattage.

Use the charts provided in chapter 4 to help you through this decision on voltage drop and wire size. My recommendation is that unless you're on a very tight budget, you follow the example of the high-end builders and use a 3 percent voltage drop for everything. You can't go wrong.

## Wire Type

Once you have determined the gauge of the wire you'll need in your new circuit, think about the wire insulation requirements and again refer to chapter 4 for help determining what's required.

A time-saving alternative to running separate wires for the hot and ground sides of your new piece of equipment is quality marine-grade duplex wire that has the two conductors bonded together much like a household extension cord. (Household wire, of course, should never be used on a boat; the insulation is not rated for the marine environment.) Duplex wire has a double layer of insulation, and it's much easier to fish through small holes and tight places than individual wires. A single run of duplex wire is slightly more expensive than a double run of single wires but usually not enough to offset the convenience and other advantages it offers.

If you're trying to match ABYC color-coding recommendations, you might have trouble finding duplex with the correct colors for the circuits you're working with. Be diligent; the better vendors stock the common colors, and they can order other colors for you. They may ask you to order an entire roll, though, which may not be practical in some cases. If you can't find the colors you want, use the alternative methods for labeling wires I discussed in chapter 4.

## Fuses and Circuit Breakers

Once your wiring has been selected, you must select the appropriate fuse or circuit breaker for your new circuit. This can be a little tricky. Remember that the circuit protection may be rated to as much as 150 percent of the amperage-handling capacity of the smallest wire in the circuit. This means that if you connect a new accessory with a continuous draw of 5 amps, you would use a fuse or breaker rated not necessarily at 150 percent of 5 amps (7.5 amps), but rather at 150 percent of the wiring capacity. Let's take a closer look at this problem.

The wire must be rated at the engine-room specification if *any* length of the wire goes through this space, regardless of length. Keep in mind that the following ampacity figures are for wire with an insulation rating of 105°C, which is the most common type found in marine supply houses.

If your new 12-volt accessory were going to be mounted 10 feet away from your boat's main distribution panel (measured along the wiring), you would have a total run of 20 feet. Using the 3 percent voltage-drop criterion and referring to figure 4-3 on page 44, you can see that the correct wire to use is 14 AWG. By using the ampacity table, figure 4-7 on page 48, you can see that 14 AWG wire has an ampacity of 35 amps outside the engine room, and just under 30 amps inside the engine room.

Well, in this example, even though the actual load is only 5 amps, we have connected the load to a wire with a base ampacity of, let's say, 30 amps (we'll use the engine-room rating here). We could use a circuit breaker or fuse rated as high as 45 amps (150 percent of 30) and provide adequate protection for the circuit's wiring. However, we don't need that much protection, and in this case a common 10-amp breaker or fuse would be quite appropriate and would provide safe, conservative protection for the circuit. Remember, when installing overcurrent protection, it's the circuit wiring you're protecting. Any protection for the equipment the circuit is supplying will be done at the equipment (with the exception of motor loads as discussed in chapter 4), which may be internally protected, but in fact usually is protected by a fuse or breaker in the circuitry.

This explains why most electronic equipment has an individual fuse in addition to the fuse or circuit breaker on the circuit. The main fuse or circuit breaker on each circuit is there to protect the wiring that's common to all equipment on the circuit, and the internal fuse is there to protect each individual piece of equipment. If, in the example above, there were two other pieces of equipment sharing the circuit with our 5-amp device, one drawing 1 amp and another drawing 2 amps, you would have a total of 8 amps on the circuit. You could then have the 10-amp main fuse or circuit breaker for the wiring and three individual fuses of 5, 2, and 1 amp each to protect the equipment.

## Panel Feed Wire

An additional consideration, especially if you're going to be adding heavier loads or multiple additional loads to your distribution panel, is the size of the wire and the rating of any circuit breakers or fuses feeding the distribution panel. Keep in mind that the builder may have based the size of the positive and ground wires to the panel only on the factory-installed equipment, even though the panel may have blank sockets where additional breakers and circuits could be added.

Distribution-panel ratings are based on the sum of the ratings of all the circuit breakers installed on the panel. The ampacity of the conductors feeding the panel must match that total amperage. Thus, a panel with two 20-amp breakers, five 10-amp breakers, and five 5-amp breakers (not an uncommon arrangement) would need a master circuit breaker or fuse and a feed wire that could handle 115 amps if everything on the boat were turned on at once.

The ABYC also says that if the panel has a master circuit breaker (on the panel) rated at no more than 100 percent of the total rating of all the breakers on the panel, the conductors feeding the panel can be protected at up to 150 percent of the amperage of the feed conductors. If the main panel has no master circuit breaker, the fuse or circuit breaker for the feed wire may not be rated at more than 100 percent of the conductor ampacity. This means that you must be sure the breaker protection and the wire size are appropriate for any additional circuits you decide to wire into the existing distribution panel on your boat. To determine if a wiring upgrade feeding your panel is needed, get the AWG size for the positive feed and DC negative (ground) lead from the insulation, and use the ampacity table in figure 4-7 to see if you need to make any changes.

## Color-Coding and Wiring Diagram

Any wiring you add to your boat needs to be properly identified. Color coding, in accordance with the ABYC standards, can help identify the function of individual wires, but you should also draw up a wiring diagram of the circuit you've added and put it with the other paperwork in your boat's information package. If you already have a master wiring diagram, making an addendum to it now will make life a lot easier three seasons down the waterway when the new circuit starts to act up. For a list of recommendations on alternate wire identification, refer to chapter 4.

Once you deal with all of the above, you're ready to install your own DC accessories. Some common additions follow, with my personal step-by-step approach to installing each accessory outlined. After reviewing these examples, you should be ready for just about any circuit you may wish to add to your boat.

## Installing a New Cabin Light

If you're installing a conventional incandescent light or one of the newer halogen lights, don't worry about polarity. These light bulbs really don't care which way the electricity flows through them. If you're adding a low-voltage fluorescent fixture, however, you'll have to observe any positive or negative wiring indicated by the manufacturer. Circuits with dimmer switches (rheostats) and light-emitting diodes (LEDs), which are commonly used in instrument lighting and are even available now as replacements for conventional low-voltage light bulbs, are also sensitive to polarity.

Some of the companies that make light fixtures recommend the correct fuse to use and the appropriate wire gauge based on the length of the wire run. If you don't have these specifications, you must figure these numbers out for yourself. The packaging should at least tell you the operating voltage of the bulb in the fixture, so you'll have at least one of the needed values. Also, the wattage will be given with most light fixtures. By using the wattage equation from chapter 1, you can easily calculate the amperage by dividing the wattage by the voltage. The result will be the amperage the fixture will need. For example, a 20-watt bulb on a 12-volt circuit will draw 1.7 amps ($20 \div 12 = 1.7$).

Once the amperage is known, measure the distance of the run from the distribution panel to the new fixture and back again. A quick reference to the table will give you the wire size to use for the job. Since this is a cabin light, you should use a dark blue wire to the light and a black or yellow (preferably yellow) wire for the return to the panel.

One precaution regarding fixtures of this type: Often a manufacturer provides a short length of wire lead from the fixture to facilitate attachment to your wiring harness or new circuit. Typically these leads will be 16 AWG. Regardless of which gauge wire you select to run from your distribution panel to the new fixture, you must always rate the circuit overcurrent protection at the ampacity of the smallest wire in the circuit. In this example it would be the 16 AWG wire supplied with the fixture, assuming you use a 14 AWG feeder and ground return wire for a long run.

### Step-by-Step Instructions

So, with the basics above in mind, my step-by-step approach to adding a new cabin light looks like this:

1. After selecting a light fixture you like and making sure that the voltage is the same as it is on your boat, find the wattage of the bulb.

2. Once the wattage is known, determine the amperage requirements for the fixture. In the above example, a 12-volt, 20-watt bulb would require 1.7 amps. Always round up, so in this case the amperage requirements would be 2 amps.

3. Use the table of wire gauges in figure 4-3 on page 44 for acceptable voltage drop and length of wire run. If the amperage requirements are less than the minimum specified on the table, use the gauge indicated for the minimum value (5 amps). In any event, never use wire smaller than 16 AWG when adding anything to your boat, no matter how little current is drawn by the equipment you're installing. Wire smaller than 16 AWG is only used for electronic control circuits and small connecting links on the back of instrument panels and the like.

4. Select the switch or circuit breaker on the distribution panel you'll be using to feed this new circuit.

5. Determine that the amperage rating of the fuse or circuit breaker is appropriate for the total of all circuits or loads being fed by that breaker. For example: In this case you may already be servicing several cabin lights in addition to the one you're adding. Total circuit protection at the panel must cover the amperage of all the lights on any given circuit. The fuse or circuit breaker must not be rated at more than 150 percent of the ampacity of the smallest wire used, which

could well be the pigtail on the back of the fixture, not the feed wire.

6. Check the total load on the distribution panel, and if the wire and circuit protection on the panel are not large enough, change them to a larger size before doing anything else.

7. Once wire gauge and circuit protection ratings are determined, string the wire from the distribution panel to the location of your new cabin light. Don't forget to support your new wiring at least every 18 inches, and preferably more frequently than that. If the wire must go through an area where chafe protection is needed, provide it as shown in figure 4-20 on page 59.

8. Connect the ground wire from your new light to the negative bus bar on the back of the distribution panel and the positive wire to the switch or circuit breaker output terminal. You might need a two-to-one connector to tie into a breaker or fuse on the panel.

9. At the fixture end of the wire, use crimp-type butt connectors to attach the new light to the feeder wires. If the wire on light-fixture pigtails is more than two AWG sizes apart, use one of the new-style step-down butt connectors available through West Marine or any good electrical supply house.

10. Finally, flip on the switch. Is there light? If so, your new circuit is a success. Mount your new fixture in position and enjoy.

Figure 9-1 provides a wiring diagram showing what your new light circuit might look like in a typical installation. (Individual switches are not illustrated at the light fixtures.)

## Installing a New Bilge Pump

To install a new bilge pump, first establish the gph (gallons per hour) rating of the pump you'll need based on the volume of the area the pump will service, the height from the base of the pump to the point of discharge, and other factors.

With bilge pumps, depending upon several variables, the actual amount of bilge water the thing will move overboard will vary considerably from the rating embossed on the pump. Aside from mechanical variations in pumps, you'll need a circuit with a 3 percent maximum voltage drop if you're going to get anything close to the rated output of the pump. Excess voltage drop here will affect pump motor speed and the volume of water it will move.

According to the ABYC and the chart in figure 2-5 on page 16, a bilge-pump circuit should have a brown positive wire, and either a black or a yellow ground-return wire is acceptable.

Because this load is a 12-volt motor, the bilge pump must be protected with a fuse rated at no higher than the manufacturer's recommendation. In my own tests, I have experimented with fuses as little as 1.5 amps over the rating recommended by the pump manufacturer. In these tests I locked the pump's impeller to simulate an actual installation and let the pump run. Figure 9-2 on page 141 is a photograph of the result of one test. As you can clearly see, the body of the pump is melted away and badly deformed. The wires feeding the pump, on the other hand, are unscathed.

Why does this happen? Why is the pump itself destroyed, generating enough heat to torch the boat while the wires remain intact? When a motor seizes, it works

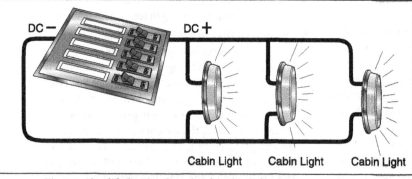

*Fig. 9-1. Simplified wiring diagram of a cabin light circuit.*

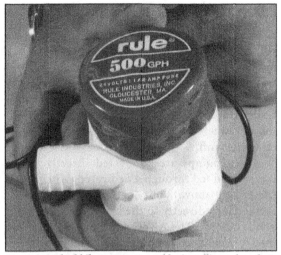

*Fig. 9-2. Melted bilge pump, caused by installing a fuse that was overrated for the motor. Notice that the wiring survived unscathed.*

against the seized impeller and heat builds up within the motor windings. As the motor heats, the internal resistance increases and the current flowing through the circuit feeding the motor actually *decreases*. You can see how this works by using Ohm's law and swapping around some numbers. If source voltage stays the same and resistance goes up, amperage goes down. In this case, the amperage decreases to less than the rating of the fuse. Both the wiring and the fuse remain intact, but current will continue to flow to the motor until it destroys itself. Therefore, never change the fuse on a bilge pump or any other motor circuit for one with a higher amperage rating than what is recommended by the manufacturer.

Do you remember from chapter 4 that a slow-blow fuse is often used in motor circuits? These accommodate the very high start-up amperage used by electrical motors. Check the manufacturer's recommendations for all motor circuits on board your boat, and have the appropriate spare fuses in your spares kit. Installing just any old fuse on a motor circuit could be an especially bad move. It could literally cause a meltdown of the motor as well as a lot of unnecessary correspondence between you and your insurance company.

Now that you have determined the gauge of wire and the size of the fuse you'll need for your new bilge-pump circuit, remember that the insulation of the wire should be moisture-, fuel-, and oil-resistant in case a spill or leak ends up in the bilge. Not that you'd pump the spill out with the bilge pump, of course, but the reason for this precaution is so that while you're removing the oil by other means you won't damage the wiring to the pump.

Next, remember that any wire terminals exposed to bilge water require a waterproof connection. A good choice for joining wires in the bilge or in other wet areas is the new crimp-type connectors that have a sealing heat-shrink jacket, as shown in figure 9-3.

## Securing the Wires

To remain in compliance with the ABYC standards, secure the newly installed bilge-pump wires at a minimum of 18-inch intervals. The truth is that this standard is quite lenient, and most quality builders secure their wiring at 4- to 6-inch intervals.

Good choices for securing your wiring are the "p" clips or screw-footed tie-wraps, available at any marine supply house. Look through the selection at a good electrical supply retailer, and you'll find a multitude of ingenious options for keeping your wires where you want them.

*Fig. 9-3. Heat-shrink-type crimp connectors. These are expensive, but worth every penny if you can get your hands on them.*

## Dedicated Bilge-Pump Switch Panels

Now that you've got some of the basic supplies assembled, decide if you want to tie this new circuit into the distribution panel or connect it directly to one of your batteries with an optional, dedicated bilge-pump switch panel, as shown in figure 9-4. These switch panels offer an integral fuse and a choice of manual or automatic operation. The better units (as shown) also have a pilot light that lights up when the circuit is on. Be careful here, though: I have found many of these switch panels with 10-amp fuses installed in the holder. If you have one of the smaller pumps, this is a problem; they often require as little as a 1.5-amp fuse. A 10-amp fuse would never do for a pump with a locked rotor; the fuse would surely allow the pump to burn up. Always double-check the fuse rating when installing one of these switch panels.

Although the bilge-pump switch panel described above could be made from various off-the-shelf components by a boatowner who had the inclination and time to do it, these assemblies are so reasonably priced that I generally use the standard switch panel—after making sure the fuse is adequate, of course.

*Fig. 9-4. Bilge-pump master switch panel.*

## Connecting the Pump to Power

There are several points to consider as you determine where you want to connect your new bilge pump to a power supply. If you connect it to the main distribution panel, the pump will be off when the master switch is thrown. This might be fine for a boat on a trailer, but less so for one kept at the dock or on a mooring where the pump needs to be on while everything else is off.

Often pumps are connected directly to the battery and fed through a dedicated switch panel (described above), but loading up a series of connections directly to the battery is simply not good practice. The ABYC suggests that no more than four conductors be attached to any one terminal. If your battery has a stud-type battery post, you'll be limited by that restriction. Also, locating fuses near the battery is a mistake due to the potential accumulation of corrosive vapors near the batteries. The resulting corrosion of the fuse and fuse holder can cause excessive voltage drop and all the problems associated with it.

I'm not suggesting that you not attach your new pump directly to the battery—it is often the best option—but if you do, use the ABYC standard to your advantage. You can mount the fuse as far as 72 inches away from the battery (as long as the wiring is sheathed in addition to its insulation) and still be in compliance with the standard.

Another option is to use a single appropriately sized wire to feed an auxiliary fuse panel connecting all the onboard equipment you want, feeding directly from the battery rather than through the main distribution panel. Locate it far enough away from the battery to avoid the corrosive fumes but close enough to comply with the ABYC standard. Companies like Ancor, Newmar, and Blue Sea Systems make perfectly suitable fuse panels for this purpose.

## Automatic Float Switch

Once you've decided how you're going to provide power to your new circuit, you need to decide if you want to install an automatic float switch for your new pump. Since most installations do use an automatic float switch of some type, I'll illustrate that setup here.

Figure 9-5 shows the basic parts to this new circuit laid out and ready for the installation of the pump and the switch.

## Tools

Tools you'll need for this installation will include the following, some of which are assembled in figure 9-6:

▶ a wire cutter, a wire stripper, and a set of quality crimping pliers (described in chapter 1)

▶ a heat source for shrinking the heat-shrink tubing (a Bic lighter will do the job, but a heat gun is better, and safer)

▶ slotted and Phillips-head screwdrivers to match the screws you'll use to mount the panel, float switch, and pump assembly

▶ an electric drill with an assortment of drill bits

▶ a small saw—either a hole saw or an electric jigsaw, depending on how you decide to mount your master switch—to cut out a hole for the switch panel

Last, but certainly not least, you'll need a wiring diagram to help you lay out your new bilge-pump circuit. All of the major manufacturers of bilge pumps and switch panels supply this vital information as part of their installation instructions. They'll often include a recommended wire gauge to use for a certain length of wire run, saving one step in the installation process. However, I have noticed that the recommended wire size provided by some manufac-

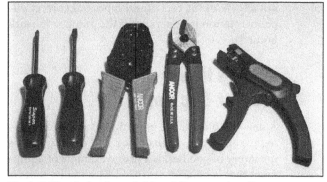

*Fig. 9-6. Electrical tools needed for a bilge-pump installation.*

turers of bilge pumps tends to be larger than what is allowed by the sizing chart in figure 4-7. My advice here is clear: for warranty and liability reasons as well as your own peace of mind, whenever there is a disagreement or conflict among different sources of information, always go with the recommendations of the manufacturer, even if it seems like overkill. Remember, a wire that is too heavy will never do any harm (up to a reasonable point, of course), whereas a wire that's too small can destroy your boat.

Figure 9-7 shows the diagram that comes with a popular pump assembly available from Rule Industries.

The pump motor shown here is, like most bilge pumps, polarity sensitive. Reversing the positive and ground return wires on the pump motor will cause the pump to run backwards. Most bilge pumps (but

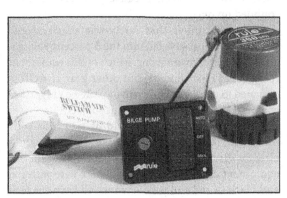

*Fig. 9-5. Basic circuit components.*

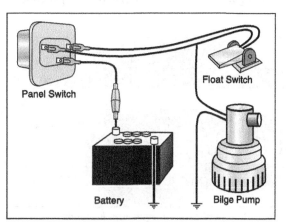

*Fig. 9-7. Wiring diagram for a bilge pump.*

not all) are of the centrifugal type, and correct impeller rotation is imperative if the pump is to work properly.

## Adding a New Compact-Disc Player

A new CD player, like any other electronic equipment you decide to install or add to your boat's inventory of goodies, is a prime example of equipment that is polarity sensitive. Essentially, motors and any equipment that contains any type of solid-state circuitry all fall into this category. It pays to be quite cautious here, as mixing the positive and negative conductors can burn out internal components of valuable equipment quicker than you can snap your fingers.

Having said that, the rest of the installation of a CD player is relatively easy, especially if you have found the above descriptions of the installation of the cabin light and bilge pump easy to understand.

Really, the most difficult part of installing a CD player is figuring out where you want to mount it and cutting the hole in the panel for the face plate. Some electronic equipment today will have a heat sink mounted on the back chassis, as shown in figure 9-8. This heat sink does just what the name implies; it radiates heat away from the parts within the equipment it's designed to protect. Make sure that the airflow past this heat sink is adequate to provide necessary cooling when the equipment is in use. Proper cooling

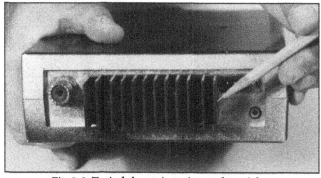

*Fig. 9-8. Typical electronic equipment heat sink.*

of the equipment will improve its longevity and performance. How much cooling air is enough? Not much; just don't stuff your valuable CD player into a tiny hole with no room for air to circulate.

Once you decide on a good location for your new CD player and cut the necessary mounting holes, you're ready to wire it in. I'm sure you remembered to check the packaging before you left the store after buying the player. Quite often the installation instructions include a template for the mounting cutout. Having this template will save a lot of time and ensure that you get a proper installation with a minimum of fitting.

As with any electrical equipment, always follow the fuse recommendations provided by the manufacturer. Most CD players come with a two-wire harness about 18 to 24 inches long with an in-line fuse holder already installed on the power lead. Typically, these leads are made with 16 AWG wire. Since most such equipment (but not all) draws less than about 1.5 amps, 16 AWG is usually large enough for runs of up to 30 feet (where the CD player is located 15 feet away from the power source). If the distance from the power goes over 15 feet, step up to 14 AWG.

In this example, using the 3 percent voltage drop from chapter 4 for a circuit length of 30 feet, 1.5 amps falls below the 5-amp minimum column in figure 4-3 on page 44. Remember to always round up in wire size and use the 5-amp column calling for a 12 AWG wire for a 30-foot run. As soon as you move over to the 40-foot column, the table calls for 10 AWG wire. If the run were, say, 32 feet I would stick to the 12 AWG, because you have already rounded up once.

Also, remember that safety-related electronic equipment will always fall into the 3 percent voltage-drop category for wire sizing. Much of this equipment (particularly fish-finders, but other gear as well) is designed to work in a fairly narrow voltage range. (See chapter 12 for more details on this subject.)

Your new CD player should be tied into your main distribution panel just like the cabin light already discussed. Since it falls into the general-equipment category, the use of duplex wire with red and black or red and yellow wires will keep the feed wire in compliance with the ABYC's color-coding scheme.

A 10-amp circuit breaker or fuse at the panel will be a good choice here as long as the manufacturer-supplied fuse and holder are not removed from the circuit. Remember that the panel fuse will protect the wiring to the CD player, and in the case of 16 AWG wire, the basic ampacity for 105°C-rated wire (the most common) is 25 amps, so a main breaker rated at 10 amps is safe and, in fact, conservative.

Since the factory-supplied harness that came with the CD player probably came with quick-disconnect bullet-type connectors, you can use the same type to splice into the harness you're running from the panel to the player. These bullet-type connectors come in male and female halves, and are a good way to ensure that the polarity of the equipment is observed. Just make sure the correct connector ends up on the appropriate wire.

Many installers cut off these bullet connectors and replace them with straight butt-type crimp connectors, feeling that these might be less likely to corrode. The truth is that this is not such a great idea, for several reasons. First, the standard male and female bullet connectors enable a quick disconnect in the event you need to remove the CD player for service or whatever reason, and the connector can be reused when you reinstall it. Second, most bullet connectors that I've seen have a rubber seal to minimize water intrusion. Last, these connectors are a good way to ensure that polarity is observed, regardless of wiring color.

Figure 9-9 shows the bullet-type plug connector in question.

For the installation of the wire for your new CD player, follow the same ten steps for installing the cabin light, and you'll be ready to go with the main wiring for the player. (Review the Step-by-Step Instructions earlier in this chapter.)

Keep in mind that many pieces of electronic equipment today will have two positive feed wires, one switched and the other intended to supply a constant DC current. This is to maintain any internal memory the equipment may have for such things as preselected radio stations. So when selecting your power for the memory function on your player (if needed—check

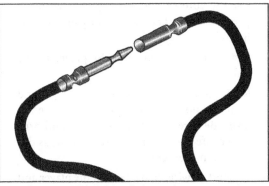

*Fig. 9-9. Typical "bullet-type" electrical connectors. These are useful if installed as opposites on the positive and negative return wires in preventing a reverse-polarity situation that can damage sensitive electronic equipment.*

your owner's manual), remember that this connection must be live at all times, and probably the best source of power will be at the feed side of your main battery switch or at the battery itself.

## Adding Speakers

When it's time to connect the speakers for your newly installed CD player, regular speaker wire, available from Radio Shack and other stereo-supply houses, will do the job. However, because of the better insulation, a better choice would be the marine-grade duplex wire already mentioned.

The ABYC doesn't address speaker wires in its color-coding scheme, so select duplex wires with different color schemes to help identify left and right speaker leads. When running these leads, remember to observe polarity, and don't mix up the wires. As with any wiring on board, speaker wires should be supported at least every 18 inches.

Once wire gauge and circuit protection decisions have been made, the six-step list that follows will guide you through the installation of the CD player and speakers. Remember that when locating the speakers, the magnets contained within them will affect things like compasses and any electronic compass sensors you may have on board. Keep the speakers at least 16–18 inches away from compasses and sensors!

1. Use the cutout template supplied with the player and speakers to cut out your mounting holes.

2. Install your speakers and the player in the holes.

3. Route all wiring from power sources, ground connections, and any speaker or antenna leads. Be sure to secure the wiring and provide chafe protection where needed, as described in chapter 4.

4. Connect all wires to the back of the player and to the speakers, carefully following the printed instructions supplied with the equipment as to which wire goes where.

5. Test the operation of the equipment. In other words, turn it on and see if it works.

6. Finish mounting the equipment chassis in the mounting hole. Enjoy!

Figure 9-10 provides a wiring diagram for this installation that includes the speaker wiring.

If you keep the points mentioned here in mind for all of your DC circuit additions and carefully follow the steps outlined, including the tables and charts in chapter 4, you should have no problem adding your own equipment to your boat in a safe and professional manner.

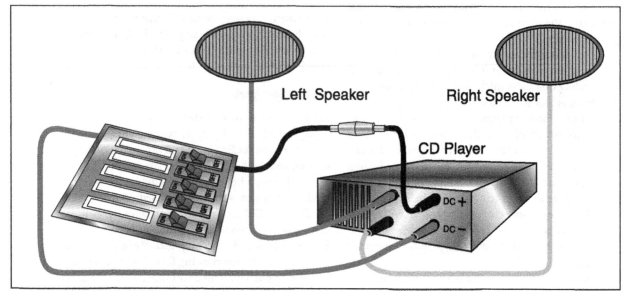

*Fig. 9-10. Basic wiring diagram for a new CD player.*

# Chapter 10

# Engine Instrumentation Problems and Solutions

Often taken for granted, many times ignored; on many boats, that's the general lot of the vast array of expensive and delicate engine and navigation instruments. The truth is that all your instruments should be taken quite seriously and considered an important part of the safety equipment on board your boat. If your engine suddenly stops running 20 miles from shore, you could be in serious danger. That incoming thunderstorm could catch you in gale-force winds, or a strong current could push you into shoal water before you have time to set an anchor.

It is very important to monitor your instruments constantly, because they may provide the early warning you need to avoid this sort of emergency. Your instruments are also the primary communication channel between you and your engine, and they will keep you informed about just what is going on inside that very expensive and important piece of mechanical apparatus.

Understanding what the instruments are trying to tell you is also important. It doesn't do much good to look at instruments if you don't know what all those dials and numbers mean. For the beginner, misinterpretation of instrument readings can lead to a lot of false worries. For example, on dual-helm boats, different instrument readings for temperature, oil pressure, and rpm are not at all uncommon between helm stations. The same is true with the instruments on twin-engine boats: duplicate instruments for each engine often give conflicting readings. This is normal and no problem once you understand what is going on.

## Mechanical Gauges

Many older boats use mechanical gauges, and much of the information provided in this chapter on electrical troubleshooting will not apply to these instruments. It's a good idea to determine what kind of gauge you have before a problem does crop up so you'll have some insight into what the best plan of action may be. Look at the back of the instrument. If it has nothing but wires connected to terminals, it's an electrical instrument. However, if you see any kind of non-electrical tube or cable in addition to one or two wires, you probably have mechanical gauges. (The wires are for the instrument lights.) Many boats have a combination of mechanical and electrical gauges.

Most small to medium production boats built today use only electrical gauges, mostly because they are a lot cheaper and easier to install than mechanical ones. Since this book is intended for outboards and smaller powerboats generally powered by IO drives or gas inboards, I'll focus on problems with the electrical instruments on these boats and leave the mechanical gauges alone.

## Common Instrument Interpretation Problems

There are several things to think about when you're viewing your boat's instruments. For example, consider the actual accuracy of the instruments. For reasons that will be pointed out shortly, the readings you get from your instruments could be slightly different than what's really going on in your engine.

The quality of instruments used on boats varies widely among boatbuilders. In fact, discrepancies between readings on different gauges and the actual readings at the engine are quite common. What you, as a boatowner, should be looking for as you monitor your engine's vital signs is any change from the established norm for your particular engine. Any change in the reading of a gauge is a surefire indication that something is up, and it could be a problem.

As already mentioned, another common situation on boats with dual helms or dual engines (or both) is a variation in instrument readings between stations or between engines. Often, one gauge set will read differently from another—not by much, but different nonetheless. The obvious question is, is this a problem? The answer is no. I have wasted hours trying to match gauge readings on boats with duplicate instruments. Unless I was very lucky or was working on exceptionally high-quality instruments, my results were less than satisfactory. The best gauges have calibration screws that enable you to fine-tune the actual readings, but don't count on finding these expensive gauges on a typical production powerboat.

Some manufacturers (VDO and MerCruiser, for example) offer sending units designed for two gauges for use on dual-helm boats. Any discrepancy between the two gauges working on a common sending unit is caused by voltage drop, the phenomenon mentioned throughout this book. Since you have read this far, you know that due to the increased resistance to electrical flow in a long wire, the length of a wire has a direct effect on voltage drop. Well, this extra resistance directly affects the instrument reading at your console, because most instruments rely on variable resistance created by an engine-mounted sensor to give you readings.

Differences in the lengths of connecting wires on instruments at upper and lower stations, combined with manufacturing tolerances in gauges and sensors, ultimately control the actual reading you get at your instruments. Don't panic if you see slight variations from one gauge to another. This is a normal condition, and repeated trips to your mechanic or boat dealer to solve the problem will almost always prove futile. Remember to look for relative changes in your normal instrument readings; that's what's important.

# Abnormal Instrument Readings

At some point your instruments will indicate that a condition other than the norm exists. It might be high engine temperature, low oil pressure, erratic rpm, or dozens of other deviations from your normal readings. Often when there is a change in one instrument there is a corresponding change in others. Falling oil pressure might be accompanied by rising engine temperature and falling rpm, for example.

When this occurs, you must respond quickly and verify that a problem does in fact exist. Ask yourself: Is there *really* a problem, or is the gauge just acting up? Initially, you must assume that a problem does exist and immediately shut down your engine until you can verify that it's OK.

Verification of engine condition requires some mechanical expertise on your part, and if you're in doubt, you may need to consult an experienced mechanic. This works fine at the marina, but offshore it won't be possible to call a mechanic, so some basic tips are in order. If your boat has an outboard engine, my book *Outboard Engines: Maintenance, Troubleshooting, and Repair* will surely help you solve most common problems. If yours has an IO or inboard engine, the following steps should point you in the right direction.

## Low Oil Pressure

When your oil-pressure gauge gives you a low-oil-pressure reading, immediately shut down the engine and check the engine oil level. Refer to your owner's manual to determine the correct level, if you don't already know it. While you're at it, look for any signs of leaking oil.

If the oil level is correct, an oil-pressure problem is quite unlikely unless your engine has many hours on it (over 1,000 hours for gas engines and even more for diesels). Excess engine noise, such as ticking sounds coming from the top of the engine block, is a sure indication that a problem exists, and you may not be able to get the boat home without assistance. If in doubt, radio for help; the chance of causing extreme engine damage here is great and not worth the risk.

## High Engine Temperature

If excessively high engine temperature is indicated by your temperature gauge and the rise occurred suddenly, you should back off the throttle to an idle and see if the temperature reading begins to drop. Often it will, and it's preferable to let the temperature stabilize before shutting off the engine to scope out the problem. Suddenly shutting down an overheated engine can cause extreme shock to the engine's pistons, inducing the engine to seize. Once the engine has had a chance to catch its breath and stabilize somewhat, shut it off and let it cool down enough so you can check the level of cooling water if you have a fresh-water-cooled engine. Next check for a broken fan belt on the water pump. If the belt is in order, the most likely cause for overheating is a blocked water intake to the engine's cooling system.

Follow the steps outlined in your workshop manual to determine if adequate cooling water is entering the system. Often the problem is a piece of debris that's drawn to the intake port by the suction of the water pump. In many cases, stopping the boat and backing down for 10 or 20 feet will dislodge the foreign object, and all will be well. In any event, you should spend some time reviewing your engine workshop manual, getting familiar with the cooling system and troubleshooting procedures *before* problems develop. Carry spare water-pump impellers and fan belts at all times.

## Low Voltage Reading

If your volt gauge suddenly shows a lower-than-normal or a higher-than-normal voltage reading, you can easily verify the accuracy of the gauge by doing an open-circuit voltage test at your battery. Use your multimeter and take the reading with the engine running as outlined in chapter 5.

## Low or High RPM

Irregular engine rpm usually shows up as an erratic reading or no reading at all on the tachometer. If the engine is running normally in spite of the erratic reading, get the boat back to shore and follow the electrical troubleshooting steps outlined in the next section of this chapter.

## Trim-Gauge Problems

Of all the instruments on a boat with an inboard/outboard engine, the trim gauge is the one with the highest failure rate. This is because the sending units on these boats are often located underwater on the side of the engine drive unit. Here they are exposed to the worst environment any electrical equipment can experience.

Faulty trim-gauge readings always indicate an electrical malfunction and have nothing to do with the function of the drive itself. To be safe, take a look over the transom just to be sure the drive is down before starting the engine.

On inboard engines, hydraulic trim tabs operated by an electric servomotor control trim. They have a comparatively low failure rate, because all the electrical components are located inside the hull and are not exposed to seawater.

## Fuel Gauge Problems

Common sense should assist you with any erratic reading on your fuel gauges. As soon as you buy a new boat, you should establish an approximate fuel-consumption rate. Calculate the gallons of fuel used by your engine per hour of running time at different rpms. Based on that usage and the capacity of your fuel tank, you should be able to estimate the amount of fuel in your tank and use that estimate to judge the accuracy of your fuel gauge. For example, if you burn 10 gallons per hour at 3,000 rpm and have a 50-gallon fuel tank, you can safely operate your boat for four hours and still have an emergency reserve, no matter what your fuel gauge tries to tell you.

Problems with fuel gauges, like problems with trim gauges, are almost always the fault of the tank sending unit. The test procedure for this will be found later in this chapter.

# General Instrument Troubleshooting

The pros say that whenever an instrument problem crops up, you should always verify that a problem does in fact exist by swapping the engine gauge with a quality shop gauge, which is often a mechanical gauge. This is good advice, but unless you have a personal friend who's a mechanic (which is a great idea), you probably won't have ready access to a set of quality shop gauges. The tips that follow will help you around this deficit and to successfully solve most instrument problems. Remember, if you still have doubts about your abilities to attack your instrument problems after reading the steps outlined here, your best bet is to call in a pro who has the equipment to do the job properly.

## Troubleshooting the Tachometer

Tachometer circuits come in several types, depending on the engine used in your boat. The primary differences are between those used on gasoline and on diesel engines. Modern diesel tachometers are generally connected to the back of the engine alternator at a terminal labeled "tach." This terminal senses the AC pulses inside the alternator and sends them to the tachometer where the pulses are translated into engine rpm.

The tachometer on most gasoline engines gets its signal from various points in the ignition system. The only way to be really sure where your tachometer is getting this signal from is to use your wiring diagram and service manual. On gasoline engines, the sensing wire is usually gray.

If there is any break in this wire between the ignition circuit and the back of the gauge, the tachometer will not give a reading. Any short circuit in this wire can short out the ignition system and cause the engine to quit.

Figure 10-1 shows a typical diagram for a tachometer circuit on a gasoline engine. In addition to the gray sender wire, wires provide battery power to the instrument and a return to ground. Figure 10-2 shows the battery power to the tachometer being checked with the ignition key on. Where the ABYC color-coding is used, this wire will be purple. Note that a small jumper is built into the gauge to connect power to the instrument light.

If no power is available at this wire when the ignition key is on, make sure that the lanyard safety key is installed, if the boat has one (all newer boats have one). If it is, using the methods previously described, check all the connections and the condition of the lanyard switch. Continuity tests and voltage tests may be used here.

Next, verify the continuity of the ground with your multimeter. Check between the "GND" (black wire) terminal on the back of the tachometer and a good ground on the back of the instrument panel, as shown in figure 10-3 on page 151.

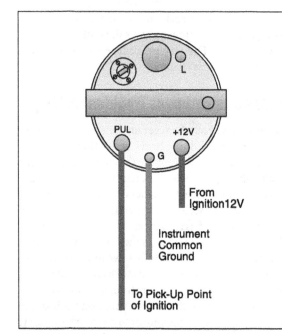

*Fig. 10-1. Wiring diagram of a typical tachometer circuit.*

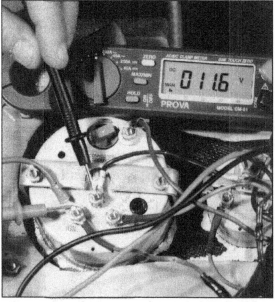

*Fig. 10-2. Testing battery power to the tachometer. This test is to determine if the instrument is getting voltage to run. My red meter lead is connected to the gauge terminal marked "IGN," which will usually have a purple wire attached. My multimeter's black lead is connected to a common "GND" terminal on the gauge. These will almost universally have black insulated wire connected to them.*

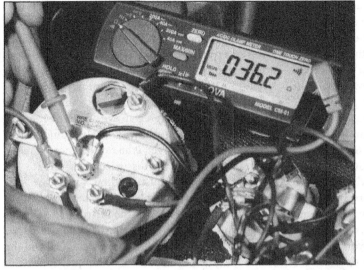

Fig. 10-3. *Verifying instrument ground continuity at the tachometer. As with all boat circuits, the power feed is only as good as the ground return. Here I'm checking for a good ground for the instrument. My meter leads are connected to the "GND" terminal on the tachometer and to a common ground stud on the back of an adjacent instrument. Since we're checking for continuity, it really doesn't matter which lead goes where.*

Fig. 10-4. *Tachometer calibration. The circular scale on the back of the tachometer shown here is used to select the appropriate calibration for your engine. This is most often done with a mini-slotted screwdriver and turning the setting screw inside the instrument to the appropriate point on the dial.*

If you find continuity in the ground wire, good ground for the gauge exists, and the powering circuitry for the instrument is in good order. Next, use your engine wiring diagram to determine where the tachometer gray wire connects to your ignition system. With the ignition key off, determine if you have continuity between the connection point on the back of the tachometer and the point on the engine where it terminates (usually at the ignition module). If continuity exists here, and the power and ground circuits are functioning normally, the only remaining possibility is that there is a problem in the gauge itself, and a new unit should be installed. (Note: One slight possibility is that the tachometer is not getting a signal from the ignition system via the gray wire from the ignition system itself, but this is extremely rare and almost always associated with an ignition-system problem as well.)

If you need a new tachometer, make sure to follow any calibration instructions provided with the gauge. Manufacturers generally provide one gauge for four-, six-, and eight-cylinder engines. The correct number of cylinders should be set using a small calibration screw on the back of the gauge as shown in figure 10-4. Select the setting that corresponds with the number of cylinders on your engine.

If you have a diesel or gasoline engine that uses the previously mentioned "tach" sensor at the alternator, you still need to verify that the tachometer is getting 12 volts with the key on and that it's connected to a good ground.

If you find that everything I have mentioned so far is in order and your tachometer is still not reading, the problem may be an open circuit in the sensor wire from the alternator to the tachometer or a fault within the alternator itself. Since this sensor wire is sensing voltage from within the alternator, no signal here means no voltage inside the alternator. The basic checks of the charging system described in chapter 6 will help isolate the reason that your tachometer quit.

One caution here, however: On many diesel engines, a separate oil-pressure sender on the engine switches the field voltage (see chapter 6). This way, even if the ignition key is left on, the alternator will not get excitation voltage to the field windings until the engine is actually running and oil pressure closes the circuit. These senders have a high failure rate and are often the cause of alternator failure on a diesel.

Check the engine manual to see if you have one of these switches. If you do, in order to check for field voltage at the "F" terminal on the back of the alternator, either bypass the oil-pressure switch with a jumper wire or do the voltage test with the engine actually running.

If no voltage is found, then the switch on the engine is not getting voltage from the ignition switch or the oil-pressure switch is defective. To check, follow the procedures outlined throughout this book for testing any switch. If voltage is getting to the alternator, and all the other procedures from chapter 6 for testing the alternator have been followed, a problem with the alternator or the internal voltage regulator is indicated. Remove the alternator and send it out for overhaul.

Once you have determined that the alternator is not the cause for your tachometer failure, verify the continuity of the wire connecting the tachometer to the back of the alternator. Disconnect the wire at both ends (at the tachometer and at the back of the alternator) and use your multimeter. If you find continuity, the problem is within the tachometer itself. If you don't, there is a break in the wire that should be located and repaired.

## Voltmeter Checks

In recent years, console-mounted voltmeters have replaced or (on expensive instrument panels) supplemented ammeters as indicators of battery condition and state of charge. This change has taken place for economic reasons more than anything else. Voltmeters are less expensive than ammeters, and they are much cheaper to install. Ammeters require heavy wires or expensive shunts (see chapter 3), whereas voltmeters for the largest batteries can be installed using 16 AWG wire. Voltmeters impart slightly different information than ammeters, but they are a very useful way of keeping an eye on your battery. A digital voltmeter coupled with an electronic battery charger, or smart charger, is an excellent way of monitoring the charge cycles discussed in chapter 6.

If your voltmeter quits reading, simply use your multimeter to verify that battery voltage is getting to the terminal at the back of the instrument and that the ground lead is properly attached and connected to ground. If power feed to the gauge is OK and the ground is good, there should be no questions here; the gauge is bad and needs replacement. A gauge reading higher than normal indicates a charging-system problem—probably with your voltage regulator. To solve this problem, follow the procedures outlined in chapter 6.

Figure 10-5 on page 153 shows the voltage and ground verification checks being made at the back of a typical voltmeter.

## Temperature, Fuel, and Oil-Pressure Gauges

Engine service manuals generally combine these engine instruments into one group for diagnostic purposes, because they all operate on the same basic principle: they all use a variable resistance to ground to generate the instrument reading. Figure 10-6 on page 153 shows a simplified wiring diagram that illustrates how these gauges work.

### Temperature Gauges

Like all other gauges (except the mechanical ones), the temperature gauge needs battery power and a good ground to function. If the gauge stops functioning, a simple way to verify that the electrical circuits are in order is to disconnect the wire at the sending unit (the variable resistor on the engine) and short the wire to ground with your ignition switch on. If the needle moves all the way to the right (to maximum temperature), the problem with the circuit is a faulty sending unit, which should be re-

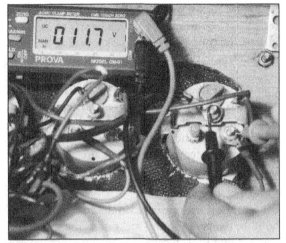

Fig. 10-5. *Verifying voltage and good ground at the voltmeter.*

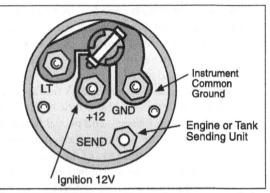

Fig. 10-6. *Simplified wiring diagram for temperature, fuel, and oil-pressure gauges.*

placed. If there is no change in the position of the needle, trace the power to the instrument and verify the continuity of the ground lead. Replace or repair these wires as needed.

If both of these leads are in good order and behaving as they should, the fault is in the instrument itself. Figure 10-7 shows the wire disconnected at the sending unit and shorted to the engine block. This is what your dash-panel-mounted instrument should read if the fault is simply with the sending unit, which is the most common difficulty. This test is for a *one-wire* sending unit. If your unit has two wires attached to it, disconnect one of the wires from the sender and touch it to the terminal on the sender for the other wire. Watch the gauge with the ignition on, or get someone to watch the gauge needle for you. If the needle moves as you connect these leads, the problem is in the sending unit.

## Fuel Gauges

Fuel gauges are wired exactly as temperature gauges but use a different type of variable resistor as the sending unit. The senders are located inside the fuel tank; you need access to the top of the tank to locate the senders and the wiring. To test the sender, turn the ignition key on, disconnect the wire from the sender, and ground it at either the black lead on sender or directly to the tank. Observe the gauge.

Fig. 10-7. *Testing the temperature sending unit. With the wire to the sender removed, I'm grounding it out on the engine block with the ignition key in the "on" position; the needle on the temperature gauge on the dash panel should read at the maximum side of the gauge.*

Senders on metal tanks often have only one wire, and the sender grounds to the tank itself. Disconnect the wire and ground it on the tank. In either case, if the needle moves so that the gauge reads full, the sender is bad and must be replaced.

In some instances fuel gauges work fine at some fuel levels and not at others. This erratic reading is a function of the sender design, and partial failure is not uncommon. To check, remove the screws holding the sender in place on the top of the tank and lift it out. Next, attach a jumper lead between the tank ground lead and the grounding connection on the sender. Again, with the ignition key on, move the float on the sender up and down while carefully observing the gauge on your instrument console. You may need an extra set of eyes to help you here, depending on the distance between the sender and the gauge. If the needle on the gauge acts erratically as you move the float assembly up and down, the float sender needs replacement.

Figure 10-8 shows a sender removed and being tested. An important safety note here is to carefully inspect the condition of the gasket sealing the float mechanism to the tank. If any doubt exists as to its condition, replace the gasket. A fuel leak here is extremely dangerous and cause for immediate concern.

If your tests of the fuel-gauge sending unit cause no movement of the needle on the gauge, verify that you have power and good ground at the instrument, just as with the temperature gauge already described. If this fails to locate the problem, replace the gauge.

## Oil-Pressure Gauges

Oil-pressure gauges are tested in the exact same way as both the temperature and fuel gauges mentioned already. Figure 10-9 on page 155 shows the location of a typical oil-pressure sending unit on a General Motors "V" block used widely by MerCruiser, OMC, Volvo Penta, and other marine-engine manufacturers. For the exact location of the sending unit on your engine, refer to your engine workshop manual.

### Trim Gauges

As mentioned earlier, trim gauges, generally found only on outboard and IO boats, have an extremely high failure rate, because the sending units on these boats are located underwater on the engine drive unit.

These sending units are sealed and use two wires to connect the sender to the inside of the boat. The wires are fed through the drive unit's gimbaled bracket assembly, disappearing behind the engine where they are extremely difficult to get at. Besides the difficulty of getting to the wires, the hole where the wires pass through the transom must be properly sealed to prevent seawater from leaking into the boat. Unless you're an experienced technician, I do not recommend attempting to replace these senders on your own. This is a good job for a professional with experience not only in the replacement of trim-gauge sending units but their proper adjustment as well.

Finally, if you have any real doubt about the accuracy of your gauges, you should consult a professional with the mechanical and elec-

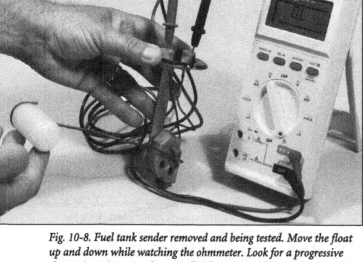

*Fig. 10-8. Fuel tank sender removed and being tested. Move the float up and down while watching the ohmmeter. Look for a progressive change in resistance value. Any "OL" readings while performing this test indicate a "dead" spot in the sender, and it will need replacement.*

tronic shop gauges necessary to verify exactly what's going on with your engine. Once proper operation has been verified in this manner, record the normal readings of your gauges. Remember, while underway you're looking for readings outside these pre-established norms.

If you follow the steps outlined in this chapter, you'll have the confidence and ability to tackle and repair most instrument failures that crop up on your boat. Remember that, as with all the other sections of this book, you should never attempt to go too far with your diagnosis and repair without the aid of your workshop manual. Also remember that the basic electrical troubleshooting and repair procedures already discussed will carry you through any diagnosis of instrument problems.

## The Future

Figures 10-10a and 10-10b show how far we have come since the first edition of this book. New boats today will likely be equipped with a networked system for distributing engine data, among other things. The Mercury Marine SmartCraft display in figure 10-10a is an integrated part of that system, and effectively replaces the traditional gauges discussed in this chapter. The data come from an engine-mounted computer like the one shown in figure 10-10b. All wiring is done through proprietary harnesses with multiple-pin plug assemblies as in figure 10-10b. Troubleshooting instrumentation problems on these systems is a bit more

Fig. 10-9. An oil-pressure sending unit on a GM V8 engine. On this engine it's located next to the ignition distributor.

complicated than some of the procedures described for conventional instruments. But with an ohmmeter, you can check continuity of the pin connections from one end of the harness to the other and at least determine if there is a problem with the harness or a plug assembly. Beyond that there is not much you can do without specialized equipment that goes beyond the scope of this book. One resource for those that want to learn more about these systems is my latest book, *Advanced Marine Electrics and Electronics Troubleshooting*.

Fig. 10-10a. SmartCraft display.

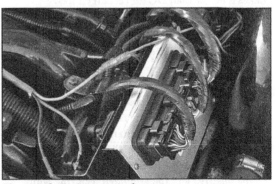

Fig. 10-10b. Engine-mounted computer.

# Chapter 11

# Alternating Current and AC Equipment

## What Is Alternating Current?

Throughout this book on electrical systems for powerboats, I have been talking about direct-current electricity, simply because more than 90 percent of all systems on most boats use DC power. Of course, most of us already know what alternating current is, but let's run through it one more time for review.

Most technically aware boatowners know that AC is the stuff that can kill you, and that DC electrons flow in one direction whereas AC electrons reverse direction. I will discuss AC dangers and safety later on, but let's first take a closer look at the second item, this apparent difficulty that AC electrons have in making up their minds which way to go. In chapter 5, I discussed the manner in which direct-current electrons flow through a circuit from the negative pole of a battery (the *cathode*) to the positive pole (the *anode*). With alternating current, of course, the anode and the cathode repeatedly and rapidly reverse positions. Instead of flowing in a continuous stream from one end of the circuit to the other, the electrons in an AC circuit travel only a short distance before changing their minds and rushing back to where they started. They do this over and over again, and while the electrons in an AC circuit get nowhere, the power they generate has some important qualities that makes it better than DC for certain chores.

Before I go any further, let's get some more basic terminology out of the way.

### Basic AC Terminology

▶ *Polarity.* Obviously, with the anode and cathode continuously reversing positions, our old concept of opposing plus and minus terminals, or poles, no longer works for AC. Many electricians who should know better (almost all of us, in fact) refer to the hot lead (the black one) in an AC circuit as the *positive* and the grounded lead (the white one) as the *negative*. In actuality, each wire takes turns being positive, then negative, several thousand times a minute. If you choose to use this positive/negative distinction to describe AC wires, you must keep in mind the fact that there is no true polarity in an AC circuit, as there is in a DC circuit.

Ironically, because of the physics involved, the proper wiring of AC circuits (or *polarity*, if you like) is even more critical than it is in DC circuits, as we will discover a little later on.

▶ *Frequency.* The frequency of an AC circuit is simply the rate at which the current reverses itself. In most American countries the standard is 60 cycles per second, which means that the electrons hop back and forth 60 times every second. Frequency is measured in Hertz (Hz), so the standard in the United States is called 60 Hz service. (Europe and Asia use 50 Hz service.)

On boats, frequency is particularly important when dealing with generators, as we will see.

▶ *Resistance.* Resistance, as you'll recall, is an important component of any DC circuit. It's equally important with an AC circuit, but it carries the added influence of *induction* (the generation of an electrical current in a wire exposed to a magnetic field). Induction becomes important with AC because of the higher voltages (remember how the strength of a magnetic field increases with an increase in voltage?). Also, the tendency of resistance in a DC circuit to cause a buildup of heat, which in turn causes an increase in resistance, is not as important in an AC circuit; the reversing electrons just don't get a chance to generate a lot of heat before it's time to turn around and go back to where they started. This makes AC much more efficient than DC when higher voltages are needed, and it's one of the big reasons we use it at all.

▶ *Impedance.* Impedance is the combined effect of resistance and induction. The place you'll hear the word used the most around boats is when working with your radio antennas (see chapter 12).

▶ *Voltage drop.* The efficiency of AC is also the reason that voltage drop, which I have repeatedly stressed as one of the most important considerations in any DC circuit, just isn't important in an AC circuit. Also, because of the higher voltages used in AC, a much lower amperage is needed to do a given amount of work (remember Ohm's law?), which further reduces the importance of resistance and voltage drop.

▶ *Waveform.* Most working electricians will have access to an *oscilloscope*, a testing device that shows the track of an electrical impulse as it reverses direction through a single cycle in an AC circuit. The resulting sinusoidal wave shows the variation in voltage from zero up through the peak at about plus 170 volts, then back to zero, then down to a minus 170 volts, then back to zero. This fluctuation averages out to 120 volts, and is why I suggested earlier that if you intend to work with AC electricity even a little, you should invest in a true RMS (root-mean-square) multimeter. The cheaper meters (average-responding type) read the peak voltages without consideration of the time the circuit is at zero voltage, and are only effective for measuring true sinusoidal AC wave forms.

When working on boats, waveform is most important when considering inverters. No, you don't have to run out and buy an expensive oscilloscope. Just knowing what a waveform is and why it's important is plenty for now.

## AC on Your Boat

Just a few years ago, any use of alternating current on board any small boat (under 35 feet or so) was extremely unusual. Some of the fancier boats did have a dedicated battery charger (Constavolt was a popular one), but the best of these were expensive and inefficient, and the good ones weighed nearly 100 pounds. My, how times have changed! Today it

seems that even the smallest of boats is coming through with at least a rudimentary AC system.

Boaters now demand onboard systems to run a shore-power-fed battery charger and electric hot water. In New England, where I live, small boats might have an electric space heater in the cabin. Even 23- to 27-foot-long walk-around fishing boats and weekenders, on which designers wouldn't have dreamed of installing an AC system just 10 years ago, now have several outlets in the cabin as standard equipment.

Boaters are demanding more of the comforts of home, and builders are doing everything they can to oblige the craving for luxury. With all of this increase in AC equipment on boats comes the need to have a basic understanding of how alternating current works and how it gets integrated into your boat's total electrical system. AC power will come on board your boat from one of three sources: a direct plug to shore, an AC generator, or a DC-to-AC inverter. Since both the AC and DC systems are run closely together throughout your boat, you need to make sure you know which system you're working with and how to identify the key components of each system. Never forget that alternating current can kill you!

## AC Safety

Alternating current can be extremely dangerous if it's not handled with care and common sense. The hazard of a lethal electrical shock is real and present any time you have AC on your boat, and a poor-quality AC installation is as much of a fire hazard as a bad DC installation. Happily, the basic rules for handling alternating current on your boat are clear, and these systems rarely cause a problem if these simple rules are followed.

Nearly all accidents involving AC on boats are caused by ignorance, laziness, blatant stupidity, or some combination of all three of these things. Most often a boatowner attempts to cut corners to save a little time or a few dollars on an installation, and gets hurt or damages the boat in the process. On one boat I recall, the owner thought the best approach to

AC upgrades was to hire a licensed electrician to install the AC service. The problem was that this particular electrician, although probably a competent worker on shore-based systems, had no experience with marine electrical installations. Within months after a major refit to the boat, a fire broke out on board, and the boat burned to the waterline. The insurance investigation revealed that the fire was caused by the boat's new AC shore-power system. This was a lesson hard-learned for the owner, and for the electrician!

If you're having an AC system professionally installed on your boat, ask your electrician if he or she has been certified by the ABYC to work on boats. If not, you might want to wait until they get certified, or simply look around for an electrician who has passed the ABYC certification program. Quality marine electricians are proud of this certification, and will always promote the fact that they are certified, so it shouldn't be too hard to locate one in your area.

## Basic AC Safety Rules

I could easily fill up two or three pages with safety rules that all of us should observe when working with AC, but most of these rules are common sense. A case recently came to my attention where an electrician who had forgotten his wire stripper was removing insulation with his teeth. Everything went fine until he tried to strip the hot (black) wire while holding on to the bare end of the grounded (white) wire. He woke up in the hospital with a good part of his lips burned away. Therefore, one rule might be: Always turn off the power before you strip wire with your teeth. Another, older case suggests another rule: Never change a light bulb while standing in a bathtub full of water. There are lots more, but I have covered them all with rule number 10 below. Here are a few others that apply specifically to boats.

1. Use only marine-grade products, wiring, terminal strips, and connectors on your boat.

2. Observe polarity at all times. The orientation of the hot wire (also referred to as the *ungrounded conductor*) and the ground wire (the *grounded conductor*) and color-code matches are all very important. Reverse polarity can at the least cause

certain equipment not to function, and at worst, it can destroy expensive gear.

3. When working on the AC system, disconnect the power at all times except when testing for voltage and amperage at points throughout the circuit.

4. Never work on a system with wet hands or feet or when any of the components are wet.

5. Make sure the boat is connected to a proper and tested ground, even when working with the power off. This means that whenever possible, you must avoid working on AC when the boat is at anchor or on a mooring.

6. Always wear rubber-soled shoes (deck shoes and running shoes are fine) when working on AC power. It's also an excellent idea to wear rubber knee pads, because most of your work on a boat will be done while kneeling.

7. Never work on AC service with distractions such as a television or chatty friends present.

8. Ground-fault circuit interrupters (GFCIs) should be tested at least monthly to ensure proper function.

9. The common practice of clipping off the third prong (the grounding prong) of a three-pronged plug creates a real shock hazard on board a boat, and this should never be allowed. Any cords or equipment you have where this all-important terminal has been removed should have that third terminal replaced.

10. Avoid doing obviously dumb things (such as standing in water or putting hot wires in your mouth) when working with AC.

Let's take a more detailed look at specific system layout and the key standards as established by our friends at the ABYC.

## Color Coding for AC Wiring

Unlike the DC systems already discussed, we will only be working with three colors for simple, small-boat AC wiring schemes. Larger boats using combined 120/240-volt systems use several additional colors for the extra legs of the circuitry that combine to make the higher voltage, but these systems are used only on larger yachts, and a discussion of them would go beyond the scope of this book. I'll focus on only the most common, single-phase 120-volt, 20- and 30-amp systems here.

The three colors used with AC in the United States are black, white, and green. The black conductor is used only for the AC ungrounded (positive) lead. Some people refer to this as the *hot* lead. This explains the trend toward using yellow as a DC negative conductor in accordance with the ABYC's recommendations for DC systems. There is an obvious risk of confusing the hot AC positive wire with the relatively inert DC negative wire, which has traditionally been black. Increasingly, new-boat builders are moving to the yellow DC negative wire as a means of more clearly separating the AC service from the DC service. Manufacturers are now making the yellow insulated wire available in all gauges including battery-cable sizes.

With AC, the white lead should always be the negative, *grounded* lead, and green should be the *grounding* lead, which offers shock protection to the boatowner. This green wire, which does not normally carry current, is one of the most important keys to preventing the "zap" you could receive from electrical appliances on board if they are not properly connected or if a fault occurs anywhere in the system. This, coupled with the fact that appliances will work just fine whether this wire is attached or not, is why ensuring continuity throughout the circuit all the way to the shore-power box is crucial.

## ISO Color Coding

If your boat is not built to U.S. specifications, there may be some variations in the color-coding scheme described above. The International Standards Organization (ISO), whose standards are used in many countries, prescribes the following colors for use with AC installations:

▶ For hot conductors (ungrounded), either black or brown wires must be used.

▶ For neutral (grounded) conductors, either white or light blue wires must be used.

▶ For ground (grounding) conductors, either green (as with the U.S. system) or green with a yellow stripe may be used.

If your boat is wired using the ISO system and you're making additions or modifications, it's an excellent idea to stick with the existing color code rather than changing or mixing the codes. However, in the United States you might have trouble finding wire in ISO colors, in which case you should improvise your own coding system as described in chapter 2.

## Reverse Polarity

Reversal of the black and white leads on an AC circuit creates reverse polarity, where the white wire becomes the hot lead and the black wire becomes the grounded lead. This condition can destroy polarity-sensitive equipment, such as motors, TVs, and microwave ovens, and it creates a serious shock hazard.

The bottom line here? You need to be certain that wiring color coding is matched and appropriately connected through every inch of the AC circuit, from the shore-power source all the way through your boat.

### *Testing for Polarity*

Many newer boats with AC distribution panels have a polarity-test button right on the panel. If you don't have one of these panels, you can check polarity with your multimeter every time you plug in, or you can buy a simple and cheap circuit tester (see figure 11-9 on page 167) that plugs into any standard outlet. If the indicator lights on the tester don't light up in the proper sequence, you know you have reverse polarity somewhere in the circuit, and you must shut down the circuit until you find it and fix it.

Figure 11-1 on page 160 illustrates typical AC wiring connections from the shore-power inlet on your boat through the AC panel to a standard outlet.

## Comparisons between AC and DC Circuits

As with the DC circuits discussed throughout this book, things like amperage and voltage are major

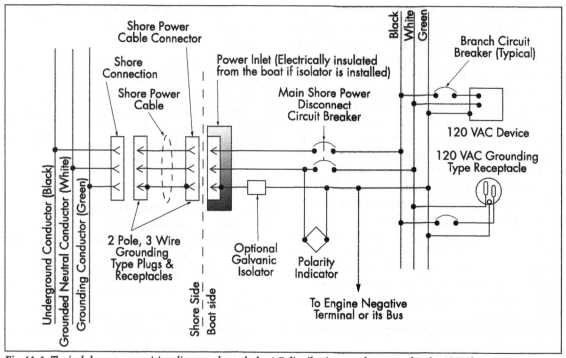

*Fig. 11-1. Typical shore-power wiring diagram through the AC distribution panel to an outlet. (© ABYC)*

considerations when wiring for AC. Unlike DC, however, voltage drop through the circuit is really not much of a factor in AC circuits. It's not that voltage isn't lost as it finds its way through an AC circuit, but for the lengths of wire runs used on the small boats discussed here and because of the physical considerations cited above, voltage drop is an insignificant factor—so insignificant that the ABYC doesn't even take it into consideration in its electrical standards for AC circuits. Wire sizing of AC circuits is easier as a result of this disregard for voltage drop, with amperage requirements being the only consideration when designing circuits.

Wattage, however, is an additional element we must take into account here. In chapter 1, you'll recall, I discussed the Ohm's law equation and an additional variation for watts, the unit of electrical power. If needed, go back and refresh your memory on this process, because the wattage equation really has some practical use when dealing with AC.

In the United States, as a requirement of the Un-

derwriters Laboratory (UL) rating of AC equipment, each electrical device must be marked with either the operating voltage and amperage, or the operating voltage and wattage. Typically wattage is given. Knowing this, you can easily find out the amperage of a given appliance by dividing wattage by the operating voltage.

This vital information is step one in the determination of overcurrent protection ratings as well as wire sizing. No adjustment, or *de-rating*, of the ampacity of the conductor for length of wire run is necessary as it is with DC circuitry.

With AC, a different criterion comes into play. Heat generated by whatever electrical resistance is present will require de-rating the wire gauge. Bundling of AC conductors requires that wire sizes be increased. Also, as with DC, wires routed through engine rooms must be larger than those used outside the engine room, to deal with the higher temperatures.

Figure 11-2 shows what a typical bundle of AC ca-

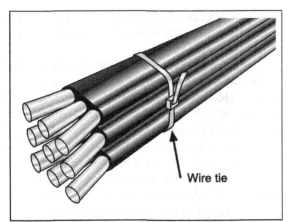

*Fig. 11-2. An AC wiring bundle.*

bles would look like in your boat. Figure 11-3 is a table from the ABYC's section E-11 showing the ampacity of a typical length of triplex AC boat cable.

Remember that the green conductor does not normally carry current and is therefore excluded from the process.

Another common question that comes up has to do with routing AC and DC wiring in the same bundle. Although the ABYC allows this practice as long as the wiring in question is separated by an appropriate sheath, which can be the outside skin of a typical length of AC boat cable, it's much better to keep AC and DC wires in separate bundles. The possibility of cross-induction (remember, any wire with current

## TABLE VIII-A-ALLOWABLE AMPERAGE OF CONDUCTORS WHEN NO MORE THAN 2 CURRENT CARRYING CONDUCTORS ARE BUNDLED

| CONDUCTOR SIZE (AWG) | TEMPERATURE RATING OF CONDUCTOR INSULATION | | | | | | | | | | | | |
|---|---|---|---|---|---|---|---|---|---|---|---|---|---|
| | 60°C (140°F) | | 75°C (167°F) | | 80°C (176°F) | | 90°C (194°F) | | 105°C (221°F) | | 125°C (257°F) | | 200°C (392°F) |
| | $OS_1$ | $IS_2$ | $OS_1$ | $IS_2$ | $OS_1$ | $IS_2$ | $OS_1$ | $IS_2$ | $OS_1$ | $IS_2$ | $OS_1$ | $IS_2$ | $OS_1$ OR $IS_2$ |
| 18 | 10 | 5.8 | 10 | 7.5 | 15 | 11.7 | 20 | 16.4 | 20 | 17.0 | 25 | 22.3 | 25 |
| 16 | 15 | 8.7 | 15 | 11.3 | 20 | 15.6 | 25 | 20.5 | 25 | 21.3 | 30 | 26.7 | 35 |
| 14 | 20 | 11.6 | 20 | 15.0 | 25 | 19.5 | 30 | 24.6 | 35 | 29.8 | 40 | 35.6 | 45 |
| 12 | 25 | 14.5 | 25 | 18.8 | 35 | 27.3 | 40 | 32.8 | 45 | 38.3 | 50 | 44.5 | 55 |
| 10 | 40 | 23.2 | 40 | 30.0 | 50 | 39.0 | 55 | 45.1 | 60 | 51.0 | 70 | 62.3 | 70 |
| 8 | 55 | 31.9 | 65 | 48.8 | 70 | 54.6 | 70 | 57.4 | 80 | 68.0 | 90 | 80.1 | 100 |
| 6 | 80 | 46.4 | 95 | 71.3 | 100 | 78.0 | 100 | 82.0 | 120 | 102.0 | 125 | 111.3 | 135 |
| 4 | 105 | 60.9 | 125 | 93.8 | 130 | 101.4 | 135 | 110.7 | 160 | 136.0 | 170 | 151.3 | 180 |
| 3 | 120 | 69.6 | 145 | 108.8 | 150 | 117.0 | 155 | 127.1 | 180 | 153.0 | 195 | 173.6 | 210 |
| 2 | 140 | 81.2 | 170 | 127.5 | 175 | 136.5 | 180 | 147.6 | 210 | 178.5 | 225 | 200.3 | 240 |
| 1 | 165 | 95.7 | 195 | 146.3 | 210 | 163.8 | 210 | 172.2 | 245 | 208.3 | 265 | 235.9 | 280 |
| 0 | 195 | 113.1 | 230 | 172.5 | 245 | 191.1 | 245 | 200.9 | 285 | 242.3 | 305 | 271.5 | 325 |
| 00 | 225 | 130.5 | 265 | 198.8 | 285 | 222.3 | 285 | 233.7 | 330 | 280.5 | 355 | 316.0 | 370 |
| 000 | 260 | 150.8 | 310 | 232.5 | 330 | 257.4 | 330 | 270.6 | 385 | 327.3 | 410 | 364.9 | 430 |
| 0000 | 300 | 174.0 | 360 | 270.0 | 385 | 300.3 | 385 | 315.7 | 445 | 378.3 | 475 | 422.8 | 510 |

₁Outside engine spaces (OS)

₂Inside engine spaces (IS)

*Fig. 11-3. ABYC ampacity table for a single run of triplex. (© ABYC)*

flowing through it generates a magnetic field) is real and may cause problems with sensitive electronic equipment, as we'll see in the next chapter.

### Marine versus Residential Materials

Many boatowners who want to add AC service to boats that came with only a simple DC setup as standard equipment, head for the nearest residential electrical supply house to get the gear for their new circuit. Some people have undoubtedly seen boats that came right from the factory with this residential gear installed; Square-D switch boxes, panels, and breakers, as well as the solid-copper wire known as Romex, have been used in original-equipment installations by various boatbuilders over the years. Virtually none of this household gear meets current ABYC standards, and it's definitely not recommended that household AC gear be used on board your boat. In fact, if your boat has household-rated AC equipment, one of your first orders of business should be to remove it and replace it with appropriate marine gear. Remember what happened to the boat and licensed electrician mentioned earlier? You could be next!

Some appropriate exceptions to this rule on marine-grade versus household material are the commonly available plastic outlet boxes, face plates, and plug assemblies that all work just fine on boats as long as they are the all-plastic type. Even with these, however, it's best to throw away the steel screws that usually come with the equipment and substitute stainless or brass screws instead.

### Wire for AC

Most 120-volt AC circuitry on small powerboats will use 12-gauge, tinned triplex boat cable for the entire wiring scheme, regardless of the length of the run or the anticipated load. You can, of course, legally and safely use 14-gauge wire for your AC circuits (as many builders of budget boats do), but since the savings amount to about $30 for a 100-foot roll, you might as well go ahead and use the heavier and slightly safer wire. Tinned triplex with AC color-coding (black, white, and green) is available from West Marine and most other chandlers.

I've said it before, and I'll say it again: Don't use Romex or any other solid-copper wire on your boat. If you have any already installed, replace it with proper boat cable.

As for the insulation temperature rating of AC wiring, rated boat cable from a marine supply store will probably have a 105°C rating, although there is still some 90° cable available, and many boats already wired have this lower-rated wire in use.

Figure 11-4 on page 163 shows the ampacity for a group of two to three of these triplex cables bundled together. The higher ratings in the tables are specialty cables not readily available, and the lower ratings are not commonly available either. For any new work you're doing, the 105° cable is more than adequate for typical small-boat installations.

# AC Overcurrent Protection

As for rating and location in circuits of overcurrent-protection devices (fuses and circuit breakers), the same basic rules apply for AC circuits as for DC circuits. An exception is the rating and location of breakers for feeder wires from the shore-power inlet on your boat to your main AC distribution panel. Refer back to chapter 4 to refresh your memory regarding the 7–40–72 inch location rule and the 100–150 percent rule. The ABYC allows a run of up to 10 feet between the shore-power inlet and the main circuit breaker on the main feed conductors to your boat's AC distribution panel. On boats of the size for which this book is intended (up to about 35 feet), this will usually mean the main breaker will be located on the AC distribution panel itself. For larger installations where the distance between the inlet on the boat and the panel exceeds 10 feet, a circuit breaker is required on the feed wire before it reaches the panel. These breakers must be of the trip-free variety, just like those used for DC, so they can't be held closed by the operator. This means you must use only marine-rated circuit breakers for any replacements to existing services as well as for any new circuits.

### AC Circuit-Breaker Types

Circuit breakers for use with AC systems must be of the trip-free variety, as already stated. But an addi-

## TABLE VIII-C-ALLOWABLE AMPERAGE OF CONDUCTORS WHEN 4 TO 6 CURRENT CARRYING CONDUCTORS ARE BUNDLED

| CONDUCTOR SIZE (AWG) | TEMPERATURE RATING OF CONDUCTOR INSULATION | | | | | | | | | | | | | |
|---|---|---|---|---|---|---|---|---|---|---|---|---|---|---|
| | 60°C (140°F) | | 75°C (167°F) | | 80°C (176°F) | | 90°C (194°F) | | 105°C (221°F) | | 125°C (257°F) | | 200°C (392°F) |
| | OS₁ | IS₂ | OS₁ | IS₂ | OS₁ | IS₂ | OS₁ | IS₂ | OS₁ | IS₂ | OS₁ | IS₂ | OS₁ OR IS₂ |
| 18 | 6.0 | 3.5 | 6.0 | 4.5 | 9.0 | 7.0 | 12.0 | 9.8 | 12.0 | 10.2 | 15.0 | 13.4 | 15.0 |
| 16 | 9.0 | 5.2 | 9.0 | 6.8 | 12.0 | 9.4 | 15.0 | 12.3 | 15.0 | 12.8 | 18.0 | 16.0 | 21.0 |
| 14 | 12.0 | 7.0 | 12.0 | 9.0 | 15.0 | 11.7 | 18.0 | 14.8 | 21.0 | 17.9 | 24.0 | 21.4 | 27.0 |
| 12 | 15.0 | 8.7 | 15.0 | 11.3 | 21.0 | 16.4 | 24.0 | 19.7 | 27.0 | 23.0 | 30.0 | 26.7 | 33.0 |
| 10 | 24.0 | 13.9 | 24.0 | 18.0 | 30.0 | 23.4 | 33.0 | 27.1 | 36.0 | 30.6 | 42.0 | 37.4 | 42.0 |
| 8 | 33.0 | 19.1 | 39.0 | 29.3 | 42.0 | 32.8 | 42.0 | 34.4 | 48.0 | 40.8 | 54.0 | 48.1 | 60.0 |
| 6 | 48.0 | 27.8 | 57.0 | 42.8 | 60.0 | 46.8 | 60.0 | 49.2 | 72.0 | 61.2 | 75.0 | 66.8 | 81.0 |
| 4 | 63.0 | 36.5 | 75.0 | 56.3 | 78.0 | 60.8 | 81.0 | 66.4 | 96.0 | 81.6 | 102.0 | 90.8 | 108.0 |
| 3 | 72.0 | 41.8 | 87.0 | 65.3 | 90.0 | 70.2 | 93.0 | 76.3 | 108.0 | 91.8 | 117.0 | 104.1 | 126.0 |
| 2 | 84.0 | 48.7 | 102.0 | 76.5 | 105.0 | 81.9 | 108.0 | 88.6 | 126.0 | 107.1 | 135.0 | 120.2 | 144.0 |
| 1 | 99.0 | 57.4 | 117.0 | 87.8 | 126.0 | 98.3 | 126.0 | 103.3 | 147.0 | 125.0 | 159.0 | 141.5 | 168.0 |
| 0 | 117.0 | 67.9 | 138.0 | 103.5 | 147.0 | 114.7 | 147.0 | 120.5 | 171.0 | 145.4 | 183.0 | 162.9 | 195.0 |
| 00 | 135.0 | 78.3 | 159.0 | 119.3 | 171.0 | 133.4 | 171.0 | 140.2 | 198.0 | 168.3 | 213.0 | 189.6 | 222.0 |
| 000 | 156.0 | 90.5 | 186.0 | 139.5 | 198.0 | 154.4 | 198.0 | 162.4 | 231.0 | 196.4 | 246.0 | 218.9 | 258.0 |
| 0000 | 180.0 | 104.4 | 216.0 | 162.0 | 231.0 | 180.2 | 231.0 | 189.4 | 267.0 | 227.0 | 285.0 | 253.7 | 306.0 |

₁Outside engine spaces (OS)

₂Inside engine spaces (IS)

*Fig. 11-4. ABYC ampacity table for a bundled run of up to three triplex cables. (© ABYC)*

tional consideration is whether or not they need to be of the single- or double-pole configuration. Almost all circuit breakers used with DC systems are single-pole breakers with two terminals on the back designed to be connected in series with the DC positive feed wire. A notable exception is with some DC panel master breakers where two single-pole breakers will be ganged together.

For all AC circuits, the main circuit breaker must be of the *double-pole type*. With this type, the breaker will have four terminals and be designed to simultaneously trip both the black AC positive conductor and the white AC negative conductor. This added safety measure provides protection even with reverse polarity. So in effect, even if the wiring entering the boat from the dock is set up incorrectly, the breaker will still do its job.

If your boat's AC distribution panel is equipped with a reverse-polarity indicator, you may use single-pole breakers for any branch circuits on the panel or downstream from the panel. If you're buying a new distribution panel to add AC to your boat, be sure to get one equipped with this reverse-polarity indicator. Any money saved on the panel by not getting this feature will be false economy in the long run—the incidence of reverse polarity at marina shore-power boxes is just too high! Figure 11-5 on page 164 shows both a single- and double-pole breaker of the approved type. Figures 11-6a and 11-6b illustrate how these two types of circuit breakers are wired into an AC circuit.

# Basic AC Outlet Connections

When installing a new AC outlet, the black wire to the back of the outlet must be connected to the copper- or brass-colored screw terminal. The white wire must be connected to the white or silver terminal, and the green wire must be connected to the green terminal. You must use the captive-crimp terminals described in chapter 4 for all connections to the outlet. The spring-loaded press-on terminals used for some residential outlets are for use with Romex solid-copper wire and are never appropriate for the stranded wire you must be using if you're

*Fig. 11-5. Single- and double-pole AC circuit breakers.*

adding an outlet. The screw-terminal variety of household outlet is just fine as long as a proper ring-eye, or *captive* terminal as described in chapter 4, is crimped to each wire. This connection scheme must be followed throughout the entire boat. It's easy to mess up here and have the outlet still work, but you could possibly have introduced reverse polarity to that outlet that will not be detected by your AC panel-mounted reverse-polarity indicator.

On a boat, all AC connections must be enclosed in a protective box. I've seen outlets installed on bulkheads with the back side of the outlet exposed to the inside of a cabinet or hanging locker. One metal coat hanger or soup pot sliding into the back of the outlet, into contact with the terminals, is all it would take to create an instant short circuit. The readily available and quite inexpensive plastic outlet boxes used in residential wiring are perfect for this purpose. They'll last forever, they can be easily installed from the back of the assembly (sometimes without even removing the outlet), and they prevent any short circuits or shock hazard.

Figures 11-7a and 11-7b show a typical three-pronged outlet and indicate which color conductor should be servicing each prong.

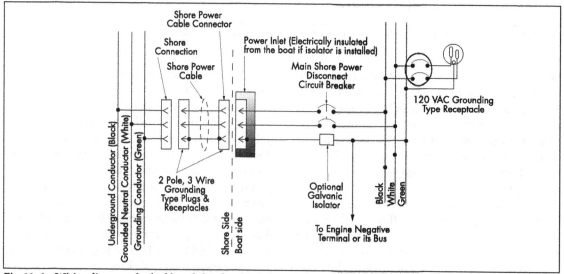

*Fig. 11-6a. Wiring diagram of a double-pole breaker (circled area) that will simultaneously trip and open the black and white conductors. (© ABYC)*

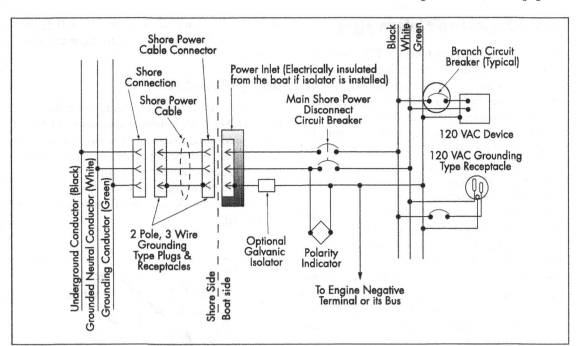

*Fig. 11-6b. Here, a single-pole breaker (circled area) is allowed in the branch feeder to both the 120-volt AC appliance and the outlet, because the boat is equipped with a polarity indicator. The breaker will only trip the black conductor. (© ABYC)*

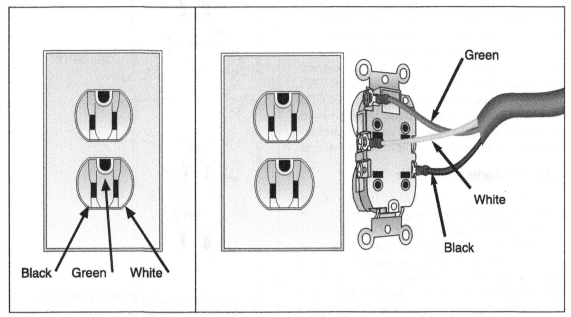

*Figs. 11-7a, b. Standard outlet for a three-pronged plug, showing which socket does what and the color of the wire going to it.*

# Ground-Fault Circuit Interrupters

Ground-fault circuit interrupters (GFCIs) are a specialized type of circuit breaker designed to trip open whenever resistance between ground and the ungrounded conductor drops below 25,000 ohms. Any time current is diverted from the white wire, such as through your body when you grab a hot AC wire, the GFCI senses the absence of grounding current and opens the circuit, hopefully in time to prevent all your friends and relatives from having to make premature calls to the florist.

Just as with home installations, boats are required to have ground-fault circuit interrupter outlets on certain branch circuits of the AC service. This type of outlet is easily identified by the test and reset buttons located on the face plate. Many novice electricians assume that the purpose of GFCIs is to protect the circuit or device a circuit is feeding. Not so! GFCIs are intended to protect people from shock, not equipment.

GFCI protection is required in areas of the boat where excess moisture or a particular shock hazard may exist. Specifically, the ABYC recommends GFCIs in heads, galleys, engine rooms, and on deck. For all practical purposes, this means you may want a GFCI on every AC circuit on your boat.

In some cases, protection for all of these areas can be provided by just one GFCI outlet, with conventional outlets installed "downstream" from the GFCI. To protect the other outlets downstream, the GFCI must be the first outlet in the circuit. On larger boats, this protection may be broken up into more than one circuit, necessitating the use of several GFCI outlets.

## Ignition Protection with GFCIs

All of this is of particular significance to boats that use gasoline as fuel and must meet ignition-protection requirements as discussed in chapter 4. Most GFCI outlets are not rated for ignition protection and therefore should never be used in engine rooms. Marine-grade GFCIs are available, but at considerable cost. This is really no problem for either the boatbuilder or you if you intend to add an outlet in your boat's engine room. Simply use a conventional outlet in the space requiring ignition protection, and tie it into a GFCI

outlet mounted in a safe area, such as in the galley. Figure 11-8 illustrates how this arrangement should be wired.

## Testing GFCI Outlets

All GFCI outlets used on boats must be tested monthly. The delicate internal mechanism of a GFCI outlet used in the harsh marine environment can corrode and cause the unit to not trip when you need it most. The simple test procedure is often overlooked, and not testing each outlet every month can cause obvious problems (it won't work when it's really needed).

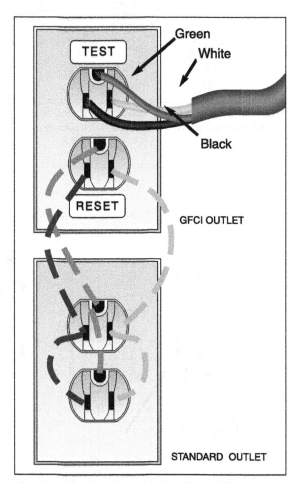

*Fig. 11-8. A GFCI outlet with a non-GFCI outlet wired in to share protection.*

To test a GFCI, simply depress the test button on the assembly faceplate. This trips the internal breaker and actually exercises the outlet's inner workings to ensure that it's functioning as it should. If the test and reset buttons feel spongy and seem to have lost their crisp snap action, odds are good that the GFCI mechanism is corroded, and the outlet should be replaced.

Another point worth mentioning here is that just because the dock box that your boat is connected to at the marina is protected by GFCI (and it always should be), you shouldn't think that you're protected from shock hazard on your boat. These dockside GFCIs are likely to be forgotten by the maintenance crew and never tested until it's too late. To be safe, always test the dockside outlets before you plug in your shore-power cord, and to eliminate any worry, upgrade your boat with this important protection as soon as you can.

## Checking Voltage, Continuity, and Polarity on AC Circuits

Sooner or later, problems will crop up with the AC circuits on your boat, and you'll need to do basic multimeter tests for voltage, polarity, and continuity. There is no need to be afraid of doing these tests on AC circuits, even for the novice, but following some basic rules, in addition to the safety rules listed above, will ensure that you won't damage your meter or end up having a shocking experience.

Besides your multimeter, several small, inexpensive testers can be extremely useful when working around AC systems. Figure 11-9 shows an LED outlet tester with a built-in GFCI test function, and figure 11-10 shows an inductive voltage sensor used for verifying the presence of AC voltage, even behind panels and through insulation. The LED outlet tester is useful in determining whether reverse polarity exists and whether or not there is an open circuit in any of the three conductors.

It is not at all uncommon for low voltage to be a problem in an AC circuit, or reverse polarity for that matter. A disconnected green grounding conductor is quite common and can go unnoticed until someone gets a shocking jolt. The good news here is that

these problems usually originate at the dock, not on the boat, and it's easy to check for them yourself.

Figure 11-10 demonstrates using the inductive AC tester to see if there is voltage present at an outlet. If the tester's LED flashes and it emits a steady beeping noise, AC is present in the circuit. The only remaining question is how much voltage. To determine that, you'll need your multimeter.

*Fig. 11-9. An LED outlet tester.*

*Fig. 11-10. Using the inductive AC tester to check voltage at an outlet.*

## Checking AC Voltage

When using your multimeter to check for AC volts, you need to remember that AC and DC volts are different as far as your meter is concerned. With either volts or amps, you must switch to the AC function on your meter before making any checks. If your meter is self-scaling (auto-ranging), the next step is to simply insert the leads into the appropriate sockets and take a direct reading on the meter, as shown in figure 11-11.

Note that in the diagram the meter's red lead is inserted into the smaller of the two slotted holes and the meter's black lead is inserted into the larger. Don't forget to turn on the appropriate branch breaker before making this test. If your meter is not self-scaling, make sure you select the appropriate scale for the voltage you're expecting to read.

When verifying voltage at an appliance, a hot-water heater for example, that's hard-wired into the circuit (permanently installed rather than plugged into an outlet), you'll need to get at the terminals in the junction box on the appliance. With the branch breaker for the appliance turned on, check for proper voltage at the appliance by touching your red meter probe to the terminal on the black AC wire and the black meter probe to the terminal on the white AC wire. Simply take a direct reading. In figure 11-12, the AC voltage supply to a typical marine hot-water heater is being verified.

A useful tip to help you when working with AC circuit testing is to get two short lengths of heat-shrink tubing at your local supply house, one white and the other black. Shrink the black piece around the red lead on your multimeter and the white piece around the black lead. This will remind you that the black lead on the AC is the positive and the black lead is the neutral when working with AC. It simply gives you a quick color reference to work with.

Slight variations in your meter readings are the norm when measuring AC voltage. In fact, a variation of as much as plus or minus 10 percent of the rated voltage is possible. If your dockmates are all using the AC system feeding the marina simultaneously, you can expect a lower voltage reading.

At peak usage times of the day (usually around breakfast and dinner) you can also expect lower readings. AC generators on board could also conceivably run to that much of a variation. This variation is not indicative of any particular problem

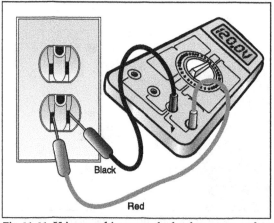

*Fig. 11-11. Using a multimeter to check voltage at an outlet.*

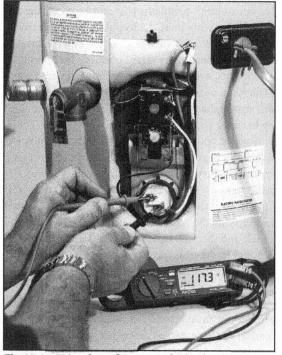

*Fig. 11-12. Using the multimeter to check voltage to a hot-water heater terminal block.*

and will not affect the performance of your onboard equipment as long as the 10 percent variation at the rated frequency (either 50 or 60 Hz) is not exceeded. By the way, multimeters that can read frequency have dropped considerably in price and are available for less than $50. If you're going to work with AC regularly, this is a good added feature to have on your meter.

## Checking AC Amperage

Checking AC amperage through a circuit can be a bit tricky. The problem is that since sheathing protects AC wiring through most of its length, it's sometimes tough to find a single conductor around which to clamp your meter to take a reading. Remember that with an inductive clamp-type ammeter you can only use one conductor to measure amperage. This applies to both AC and DC. The truth is, this is not a reading you'll be making very often, because AC appliances all provide the data needed to determine amperage. The need to actually measure amperage in AC systems is far less of an issue than it is with DC circuitry. Figure 11-13 shows an inductive AC clamp meter being used to determine current in an AC circuit.

## AC Continuity Tests

Continuity tests for AC circuits are more frequently needed than are voltage and amperage tests, and the ability to perform a good continuity test will be useful, especially when checking things like shore-power cords.

The most important point to remember when checking for continuity is to be certain the wiring that you intend to check is disconnected from the power source. The risk here goes beyond simply damaging your multimeter; it's also a shock hazard. Continuity tests can be used not only to determine the integrity of wiring, but also to check some resistive AC appliances—things such as a hot-water heater element or an electric coffee maker.

### The Ed Sherman Wiggle Test

When checking the conductor continuity in any flexible cord, such as a shore-power cord, it's a good idea to perform what I call the *wiggle test*.

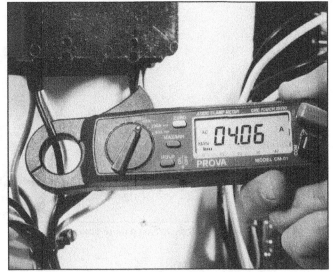

Fig. 11-13. An inductive-current clamp used to check current on an AC appliance.

These cords take quite a beating and are frequently abused. It's quite possible to get a solid continuity reading with your meter and lose continuity when the cord is flexed, especially close to the ends where the cord's three conductors attach to the plug ends. Figure 11-14 on page 170 shows a typical shore-power cord being wiggle-tested.

To do the Sherman wiggle, set your meter to the ohms scale and connect one meter probe to the prong on the plug and the other probe to the corresponding socket at the other end of the cable. You should get a very low ohms reading, near zero if all is well. Next, bend and flex (i.e., wiggle) the plug and socket ends while firmly holding the cable. Carefully observe your meter, and look for a change from a low ohms reading to an open-circuit reading of infinity, or "OL" on digital meters.

A fluctuating reading indicates a break in continuity behind the insulation at the plug end. Check all three conductors in this way to be sure they're all OK. If any momentary break in continuity is indicated, a suitable replacement end will need to be installed on the cord. Marinco, an electric supply company, makes quality replacement plugs and sockets that are available at all good marine supply houses.

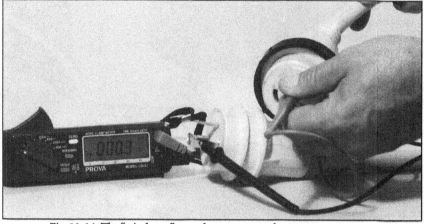

*Fig. 11-14. The "wiggle test" on a shore-power cord.*

### AC Resistive Equipment Checks

To determine if the heater element in a hot-water heater (or any other appliance using a heating element) is OK, you can also perform a continuity test. First make certain that the breaker for the heater is off, and verify that power is not present by using the inductive tester described earlier and shown in figure 11-10 on page 167. Next, attach your meter to the black and white leads, respectively, at the terminal junction on the heater and check the resistance reading through the heating element.

A resistance reading is to be expected if all is well. If you get a reading of infinity or "OL" on your meter, the element has developed an open circuit inside the heater, and the heater or the element will have to be replaced.

Figure 11-15 shows this test being performed on a good element, with a typical resistance reading shown on the meter.

## Selecting a DC-to-AC Inverter

Popular with the sailboat crowd for some time now, 12-volt-DC-to-120-volt-AC inverters are also becoming increasingly popular among owners of small powerboats. The reasons for this trend are quite simple. Space on small boats is at a premium, so a generator installation is usually out of the question. Cost

may also be a consideration. Entry into the silent world of inverter power is considerably less expensive than purchasing a generator. Noise and the exhaust fumes created by a generator are simply undesirable if a better alternative exists. Further, many of the inverters available actually work in two directions, creating the AC you want and also acting as high-end, multistage battery chargers for use at the dock when you're plugged into shore power.

At least for limited use, the DC-to-AC inverter has changed the way many small-boat owners satisfy their craving for AC power on board. Engineers have designed inverters that can produce as little as 50 watts to as much as 3,000 watts of continuous power—more than enough for most small powerboats.

*Fig. 11-15. A continuity test on a hot-water heater element.*

## Selecting an Inverter

Nothing comes without a price, and although these electronic marvels are quite capable of producing adequate AC power, they need a fairly substantial DC power source to keep them running. This in itself can be the limiting factor on some boats. Batteries are heavy, and they too take up space. When selecting an inverter and designing the system that will support it, there are some important considerations you must make to ensure your ultimate satisfaction.

Classically, people go through a period of denial about their personal AC consumption whenever the topic of inverters or generators comes up. Daily power consumption is the key to sizing not only the inverter itself, but also the battery bank that's going to feed it. Use of an inverter on board ties into much of the discussion throughout this book. Battery types, amp-hour ratings, reserve capacity, wattage—all of these factors must be given serious consideration if you hope to be successful with an inverter selection and installation.

## AC Need Analysis

The first step in inverter consideration is to perform an honest and accurate analysis of your daily AC usage. If all you want is to occasionally recharge a laptop computer or rechargeable electric-drill battery, your needs are minimal. You'll be served well by one of the small portable inverters on the market today. But, if you intend to run a TV, microwave oven, and possibly a refrigeration system in addition to supplying outlets for use with things like hair dryers and coffee makers, you're going to need an inverter that packs some real punch. What this all boils down to is wattage and how many hours per day you'll be using these appliances.

Be sure to consider usage; many of the appliances you'll be running from the inverter will be used intermittently. If you're going to be running a microwave simultaneously with a coffee maker, your total wattage needs could easily be as much as about 2,500 watts. Your inverter will need to have the power to deliver at least 2,500 watts in this scenario; the smaller 1,000-watt inverter simply won't do the job.

Determining the AC wattage you need is easy. As already stated, wattage, or possibly volts and amps, must be indicated on the appliance. If the value is given in volts and amps, simply multiply the voltage by the amperage to determine the wattage of the appliance. Make a list of all the appliances you intend to run with the inverter, and pay particular attention to the subtotals of gear you expect to run simultaneously. If money is no object, simply add up the wattage for all the appliances you expect to use. Size your inverter to handle all the possible loads you'll run simultaneously.

The bottom line here? *Don't cheat!* Remember, as already stated, people tend to underrate their AC usage, buy too-small inverters, and end up disappointed after all is said and done. This can't be emphasized enough.

Figure 11-16 on page 172 shows a sample wattage load-analysis sheet for determining the size of the inverter to select based on wattage.

Next, you'll need to make some decisions about how many hours each day you'll be running the various appliances listed in your inventory. This will help determine battery-bank size. You must also take into account the loss through the inverter as it performs its magic. This loss is really a form of voltage drop and represents the conversion of some of the DC to heat as it's inverted. Typically, inverters are about 90 percent efficient, so you can expect to lose about 10 percent of the available amp-hours from your supplying battery bank through the inverter. That, and the fact that you really don't want to discharge even the best batteries much below 50 percent of their capacity, should tell you that you're going to need some serious DC capacity (i.e., big batteries) to make this all work as it should.

Figure 11-17 on page 172 shows a typical amp-hour calculation table that should be used to determine total amp-hour consumption between battery charge cycles when plugged into shore power.

Once you have determined your daily amp-hour requirements, you need to think about how many days you might be away from shore power and how frequently you'll be charging your batteries with the

## Wattage Calculation Worksheet

| Appliance | Rated Wattage | Start-up Wattage |
|-----------|---------------|------------------|
| | | |
| | | |
| | | |
| | | |
| | | |
| | | |
| | | |
| | | |
| | | |
| | | |
| | | |
| | | |
| | | |
| | | |
| **Total wattage** | | |

Use this table to list all of your AC appliances. Find out the wattage by checking the UL labeling on the appliance. Start-up wattage applies to appliances such as refrigeration devices (refrigerators, ice makers, air conditioners). In the case of inverters, the medium- to larger-sized units all have an intermittent-output rating that's usually more than twice the rated continuous output in watts; this is to allow for the needed start-up watt requirements of these appliances. Be sure to check the specifications of the unit you're working with to make sure its rating is adequate. In the case of generators, if sized properly, a typical 20–30 percent overrating for total maximum draw will take care of this momentary need, especially since it's unlikely that you'll have all of your appliances running simultaneously for an extended period of time.

*Fig. 11-16. Wattage load analysis sheet for inverter or generator selection.*

## Amp-Hour Calculation Table for Inverter Battery-Bank Sizing

| Appliance | 5 min. | 15 min. | 30 min. | 1 hr. | 2 hr. | 3 hr. | 8 hr. | 24 hr. |
|-----------|--------|---------|---------|-------|-------|-------|-------|--------|
| 13-inch color TV | 0.5 | 1 | 2 | .5 | .9 | .14 | .37 | .110 |
| VCR | 0.5 | 1 | 2 | .5 | .9 | .14 | .37 | .110 |
| Curling iron | 0.5 | 1 | 2 | | | | | |
| Table lamp | 1 | 2 | 5 | .9 | .18 | .28 | .74 | .221 |
| 3-cu. ft. refrigerator | | | 2 | .5 | .9 | .14 | .37 | .110 |
| Blender | 2 | 7 | 14 | | | | | |
| ⅜-inch drill | 4 | 12 | 23 | | | | | |
| 20-cu. ft. refrigerator | | | 12 | 23 | 46 | 69 | 183 | 550 |
| Mid-size microwave | 7 | 21 | 41 | 83 | 166 | 249 | | |
| Coffee maker | 8 | 23 | 46 | 92 | 183 | | | |
| Vacuum cleaner | 8 | 25 | 50 | 101 | 202 | 302 | | |
| Full-size microwave | 12 | 34 | 69 | 138 | 275 | 413 | | |

*Use Time/Minutes-Hours Amp-Hours Used (Typical)*

*Fig. 11-17. Amp-hour calculation table for determining the correct size of an inverter battery bank.*

engine's alternator while underway. If you expect to be using this system for weekend jaunts at anchor, you must multiply everything by two. If you expect to be away from shore power for a week, multiply by seven, and so forth. Once this is done, go back to chapter 5 and refer to figure 5-2 on page 71, which shows typical battery amp-hour ratings. Take a common group 27 battery, for example. It has a typical amp-hour rating of about 105 amps. You can only use a little over 50 of these to prevent excessive battery discharge, so if your daily consumption requires 100 DC amps, you'll need at least two of these group 27 batteries for each day away from the dock.

Figure 11-18 shows two formulas for determining battery-bank size based on known amps or watts. Figure 11-19 lists some common AC appliances and their approximate wattage ratings.

## Installing an Inverter

After determining inverter and battery-bank sizing, you may be considering the possibility of installing an inverter on your own. The truth is, to install all but the simplest inverter with its own self-contained plug outlets goes well beyond the scope of this book and certainly the abilities of the average boatowner. There are many considerations to make, and even experienced electricians often overlook some of the fine points of the ABYC's recommendations for inverter installation. If you're thinking of adding an inverter to your boat, the best bet is to try and find an ABYC-certified marine electrician. The certified tech will be quite familiar with all the nuances of inverter installation, and the end result will be well worth the labor expense here.

Having said that, the list of general guidelines that follows will enable you to at least converse with a professional electrician intelligently to come up with an installation solution that satisfies your needs.

Presently no one makes an ignition-protected inverter. The nature of the beast is that internal switching must be accomplished during operation, and this switching process can create some arcing as the unit is working. For this reason, extreme care must be taken when selecting a location to mount the unit. If your boat is gasoline fueled, the inverter must be located in a compartment outside the engine room. Further complicating the issue is the fact that manufacturers of inverters prefer to have them mounted as close to the battery bank feeding them as possible. The reason for this is to minimize the effects of voltage drop in the DC feeder wires to the inverter.

Minimal voltage drop is a must if the unit is going to achieve the 90 percent efficiency mentioned ear-

## Formula for Determining Battery-Bank Size

**(taking inverter inefficiency into consideration)**

To find the amp-hours drawn from the batteries by any given AC appliance powered by the inverter, you must find the AC amperage or wattage consumed and apply one of the equations shown here.

$$\text{DC Amp/Hours} = \text{AC amps} \times 10 \times 1.1 \times \text{hours of use}$$
$$\text{DC Amp/Hours} = \text{AC watts} \div 12 \times 1.1 \times \text{hours of use}$$

*Fig. 11-18. Battery-bank size determination.*

## Typical AC Appliance Wattage Requirements

| Appliance | Wattage |
|---|---|
| Television | 80–100 |
| VCR | 50 |
| Stereo | 50 |
| Curling iron | 50 |
| Lamp | 100 |
| Blender | 300 |
| ⅜-inch drill | 500 |
| Orbital sander | 500 |
| Ice maker | 200 |
| Small refrigerator | 150 |
| Mid-size microwave | 900 |
| Hand-held vacuum | 1,100 |
| Hair dryer | 1,500 |

*Fig. 11-19. Common AC appliances and their wattage requirements.*

lier. Batteries give off explosive hydrogen gas when being charged and so need to be well ventilated to remove this gas.

Mounting an inverter close to batteries in an un-ventilated compartment, such as under a V-berth, is not a good choice unless adequate ventilation is added to create sufficient air exchange. Also, the inverter itself is heavy and must be securely mounted to a panel or bulkhead. Inverters must be kept cool to keep the efficiency up and to ensure the long life of the inverter itself. So again, the ventilation issue comes up. The inverter-location checklist that follows highlights these key points.

▶ Inverters must be located in a compartment separate from gasoline engines and tanks.

▶ Inverters must be located as close as possible to the batteries.

▶ Inverters must be securely mounted to a bulkhead and through-bolted with adequate backing washers.

▶ Inverters must be located in a well-ventilated location to allow for cooling of the unit and to allow any hydrogen gas that builds up as part of battery-charging to escape.

Further considerations, once a suitable spot for the inverter has been decided upon, have to do with proper circuit protection and system monitoring.

As for overcurrent protection, consider that both the AC and DC sides of the inverter will need some form of overcurrent protection installed. The output side of the inverter may have a circuit breaker built in, but it pays to double-check. As for the DC side, protection will need to be installed.

The special fuses (slow-blow) used for this purpose are generally not provided as standard with the units, but are available as an option from the inverter manufacturers. These fuses and holders are rated for extremely high amperage and are generally described as class "T" fuses. As for the location of these fuses, the 7–40–72 inch rule applies. Refer back to chapter 4 if you need to refresh your memory. Figure 11-20 shows this fuse installed in the DC positive feed to an inverter.

As for system monitoring, to comply with ABYC recommendations your inverter will need to have some form of indication installed in or very near your existing AC panel (or if none exists as yet, near the existing DC panel) to let folks know that an inverter is installed on board, and when it's on-line. This can be accomplished via the installation of a voltmeter, indicator light, or both. To simplify all this, spend the extra money and buy the inverter manufacturer's optional system monitor! You can cover all the compliance issues in one shot, and get some features built into the dedicated system monitor that are extremely worthwhile. These monitors can provide important data such as volts, amps, amp-hours consumed, and time remaining on the supplying battery bank, to name just a few of the available functions. Figure 11-21 on page 175 shows a typical inverter-monitoring system. This one is a "Link" unit from Heart Interface, now part of Xantrex.

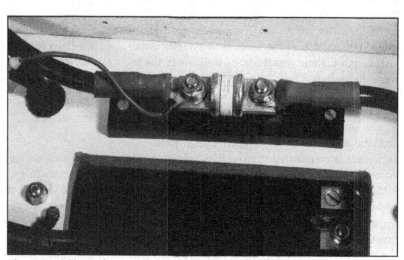

Fig. 11-20. A T-type fuse installed in an inverter DC feed cable.

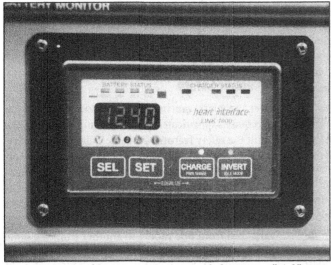

*Fig. 11-21. A typical inverter monitoring panel, the Xantrex "Link" 1000.*

## Inverter Waveform

On the subject of voltage output, there is one additional point that needs to be made regarding inverters. Most (but not all) inverters produce what is known as a *modified-square waveform*. Shore-based power supplies, on the other hand, produce what is known as a *sine waveform*. Early inverters produced a standard square waveform.

This technical mumbo-jumbo is all great information for electrical engineers and of little value to boatowners, except for several issues. First, older square-wave inverters had trouble running things like TVs, microwave ovens, and older computers, and could even damage or destroy these appliances. Today's modified-square-wave and true-sine-wave inverters have pretty much licked that problem, and the new inverters run just about anything.

The second problem caused by waveform is measuring voltage and amperage. As I mentioned earlier in this chapter and in chapter 3, the meter used to measure voltage from an inverter should be of the true RMS variety to give the best results. Typically, modified-sine-wave inverters will show low voltage when measured with an average-responding meter. This is no cause for alarm and not indicative of a fault with the inverter!

## AC Generators

Just as with inverters, advanced troubleshooting and installation procedures for AC generators go way beyond the scope of this book. These things are best left to the ABYC-certified professional marine electrician. However, some general knowledge of these workhorses is still important for the boatowner and will help to ensure that your generator is of the proper size and is performing as it should. The basic troubleshooting checklist at the end of this section will help you to at least point the service technician in the right direction if you do have trouble with your generator.

## Rating AC Generators

AC generators are rated the same way inverters are. Wattage is the key here, and the basic AC use-analysis chart for inverters will work just as well for determining your generator requirements.

The essential difference between generator and inverter ratings is that typically, generator manufacturers have rated their units in kilowatts (kW). One kilowatt equals 1,000 watts, so, for example, if your generator is rated at 4.5 kW, it's a 4,500-watt unit.

As with inverters, boaters are inclined to over- or underrate their needs with generators. Underrating will give poor electrical performance, for what should be obvious reasons by now. But a point that many people don't realize is that overrating of a generator can wreak havoc with the generator itself. Generators are designed to operate at a very specific rpm to govern and control the AC frequency. They must be able to maintain this rpm over the entire operating range of the unit under all levels of electrical load.

The problem is just that—load. Underworked generators will simply freewheel along, eventually gumming up the cylinders, valves, and rings of the engine. Slight overrating in terms of average combined wattage consumption is OK, but manufacturers recommend that a generator be rated to average 75 percent of its total wattage most of the time. Knowing this, it should be clear that running a TV from even the smallest generator will damage the unit if that's the only draw for extended periods. Generators are really only suitable for fairly serious AC loads (such as electric ranges, air conditioners, and hot-water heaters) all running simultaneously and for extended periods of at least and hour or so—for example, during preparation for the evening meal.

Other serious disadvantages of generators include the noise of the engine, those wonderful exhaust fumes permeating into the pre-dinner cocktail hour, and simply having one more engine on board to maintain.

As already mentioned, both the voltage and frequency of AC generators are carefully controlled by an engine-mounted governor that keeps engine rpm stable under all electrical loads. If you have a generator on your boat, your AC panel must have a voltmeter to be in compliance with the ABYC standards. It's a good idea from time to time to monitor this gauge. Any variation in voltage beyond 10 percent of the normal rated output for the generator that's indicated by this gauge is an indication of trouble.

Modern generators are commonly regulated to control voltage to as little as plus or minus 2 percent if all is well with the unit. As voltage fluctuates, so too does frequency. Normal frequency here in the United States is 60 Hz. Some of the better multimeters on the market have the ability to measure frequency, and this is not a bad feature to have if your boat has a generator installed or you're thinking of having one added.

## Measuring Generator Output

Verifying generator voltage and frequency is not difficult, but to ensure that any low-voltage indications on your AC panel are not due to a wiring and voltage-drop problem between the generator and the panel, measurement should be done right at the output terminals on the generator. When checking voltage and amperage at the generator, be careful of moving parts and the hot exhaust on the generator, and be sure to take your readings at the correct location as per the instructions

from the generator manufacturer. If in doubt, make sure you have the service manual at hand, and use it! Figure 11-22 shows the frequency being verified on a typical marine generator.

## Generator Safety

Over the years, marine AC generators have evolved into quite sophisticated pieces of equipment, and as a result the safety features available today are extensive. Built-in sensors shut down the generator in the event of such things as low oil pressure, engine or exhaust-system overheating, and even excessive exhaust back-pressure on some models. The problem is, different manufacturers use different systems, and features will vary even from one model to another from the same manufacturer. To familiarize yourself with your generator, get out the owner's manual, and if you intend to do any but the most basic service or troubleshooting on the unit, get the workshop manual as well.

Most inadvertent generator shutdown problems are due to loose connections, low oil pressure (is there oil in the engine?), or an overheating engine. You may have to trace through the cooling-system troubleshooting section of your workshop manual to find the solution and get the generator up and running again.

*Fig. 11-22. Checking frequency with the multimeter.*

## AC Generator Troubleshooting Guide

Aside from these basic checks, some more advanced procedures are found in the following checklist. These additional checks are too advanced for most beginners and will have to be carried out by a trained technician, preferably one certified on your particular brand of generator.

### Low Voltage

▶ Check the voltage at the generator. If the reading is OK and your panel meter is reading low, there is an excessive voltage drop in the wiring between the generator and the panel.

▶ Verify correct generator engine rpm and governor settings.

▶ Check all connections and wire terminations for integrity. First make sure the generator is off!

▶ If voltage is OK until the engine warms up and loads are applied, the generator voltage regulator and related circuitry are at fault.

▶ The voltage regulator may need adjustment or replacement.

### High Voltage

▶ Check the frequency for normal range (between 57 and 63 Hz in the United States).

▶ If possible, adjust the voltage regulator.

▶ Verify correct engine rpm and governor adjustments.

### Erratic Voltage

▶ The generator brushes could be worn or burned.

▶ There could be internal wiring problems or loose connections.

### Erratic Frequency

▶ Check for loads cycling where the generator turns the current on and off.

▶ If the frequency is erratic with all loads turned off, check the governor for proper operation. Can you hear subtle rpm changes?

### High Frequency

▶ Have the governor operation checked.

### Low Frequency

▶ Turn off all loads. If frequency returns to normal, the generator is being overworked and is probably underrated. Either give up some AC toys or prepare to upgrade to a bigger generator.

▶ Check for faulty governor adjustment.

## Galvanic Isolators

A device that has become increasingly popular in recent years on new boats is the *galvanic isolator*. The trouble with them is that most folks, including many marine electricians, haven't the faintest idea what they do. So, what are these things used for anyhow? Well, here's the definition: "A device installed in series with the green grounding conductor of the shore-power cable which effectively blocks galvanic current flow (DC), but permits the passage of alternating current (AC)."

You're probably still wondering, Yeah, but what does it do? Why do I need one?

If you spend much time at the dock plugged into shore power, you need a galvanic isolator. Here's why: Galvanic current flow is a danger at any marina, putting your boat at risk of *galvanic corrosion*. The more boats with AC shore power, the greater the risk. Your boat could be in great electrical shape, but once plugged into shore power it becomes electrically connected to its neighbors via the green grounding wire in the AC system. This connection completes an electrical circuit between multiple boats, each with potentially dissimilar underwater metals exposed to the surrounding seawater. What's created is a giant battery and the potential galvanic corrosion that can result. Further, it is also possible to transfer higher-voltage DC stray current from one boat to another in this situation. This could generate *stray-current corrosion*.

How can that be? You might have thought the AC and DC systems were completely separated on your boat. They are, except for one common point where the DC and AC grounding system are tied together. Any faults that induce current flow in this normally non-current-carrying conductor can potentially be transferred via this green wire. This stray current can cause excess corrosion, rapid deterioration of underwater sacrificial zincs, and, in the worst case, can cause underwater metal appendages from your boat to literally dissolve in seawater. A common cause of stray-current corrosion is wiring that uses a boat's electrical bonding system as the DC ground for various appliances—typically bilge pumps. Any live wire hanging in the bilge water could be the culprit.

The only direct path for stray current to flow beyond any individual boat is via the green grounding conductor in the AC shore-power system (that is, except for a leak into the water surrounding the boat). It's important to note that the galvanic isolator is designed to isolate only low-level *galvanic* DC current.

Its purpose is to block only about 1.4 volts or less, not a full 12 volts. All precautions must be taken to ensure this green wire never has high-level current trying to find ground through it unless an AC system fault occurs. The isolator is intended to block only the natural galvanic current that will try to pass due to the electrically connected dissimilar underwater metals discussed.

The isolator uses four heavy-duty diodes, often combined with a capacitor, to absorb any voltage surges that may occur. These diodes use their inherent resistance and one-way capability to effectively block any small amounts of DC flow. (Galvanic current is measured at less than 1,200 millivolts, or 1.2 volts.) If a fault in the boat's AC system develops and the green conductor must be put into real service, AC can easily overcome this resistance and will flow through the isolator.

Remember that the green wire is designed to protect against shock, and its integrity is of paramount importance. Since the isolator is mounted in series with the green wire as the first stop past the shore-power connector on your boat and is often not easily accessible, the isolator's integrity must be known at all times. A blown diode inside the isolator could have the same effect as clipping off the third grounding terminal on an extension cord, as mentioned earlier.

In consideration of all this, the current version of ABYC Standard A-28, Galvanic Isolators, mandates a status-monitoring device for a galvanic isolator. Both Guest and ProMariner make such devices, which consist of a remote panel that alarms if a failure occurs. These monitors also seem to do a very good job of identifying other electrical problems, often with the dock wiring the boat is plugged into. This has been such a problem that an ABYC committee is now considering a new type of isolator that is rated as electrically "fail safe," meaning that if a diode

*Fig. 11-23. A ProMariner galvanic isolator.*

fails, electrical continuity through the device cannot be compromised. As of this writing, the committee has not finalized a new draft of the standard for review. Rest assured that boating magazines will publicize the final decision.

If you're uncertain whether your boat even has a galvanic isolator, check with your dealer. If you can get at the wiring on the back side of your shore-power inlet, trace the green wire through to the AC master panel. If the boat has an isolator, it will be mounted here. Figure 11-23 shows a ProMariner galvanic isolator, which uses a capacitor, installed on the green wire.

## Testing Galvanic Isolators

A simple test to make sure your galvanic isolator is working as it should, once you're certain you have one, is to use the LED tester shown in figure 11-9 on page 167 to determine if an open circuit exists in the grounding conductor.

If all the connections and the wiring are intact between your AC panel and the shore-power box, an open indicates either a break in continuity inside the galvanic isolator or a problem on the dock. Have the marina operator verify the condition on the dock. If it's OK, you may have a faulty galvanic isolator. Any ABYC-certified electrical technician can check this for you if you have any doubts.

Figure 11-24 shows the correct location for the galvanic isolator in relation to your shore-power inlet and the AC panel on your boat. If your boat doesn't have a galvanic isolator installed and you spend a lot of time at the dock, it would be a good upgrade to any AC electrical system. You can do this one yourself rather easily. Just make sure that the isolator you select is rated for the proper amperage (at least the same as your boat's AC rating or more), and preferably with a built-in capacitor for added protection to the unit itself. Also remember to mount these units in a spot that's relatively easy to get at and will offer good ventilation.

Remember that this chapter is not intended to make you an expert high-voltage electrician. It's intended to give you a little confidence for basic system checks and to enable you to talk with a marine electrician as an informed consumer. If you still get nervous around shore power, stay away from it! Call in the experts.

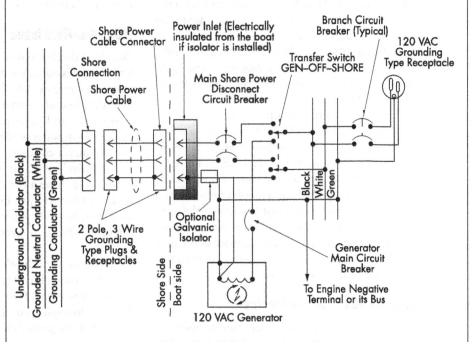

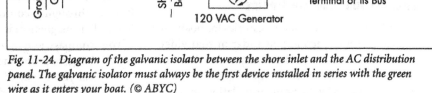

*Fig. 11-24. Diagram of the galvanic isolator between the shore inlet and the AC distribution panel. The galvanic isolator must always be the first device installed in series with the green wire as it enters your boat. (© ABYC)*

# Chapter 12

# Installing Marine Electronic Equipment

## Electronic Gadgetry

Sometimes it seems like powerboaters are the world's greatest gadgeteers. We who own boats love the electronic devices that we install on or attach to them, and from time to time (as we can afford it) one of our most pleasurable tasks is the selection, purchase, and installation of the latest piece of electronic gadgetry. Few indeed are the boaters among us who fail to install some new electronic wonder on our boats at least once a year.

My current West Marine catalog is more than 1 inch thick, and the lavishly illustrated pages are replete with images of all manner of electronic doohickeys, all of which, with very little imagination, can become essential to the safe and efficient operation of my boat. There are no less than 26 pages of marine radios and accessories, 10 pages devoted to GPS receivers, 12 pages of electronic chart plotters and navigation software, 6 pages of radar, and an entire section on lighting. Of course, you can view the entire catalog online these days, at www.westmarine.com.

You can even buy a remote-control underwater video camera with a 131-foot cable for a mere $5,999. Would I have one of these video cameras on my boat? You bet I would, and all that other stuff, too. Like nearly all boaters, if it weren't for the constraints of a small budget and a lot of common sense, I would need a bigger boat just to carry all the gadgets that I would like to install on it. All this wonderful stuff would help me navigate more safely, find that elusive lunker fish, or communicate with fellow boaters or friends on shore.

## Installing Your Own Electronics

Most aftermarket electronic accessories for boats are expensive; some (such as new radar or that video camera mentioned above) are very expensive. But one of the best ways to reduce the financial shock of new electronics is by doing the installation yourself.

Fortunately, this is a fairly easy task, and with the never-ending advances in equipment, the immediate results can be quite gratifying, provided you take into consideration certain factors that ensure a proper installation.

## Universal Installation Details

Depending on whether you're installing a depthsounder, a fish-finder, a VHF radio, a GPS receiver, or radar, many of the nuances of installing new electronics will vary, but the basic procedures for most new equipment are similar, with certain considerations in common: magnetic fields, radio-frequency interference (RFI), and the power supply. Let's take a look at these three items one at a time.

### Magnetic-Field Issue

One thing that is often taken lightly but is of extreme importance is the initial decision of where to mount your new equipment. Besides the obvious ergonomic considerations of seeing the screen or controls on the new device and perhaps keeping it from getting sprayed with water while underway, stray magnetism is a major concern. Today's small powerboats have relatively small consoles to work with and almost always have a compass mounted right in the middle of the area just in front of the helm. This is usually right where you want to mount that new radio or fish-finder to keep it in plain view and easy to use.

Virtually all of the electronic equipment you're likely to want on board emits some amount of magnetism. (Remember from chapter 3 how any current flowing through a conductor creates a magnetic field?) This magnetism is sure to upset the accuracy of your compass, and in some cases this compass error can be quite pronounced.

Several years ago, without giving the location much thought, I installed a new VHF radio on my boat. I put it about 8 inches from my steering compass, right where the old one had been. The new radio worked just fine. I could see the controls, they were easy to reach when I wanted to transmit, and the speaker was close by so I could easily hear any incoming transmission. The problem with my compass didn't show up until several weeks later when I was traveling in fog and had to use my GPS to navigate to the breakwater entrance to my homeport. I knew the GPS waypoint was accurate, so all I had to do was follow the compass course to the entrance. It was then that I discovered that my compass was 14 degrees off! Sure enough, the new VHF speakers had much larger magnets in them than my original speakers had, and the magnetic field they generated was sending my compass haywire!

## Zone of Magnetic Separation

The bottom line here is quite simple: You must maintain a *zone of separation* between your compass and any new electronic gear you install. The problem I had with my compass was caused by the new radio being too close to it. Ideally, in my experience, a separation of about 16 inches does the trick, but with highly magnetic equipment such as powerful speakers or radar, that zone of separation can conceivably extend to 3 feet or more.

You might be thinking that with your boat a 16-inch zone of separation is impossible; your console just doesn't allow that kind of room. Well, that's OK; a simple test is all that's needed to determine if you can close the zone. Temporarily power up the equipment and move it near the compass while looking for any deviation in the compass dial. By slowly and carefully moving the activated equipment closer to the compass, you can establish the actual minimum zone of separation for that particular piece of gear. Keep in mind that in some cases any device, such as one with a magnetic speaker, can have a profound effect on compass deviation without even being switched on.

In my experience, Loran and GPS receivers have virtually no effect on compasses. LCD fish-finders also seem to be fairly harmless in close proximity to compasses. (However, their CRT brothers can emit

a serious amount of magnetic interference.) Regardless, you should always check to be sure. (Note: Never "key" the mike on a VHF radio as part of this test. Keying the mike on a VHF radio with the antenna disconnected can damage the transmitter in the radio.)

Figure 12-1 shows the compass deviation being checked with a set of alligator-clip jumper leads that temporarily connect the device to a battery. (These jumpers are part of your basic tool kit from chapter 1.)

## Radio-Frequency Interference (RFI)

Another thing to consider when installing certain electrical devices, such as battery chargers and inverters, on board is what is known as *radio-frequency interference (RFI)*. Things like alternators and faulty ignition systems can also emit RFI. You may have heard one of the effects of RFI, caused by faults like a cracked distributor cap or a bad spark-plug wire, as static over an AM/FM radio. Ignition-induced RFI changes pitch in direct proportion to engine rpm.

*Fig. 12-1. Checking compass deviation with a temporary hookup to an electronic instrument.*

An easy way to isolate RFI is with a small portable transistor radio. Simply tune the radio between two AM stations (FM stations don't work as well), and you're ready to go. Turn on the electrical component you want to check, and listen for a loud hum from the radio. Move the radio alternately closer, then farther away from the component you're checking, and listen for a change in the humming noise. A good device to try this with for the first time is a battery charger. I have not found one yet that did not emit some RFI; it's quite normal for these devices.

The problem with RFI is that it can affect things like electronic compasses, autopilots, and Loran-C systems, and you'll never hear a sound. However, you could end up in Timbuktu instead of your favorite fishing hot spot!

Like the magnetism problem already discussed, you'll need to ensure that a good zone of separation is kept between devices that cause RFI and devices sensitive to it. For ignition systems and alternators, a variety of suppression devices and filters are available, and they are easy to install. All come with simple instructions. Check your local NAPA Auto Parts store or a good marine electronics distributor to get the parts for this job.

With inverters and battery chargers, you can establish the zone of separation you need using the transistor-radio method described above. Simply move the radio away from the activated device in question until no noise is heard, and your zone of separation will have been established. If you're doing this test with a battery charger or inverter, make sure the device is not only on but also under full load or output, whichever the case may be. RFI emission will vary proportionally with the amount of electrical activity within the device. In all cases it's advisable to consult the manufacturer of any electronic device you intend to install and find out about its sensitivity to RFI. While you're at it, get any recommendations they may have regarding separation zones and RFI suppression methods.

## Power Supply

Virtually all small-boat electronic equipment available today requires only a positive and a negative lead

to get the basic unit running. Some sensitive electronic equipment housed in metal cases may require a chassis ground (green wire) in addition to the negative lead (yellow or black wire). Still other equipment may have an additional hot lead (red wire) to power an internal memory. This extra lead must get power at all times and must not be switched in any way. If you have any doubt about how these leads should be connected, refer to the installation instructions for the particular equipment in question.

Remember, unlike things such as incandescent cabin lights, most new electronic gear is *polarity sensitive*. This means if you inadvertently switch the positive and the negative wires when you connect them to your power source, you could severely damage the equipment. Most manufacturers supply a red and a black lead with their equipment, indicating DC positive and negative, although white and black wires are still widely used. Always refer to the equipment installation instructions to be absolutely certain!

With the exception of VHF and single-sideband (SSB) radios and radar units, the amperage requirements for most new electronics are comparatively low, so wire gauge is not too much of an issue. Generally, on small boats, the length of the wire between the distribution panel and the equipment is not that long, so sticking with the same gauge wire supplied with the equipment (usually 16 AWG) will suffice.

Figure 12-2 shows a typical wire harness with an in-line fuse installed, as supplied with a Loran-C unit.

As for the connection to your boat, it's best to dedicate a circuit breaker at your DC distribution panel for instruments and designate separate positive and negative bus bars to connect your various pieces of equipment. Not only can direct connections to your batteries be messy, but they will add to the length of wire needed to power-up your electronic gear. Figure 12-3 on page 183 illustrates the best method to supply your equipment, by creating a dedicated branch bus from your main distribution panel. This way you can use bus bars that are adequately sized, and the addition of more equipment later on will be a much simpler task.

Once your new gear is mounted where you want it,

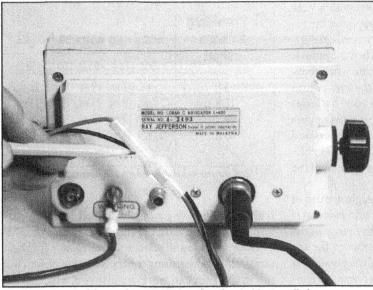

*Fig. 12-2. A typical factory harness, with in-line fuse holder installed.*

the next steps are specific to the various types of equipment. Now you have to think about other things, such as antenna or transducer placement.

## Installing a VHF Radio

Your VHF radio should be the mainstay of your onboard communication system. Although cell phones have become popular in recent years, the best way to get help when the chips are down is still via VHF radio transmission. For this reason, the VHF radio needs to be installed safely. You may need it when things aren't going so well on your boat.

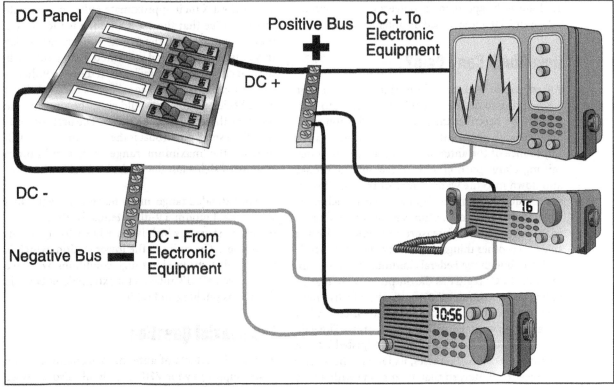

*Fig. 12-3. Dedicated bus bars to supply electronic equipment branched off the main distribution panel.*

Remember that transmission power with a VHF radio is proportional to the power supplying the radio. While transmitting, VHF power needs are approximately four times greater than when the radio is receiving. You may need to use the radio when maximum battery power isn't available; the very reason for your call for help could be that your batteries have drained enough so you can't get your engine started. Poor-quality connections and undersized wires supplying the VHF could induce excess voltage drop to the transmitter, so be sure this end of the installation is absolutely first-class!

Your next concern is the line-of-sight nature of VHF radio signals. The higher your radio antenna is mounted, the greater will be the effective range of the radio. So, when considering where to mount the antenna on your boat, try to get it as high as possible. If you venture far offshore, you may even want to consider one of the antenna mast extensions available from Shakespeare and others as a means of getting your antenna as high as it will go. The table in figure 12-4 shows the approximate range you can expect for a 25-watt VHF radio, based on antenna height.

## How Much Can I Gain?

Antenna gain is another important consideration when trying to decide which VHF antenna to purchase. *Gain* describes the power amplification available through your antenna, which refocuses the impedance of the antenna so that instead of transmitting a large portion of the signal up into the sky and down into the water, more of the signal is directed out toward the horizon where it's much more likely to do some good. Gain is measured in *decibels* (dBs), a logarithmic measure of sound and noise (plus a few other things that don't concern us here).

Even though the Federal Communications Commission (FCC) regulates the output of VHF marine radios to a maximum of 25 watts, the effective radiated power of the radio can be greatly increased by installing an antenna with a higher gain. (The gain of an antenna is fixed and can't be adjusted.) As an antenna's dB rating increases, its radiated beam gets narrower or flatter, so that an antenna with a very

| Transmitting Antenna Height | Receiving Antenna Height | | | | |
|---|---|---|---|---|---|
| | 5 ft. | 10 ft. | 25 ft. | 100 ft. | 250 ft. |
| 5 ft. | 5 mi. | 7 mi. | 9 mi. | 15 mi. | 23 mi. |
| 10 ft. | 9 mi. | 10 mi. | 11 mi. | 18 mi. | 25 mi. |
| 30 ft. | 10 mi. | 12 mi. | 13 mi. | 20 mi. | 28 mi. |
| 60 ft. | 12 mi. | 14 mi. | 15 mi. | 21 mi. | 30 mi. |

*Fig. 12-4. Antenna height versus VHF range.*

high gain will have a pancake-shaped radiation pattern oriented flat with the surface of the Earth. This can have a profound effect on your radio's transmit range without increasing the transmission power, but too much gain can work against you, especially if you're pitching and rolling in a rough sea.

The three commonly available antenna dB ratings for boats are 3, 6, and 9 dB. Figure 12-5 on page 185 illustrates their approximate radiated wave patterns. Notice that the 3-dB antenna is radiating a broader pattern than the 6- and 9-dB antennas. For this reason, a masthead-mounted 3-dB antenna is the best choice for most sailboats. If the 6- or 9-dB antennas were to be used, the sailboat's radiated signal while heeled underway would either be aimed at the moon or the bottom of the ocean. The best compromise for a small powerboat is the 6-dB antenna. It will provide the maximum range with a minimum amount of signal lost due to the boat rolling in a seaway.

For extended range, many powerboats with dual stations will mount a 9-dB antenna for the radio on the upper station, which is more likely to be used in a calm sea. The radio in the lower station, which is more likely to be used in rough conditions, will have a 6- or even a 3-dB antenna for extra reliability while the boat is pitching and rolling.

## The Coaxial Question

Besides the effects of antenna placement and the power supply to your VHF, you should also consider

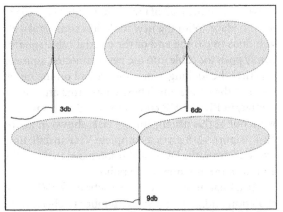

*Fig. 12-5. Wave patterns radiated by 3-dB, 6-dB, and 9-dB antennas.*

the type of cable connecting your antenna to your radio. Also, when selecting an antenna, look carefully at the factory lead coming from the base of the antenna; it should be of quality coaxial cable (described below). If not, after reading this section you may decide on a different antenna. The coaxial lead should not be the only criterion used for antenna selection, however. Internal construction and a quality plated brass base mount are also considerations.

*Coaxial cable (coax)* is designed to conduct transmitted and received energy between your antenna and radio. Coaxial cable is a two-conductor cable with a center that you can think of as the "positive" conductor. The next outermost layer of typical "coax" cable is an insulation layer used to keep the woven ground conductor separated from the center conductor. This outer conductor is sheathed by the outer "skin" of the cable. Just as with any wiring on board, the quality and amount of energy lost through this cable will affect the performance of the radio. In this case the loss is measured in dB rather than the voltage drop mentioned throughout this book. The best advice is to use the largest coax you can to minimize signal loss. Always install a high-quality lead on any antenna you buy.

There are three common kinds of coaxial cable available today: RG-58, RG-8X, and RG-8U. Just as with regular wiring, the signal loss is proportional to the length of wire. For most small powerboats, the

wire won't be much more than 20 feet long, so the loss will be minimal. The table in figure 12-6 compares the dB signal loss for a 20- and a 40-foot cable run using each of the cable types mentioned here. Notice that the loss in dB between the RG-58 and the RG-8U cable is more than double, even for a fairly short 20-foot cable run.

Besides the basic types, coaxial cable comes in different construction configurations, and these can make a difference in the long-term performance of the cable. Coaxial is basically a two-conductor element separated by a PVC insulator. For best long-term results, the center conductor should be of tinned, stranded copper. The second conductor is the braided outer shield, which should also be of tinned copper. Many manufacturers try and save a few dollars by using a solid, single-strand untinned center conductor and untinned shield. This type of coax works just fine for cable TV installations at home, but it's not a good choice for marine VHF installations.

## Cable Splices

Probably the biggest source of VHF radio problems arises out of a corroded antenna connection, either at the radio or at any point in the antenna lead where a splice is installed to extend the lead. For a simple solution to this problem, apply a light coating of silicone lubricant to the center stud and threads of the barrel on the connector itself before screwing it into place. This will provide a good watertight seal and keep the green gremlins (corrosion) away. Regardless, these connections should be checked at least once each boating season to ensure that no corrosion

| Coax Type versus Signal Loss in dB | | |
|---|---|---|
| Cable | 20 ft. | 40 ft. |
| RG-58 | –1.2 | –2.4 |
| RG-8X | –0.9 | –1.8 |
| RG-8U | –0.5 | –1.0 |

*Fig. 12-6. Signal loss (in dB) for cable runs of 20 and 40 feet, using three popular grades of coaxial cable.*

*Fig. 12-7. A Centerpin PL-259-CP coaxial (coax) connector.*

sleeves to compress all of the components of the coaxial into place. With the new solderless connectors, all you do is to cut the end of the coaxial cable square, firmly push the cable into the new connector, squeeze together the locking arms, and thread on the outer cover of the connector. These connectors are sold as Centerpin PL-259-CP connectors, and truly take the work out of this usually finicky task, shown in figure 12-7. Figure 12-8 gives a complete VHF installation overview from the DC distribution panel to the radio and from the antenna to the radio.

exists. Corrosion here will definitely create inferior VHF performance.

Eventually you may need to replace one of these coax connectors (known as PL-259 connectors). Happily, a recent breakthrough in design has eliminated virtually all of the difficulty normally associated with this task. With a standard connector you must carefully strip back precise, staggered lengths of each of the three layers of coaxial cable down to the center core. Once this is done, you carefully insert the coaxial into the connector and either solder both the center core to the center pin and the braided conductor to the outer body of the assembly, or use special

As a final note to these instructions for VHF installation and general use, remember to check your radio on an appropriate channel each time you take your boat out. This is not at all frivolous. In my experience, most failures with VHF radios occur on the transmitter side of the circuitry, not on the receiver side. So simply turning on your radio and listening to the chatter on various stations is no assurance that the radio will work as it should if the need to call for help ever arises. Be certain; always check for both transmission and reception before leaving the dock. Remember, your VHF is an important safety tool, not a toy. Respect and use proper radio etiquette at all times. You'll greatly appreciate this minor formality if you ever do need to use your radio in an emergency!

# Installing a Fish-Finder or Depth-Sounder

In terms of functionality, the latest versions of LCD and CRT fish-finders are really outstanding. The performance gains over the last 10 years with this type of equipment have been just phenomenal, and prices for quality gear have actually gone down for even the most advanced, feature-packed units. But, in the same vein as VHF radio performance, these fish-finders are only as good as the information getting to and from them. Think of the fish-finder or depth-sounder transducer as a two-way antenna that must send and receive

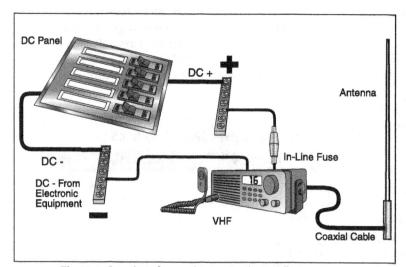

*Fig. 12-8. Overview of a complete VHF radio installation.*

signals. Rather than shooting through the air, as do VHF signals, these signals leave the underside of your boat, bounce off the bottom of the waterway, then get back to the transducer where they are translated into water depth. This is how you spot "ol' silver-sides" hiding in a clump of weeds 10 feet off the port side of your boat.

As with your VHF installation, you must consider any magnetic fields emitting from the control unit of the fish-finder or depth-sounder that could affect your compass. This is of particular concern if you have selected a *cathode-ray-tube* (CRT) instead of a *liquid-crystal-display* (LCD) device. By their nature, CRT fish-finders emit magnetism right through the face of the screen, so be sure to check this out, as described earlier in this chapter, before mounting it close to your compass.

Once you decide where to put your fish-finder or depth-sounder, make a DC positive and negative connection for powering it. The best bet is to hook it up to a dedicated bus bar. Refer to figure 12-3 on page 183 to refresh your memory on how this is done. Don't forget that, depending on the manufacturer, you may need an additional *grounding lead* to the unit's case. Be sure to check your installation manual to determine this. (Note: An easy way to figure this out is to look for a threaded stud with a wingnut on it at the back of the instrument. This is the *grounding lug*.)

## Transducer Mounting and Troubleshooting

Regardless of which brand of fish-finder you have, you'll have three choices for transducer mounting. But, if you wish to have the water-temperature-monitoring capability that comes with most top brands available today, you'll be limited to two of the three mounting options.

No matter which mounting method you decide to use, you must give your transducer a clear view below the boat that will not be clouded while underway by air bubbles or momentary separation of the hull from the water. For power-

boats the transducer should end up toward the rear of the boat at a point on the hull where the bottom is submerged at all speeds and under all normal sea conditions. You should also consider the *noise*, the air bubbles and turbulence generated by propellers and lifting strakes built into the hull. This interference can reduce transducer performance.

As a general rule, try to mount the transducer at least 18 inches (about 46 cm) away from the propeller. The face of the transducer should also be inward of the first lifting strake on the bottom of the hull by about 3 to 6 inches (7.6 to 15 cm). If your boat has a skeg or keel, mount the transducer about 12 inches (30 cm) to the side of the keel. This is not to minimize the effect of turbulence but to ensure that the transducer's conical beam is not partially blocked by the keel, reducing its performance. Figure 12-9 illustrates all of the dimensions outlined here.

One additional consideration, besides the orientation of the transducer, is the wiring harness connecting the transducer to the display unit. Even though these cables are generally much longer than needed for a typical installation, the cable length should not be altered in any way. (Factory-supplied extensions are available if more length is needed.) If

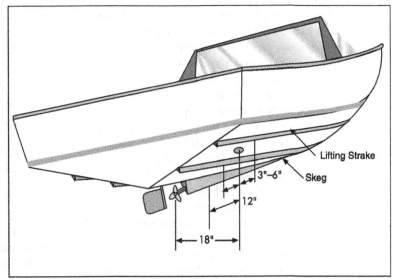

*Fig. 12-9. Transducer location, with separation zones measured out.*

you find you have excess after running the cable to your display, do not cut it and splice the connector to the shortened harness! The length of this harness is engineered to a precise resistance, and alteration will affect the performance of the unit. Coil excess wire neatly and lock it together with some tie wraps. Hide the coil behind an out-of-the-way panel away from any other electrical cables or harnesses. It's possible for this cable to be affected by *cross-induction* from other electrical cables and devices. (Remember, all wires with electricity running through them have a magnetic field around them.) Cross-inductance here will affect the sensitivity of your depth-sounder or fish-finder.

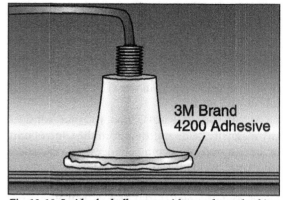

Fig. 12-10. *Inside-the-hull mount with transducer glued in place.*

### Inside-the-Hull Mount

If you aren't using a transducer with a water-temperature probe built into it, you may want to mount your transducer inside the hull. This is the simplest of the installation choices and will generally prove satisfactory, but you may experience a loss of range. If your boating keeps you in less than about 100 feet of water, this method may work well for you. This approach only works on boats with a solid-fiberglass bottom. Cored bottoms will not precisely transfer the ultrasonic waves from the transducer, and performance may be greatly hindered. If you're not sure if your boat bottom is cored, check with the builder before moving ahead on this type of installation.

If you're determined to try for an in-hull installation, do some experimenting first. Connect the transducer to the sounder's display and temporarily adhere the face of the transducer to the inside of the hull with some nonhardening adhesive, such as BoatLIFE caulk or a similar polysulfide sealer. Try the sounder for a few days under all of the conditions you're likely to encounter. If the display picture is clear and accurate, go for it! If not perfect, but still functional, try different locations inside the hull.

Avoid areas of the hull where it inclines more than about 15 degrees. Mounting the transducer at any angle greater than this will send its wave pattern to the side of the boat, and not straight down to the bottom.

Once you find the best spot for the transducer, clean away the temporary adhesive and degrease the hull with some acetone or alcohol. Lightly sand both the face of the transducer and the hull with some medium-grit (100-grit) sandpaper. Wipe down everything once more to clear the dust away. Next, apply enough fast-curing 3M 4200 polyurethane adhesive to provide full contact with the entire face of the transducer. Push the transducer into the adhesive and wiggle it slightly from side to side to break any air bubbles in the glue. Allow it to sit for about two hours to cure. 3M 4200 is much better for this purpose than the 3M 5200; it cures much more quickly than the 5200 and is a bit less tenacious, making for easier replacement of the transducer when the time comes to do so. Figure 12-10 illustrates a typical glued-in transducer.

### Through-Hull Mount

Through-hull mounting of a transducer gives excellent performance, provided the basic rules for locating it are followed. In addition to the location requirements already noted, make sure the transducer is positioned so that its face is aimed straight down and not canted to one side or the other. If you want to mount the transducer on an angled section of the hull, a *mounting pad* is required. Use an appropriate material for the fairing block (see below), and make sure the stem of the transducer is completely sealed so that water can't leak into the boat. It's also important that water not come into contact

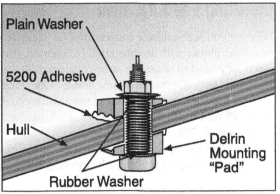

*Fig. 12-11. Through-hull mounting of transducers with fairing blocks.*

with the freshly exposed fiberglass or core material around the perimeter of the through-hull hole; a leak here exposes the laminate or core to water and can damage the laminate as water attempts to migrate into it. 3M 4200 or 5200 works well for this purpose.

As for the material to use for the fairing block, stay away from wood. Traditionally, wood has been the material of choice for this job, but today it's unnecessary and less desirable than modern materials such as Delrin or Marelon. These miracle plastics are now used for making seacocks and other through-hull fittings, and are widely used in other industries. They are available in sheet and block form from industrial supply houses. The beauty of using plastic is that it will never rot, and it won't crack on the grain as do hardwood blocks. These plastics are easy to work using regular woodcutting and forming tools. Figure 12-11 illustrates a through-hull mounting with a fairing block.

## Transom Mount

On smaller boats, the transom mount is usually the simplest and easiest of the three choices for transducer installation. Figure 12-12 illustrates a typical installation.

Virtually all fiberglass production boats built today use a plywood-cored transom. To prevent water from migrating into the core, which will eventually rot the wood, mounting screws and any holes drilled for routing the transducer cable through the transom must be sealed with 3M 5200 or a similar product. In addition, the mounting bracket must be set up so that the face of the transducer is pointing straight down, as with the two other installation options.

## Troubleshooting Fish-Finders and Depth-Sounders

For several reasons, fish-finders and depth-sounders are a bit more finicky than other types of electronic equipment. They are sensitive to voltage and will only operate within a certain voltage range, typically between 10.5 and 16.5 volts for a 12-volt unit. So, that all-night fishing trip at anchor could conceivably drain your battery to below the minimum 10.5-volt level. A faulty voltage regulator on your boat could also allow the upper 16.5-volt threshold to be reached. Depending on which depth-sounder or fish-finder you have, you might hear an alarm indicating high or low voltage, or the unit may automatically shut down. There is no problem with the unit itself, but it's a problem nonetheless.

The other fairly common problem with these units is fouling of the face of the transducer with sea growth. Barnacles and other marine growth will eventually block the face of the transducer and affect its ability to transmit and receive a signal. The solu-

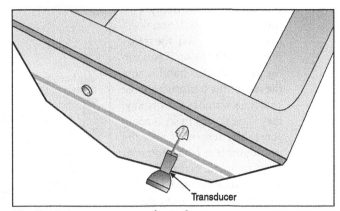

*Fig. 12-12. A transom-mounted transducer.*

tion here is simple: Either periodically wipe down the face of the transducer with a wet cloth to clear the surface, or prevent the fouling in the first place by using transducer antifouling paint, available at West Marine and other marine supply houses. I don't recommend that conventional bottom paint be used to protect these surfaces.

If your fish-finder or depth-sounder stops working altogether or begins to send mysterious signals through your display, there are several additional steps you can take to isolate the problem. First, ensure that the display unit is getting power and has a good ground, just as you would for any electrical appliance. Use your multimeter, set up to read volts, to make sure the voltage is not below your unit's minimum threshold. If it is, determine why by using all of the methods described throughout this book.

Checking your transducer may require hauling the boat so you can get at the face of the unit. If you're up to it, a brief underwater swim may be all that's needed. With the sounder turned on, you should hear a ticking noise coming from the transducer as it attempts to transmit its signal. If you don't hear a ticking sound, the transducer is faulty. Also, if you rub the palm of your hand across the face of the transducer while someone watches the display, they should get a fuzzy reading across the screen. If not, the transducer is at fault and needs to be replaced. Naturally, you should also become familiar with the controls and calibration settings for your fish-finder and depth-sounder and be sure they are set up properly.

# Installing a GPS Receiver

Whether you're installing a conventional GPS receiver or a chart plotter with an integrated GPS sensor, you essentially need to make the same considerations as you would with all other electronic devices. One thing that will make a minor difference in the installation of your GPS unit is whether or not you select a standard or differential GPS (DGPS) configuration.

Like all of the equipment discussed so far, the location for the display unit must be carefully consid-

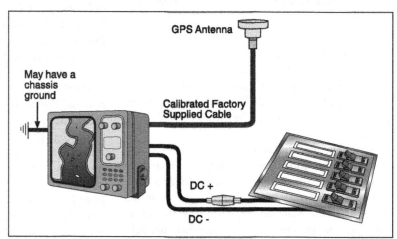

Fig. 12-13. Wiring layout for a standard GPS installation.

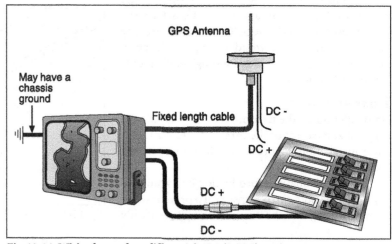

Fig. 12-14. Wiring layout for a differential GPS (DGPS) receiver.

ered. Follow the procedures described above for determining any compass deviation and getting power to the receiver. The big consideration is where to locate the GPS antenna. GPS receivers use receive-only antennas that need a clear view of the sky at all times. Even something like a Bimini top or a windscreen can affect the integrity of a GPS signal. Also, radio transmissions from other electronic equipment such as cell phones, VHF radios, and single-sideband (SSB) radios can affect a GPS signal.

The rules here are simple and not too hard to comply with, even on small boats. Basically, the ideal is to maintain about a 1-meter separation, or a little less than a yard, between transmitting antennas and the GPS receiving antenna. On most boats this is simply a matter of mounting the VHF antenna on one side of the bridge and the GPS antenna on the other. Mission accomplished! On boats with elaborate gear-mount brackets and airfoils, just keep from mounting these antennas adjacent to each other.

GPS is a line-of-sight system between the antenna and satellites orbiting overhead. The antenna scans the sky via a conical pattern that points straight up. So, unlike VHF, mounting an antenna too high can actually be detrimental to its performance in a rolling, pitching sea, particularly if you have selected the improved accuracy provided by a differential receiver. An antenna mounted too high will drive the GPS unit crazy as it swings back and forth trying to find its exact location. Low and as close to the centerline of the boat as you can get is the way to go with this installation. Any of the commercially available mounting brackets for these antennas will do just fine, but don't think you'll improve performance by using an extension pole, as you might with a VHF antenna.

If you have a differential GPS receiver (DGPS), one that also receives radio position data from land-based stations in addition to satellite signals, you may need an additional positive and negative wire to the antenna.

As with fish-finder and depth-sounder transducer cables, your GPS antenna comes with a fixed-length cable for attachment to the display unit. Don't alter its length, and keep any extra cabling coiled away from other cables and harnesses. Figure 12-13 on page 190 illustrates a typical wiring hookup for a GPS without DGPS. Figure 12-14 on page 190 illustrates a typical installation with a DGPS receiver.

## Installing Your Own Radar

In the old days, the average boatowner wouldn't have dreamed of installing his or her own radar. Today, radar manufacturers have come a long way, and owner installation is not only practical but not that difficult.

The big consideration with radar is the mounting of the antenna *(scanner)*. Four basic rules must be followed:

▶ Install the scanner on your cabintop or on an appropriate mast with a platform designed to accept the mounting bolts.

▶ Position the scanner so that the antenna gets a good all-around view with as few parts of the superstructure or rigging as possible intercepting the scanning beam. Any obstructions will cause shadows and blind sectors on the radar screen.

▶ To minimize electrical interference, don't route the cabling from the antenna near any other onboard electrical equipment or cabling, just as with other gear mentioned above.

▶ Remember that a radar antenna creates pronounced compass deviation. Keep a separation zone of about 5½ feet (1.7 m) between the radar antenna and your compass.

When installing an antenna on a powerboat, consider the average angle at which your boat cruises while underway. If the antenna is mounted perfectly level with the boat at the dock, it will tend to aim at the stars while underway. Figure 12-15 illustrates the static angle for the antenna and the effect this slightly downward mounting has on the beam while the boat is underway. To determine the exact angle of the antenna to use, spend a morning determining the amount of lift your boat goes through from a standstill to cruising speed. Once

*Fig. 12-15. Static angle for powerboat radar antenna installation.*

you have established this angle, you'll know how many degrees to tilt the forward edge of your radar antenna downward for optimum scanner performance while the boat is under way. Typically this number is around 10 or 15 degrees.

The antenna has a definite front-facing position that must be observed. Follow the manufacturer's installation instructions if you're not sure how to achieve this important orientation. Also, as with the other gear mentioned, the cable that comes with the radar is of a calibrated length that should only be altered by installing a factory-supplied harness, which is available in different lengths.

One last thing regarding the radar antenna: All closed-array scanners (those with a fiberglass enclosure) come with a condensation drain valve on the bottom shell of the antenna housing. Make sure this drain is unobstructed and working as it should at all times. Condensation buildup inside the antenna housing will destroy the expensive circuitry in there.

Once the antenna is mounted and the lead is fed

to the approximate location of the display, permanently mount the display. Again, ergonomics is important. Radar is useless if you don't have a clear, unobstructed view of the entire display. Connect the display to the dedicated instrument bus for positive and negative return, run a ground from the back of the chassis (at the wingnut and stud) to the negative bus bar, connect the antenna cable to the appropriate socket, and you're ready to go! Figure 12-16 illustrates the wiring hookups for a typical radar installation, with some of the other mentioned concerns pointed out in the diagram.

I have one last general note regarding electronic equipment: Never attempt to use this gear until you've read through the fine points of the owner's manual and documentation that comes with the equipment. In most cases, before the gear can be used effectively there is an initialization or preliminary tuning procedure that must be followed. Be familiar with these steps, and make sure you take them before you head off into the sunset. The equipment available today is good, but it's not completely magical; it needs user intervention to give the best results.

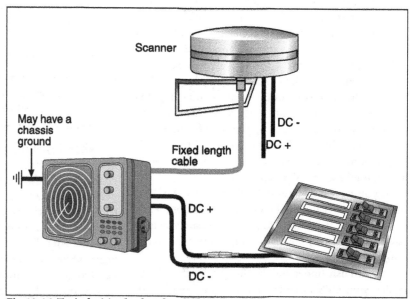

*Fig. 12-16. Typical wiring hookup for a radar system.*

# Glossary

**ABYC** American Boat & Yacht Council, Inc. The preeminent standard-making organization for the recreational boating industry. The ABYC's *Standards and Technical Information Reports for Small Craft* covers all areas of small-boat construction and repair, not just electrical matters.

**alternating current (AC)** Current that reverses direction. In the United States, the current reverses direction at the rate of 60 times per second, at 60 cycles, or 60 Hz. In Europe and other parts of the world, the standard is 50 Hz. See also *direct current (DC); frequency; Hertz (Hz)*.

**alternator** A machine that uses the principle of magnetic induction to produce electricity. Alternators produce AC, which must be rectified to DC to recharge onboard batteries.

**ammeter** A meter used to measure the current flowing through a circuit. Conventional meters must be hooked up in series with the circuit. Modern inductive-style meters simply clamp around a wire in the circuit.

**ampacity** The amount of amperage an electrical conductor or device can safely conduct.

**ampere** The unit of measure for electrical current, or rate of electrical flow past a point in a circuit. One ampere is equal to one coulomb ($6.24 \times 10$ to the 18th power) of electrons passing a given point per second. Amperage is the stuff that trips circuit breakers and fuses, and, if not controlled, can burn up your boat!

**amp-hour** A current of one amp flowing for one hour; a measure of the electrical energy stored in a battery.

**anode** The more positively charged electrode in an electrical cell.

**average-responding multimeter** A meter whose voltage and amperage readings are calculated with an averaging formula.

**battery** An electrochemical device that produces voltage, or a voltage differential across its terminals.

**battery bank** A group of two or more batteries linked together electrically.

**battery combiner** Electronic, voltage-sensitive switching device for automatically combining and separating batteries.

**battery isolation switch** A mechanical switch used to connect single or multiple batteries in parallel to a load.

**battery isolator** An electronic device that uses heavy-duty diodes to block electrical flow in one direction, effectively keeping batteries that are combined separated from each other electrically to prevent the discharge of one into the other.

**battery reserve capacity** The number of minutes a new, fully charged battery at 80°F (26.7°C) can be discharged at 25 amperes and maintain a voltage of 1.75 volts or more per cell (10.5 volts for a 12-volt battery).

**blade-type (ATO) fuse** Common fuse type using a colored plastic case for the fuse element; widely used in automotive applications today.

**branch circuit** A subcircuit fed from a main or primary circuit.

**bus bar** Metal bar used as a termination point for multiple conductors and circuits. A common point for either grounding or positive power feed.

**bus (AGC) fuse** The traditional glass cylinder style of fuse.

**cable** Wiring of any type; also *cabling*.

**capacitive-discharge ignition (CDI) unit** The "brain" of a CD ignition system.

**capacitor** An electronic component that stores an electrical charge when voltage is applied.

**carbon tracking** The carbon path etched into plastic or other insulating material by high voltage.

**cathode** The negatively charged electrode of a cell. See also *anode*.

**cell** The smallest unit of a battery. A 12-volt storage battery has six cells.

**charge coils** Coils within a CD ignition system used to step up voltage supplied to the ignition coils.

**chassis ground** The case ground for metallic-cased electrical equipment.

**circuit** A complete path for electrical flow from the positive power source or terminal to the negative or ground terminal. A complete circuit has the following key elements: a power source, circuit protection (most circuits), a switch, an electrical conductor, a load or an appliance, and a return conductor to ground (negative).

**circuit breaker** An automatic switch that "trips" when the rated current flow through it is exceeded. A bimetallic circuit breaker uses the differential thermal expansion of dissimilar metals to open the switch.

**circular mils (CM)** Cross-sectional area of a conductor.

**closed circuit** A complete circuit, one that is turned on.

**coaxial cable** Used typically for antenna leads and to interconnect marine electronic equipment. This two-conductor cable consists of an inner conductor insulated by a dielectric shield that is surrounded by a braided wire conductor and then insulated on the outside by another layer of nonconductive sheathing.

**cold-cranking amps (CCA)** The number of amps a battery at 0°F (−17.8°C) can deliver for 30 seconds and maintain a voltage of 1.2 volts per cell or more.

**color coding** One of several acceptable methods of identifying wiring in circuits.

**conductor** Any material that has a minimal amount of resistance to electrical flow through it.

**conduit** A pipe in which electrical wiring is routed.

**continuity** A complete path or circuit that will allow electrical current flow.

**continuous rating** Rated for continuous exposure as compared to intermittent exposure.

**corrosion** The process by which metals are destroyed. See also *galvanic corrosion*; *stray-current corrosion*.

**crimp** (n.) A type of connector used for terminating wire. As in captive, ring-eye, etc. (v.) To attach a crimp-type connector to a wire using an appropriate crimping tool.

**cross-induction** The inducement of electron flow in a conductor from the magnetic field surrounding a nearby current-carrying conductor.

**CRT** Cathode ray tube. Televisions and computers—before they went to flat screens—used to have CRTs.

**current** The movement of electrons through a material.

**cycles** In AC, the current shift from + to − and back to + is one cycle.

**DC ground conductor** A normally current-carrying conductor connected to the side of the power source that is intentionally maintained at boat ground potential.

**DC grounding conductor** A normally non-current-carrying conductor used to connect metallic non-current-carrying parts of direct-current devices to the engine negative terminal, or a bus attached directly to it. Its purpose is to help minimize what is known as *stray-current corrosion* and is also sometimes connected into a lightning protection system as well. This wiring, which is generally covered with green insulation and connects to things like seacocks and propeller-shaft struts, should never be used as a DC ground return for an electrical appliance.

**deep-cycle battery**   A battery designed to withstand being deeply discharged at a moderate rate of current draw over an extended period.

**de-rating**   Reduction of a nominal rating, typically used with ampacity and voltage drop tables.

**Deutsch plug**   Trade name for a high-quality waterproof plug assembly.

**DGPS**   Differential global positioning system using both satellite and land-transmitted data to calculate position.

**dielectric**   An insulating material.

**diode**   An electrical semiconductor that allows electrical flow through it in only one direction.

**direct current (DC)**   Electrical current that flows in one direction. See also *alternating current (AC)*.

**double-pole**   A classification of switch or circuit breaker that allows for the opening of two separate connections simultaneously.

**dry-cell battery**   A battery using a dry, paste-like electrolyte instead of a liquid. See also *wet-cell battery*.

**DVOM**   Common acronym for digital volt-ohm meter, also known as a multimeter or VOM.

**earth ground**   A point that is at the same voltage potential as the local earth.

**electrical potential**   Voltage.

**electrolyte**   The solution inside a battery, but can be any electrically conductive fluid, such as salt water.

**engine negative terminal**   A bolt or stud on an engine where the negative battery cable is connected.

**ferro-resonant charger**   Simple unit using a ferro-resonant transformer to convert AC to a lower voltage before being converted to DC for charging batteries.

**field winding**   The wire coils wound onto the rotor inside an alternator. When electrical current flows through these windings an electromagnetic field is created around the rotor assembly, which induces current flow in the alternator's stator windings as the rotor spins.

**float charge**   The third and final phase of battery charging. Also known as the *finish stage*.

**flywheel**   A wheel used to maintain an engine's rolling inertia between firing strokes.

**frequency**   The number of complete alternations per second of alternating current.

**fuse**   A conductive device designed to melt when amperage flow through it exceeds a rated amount.

**galvanic corrosion**   Corrosion resulting from dissimilar, electrically connected metals being immersed in an electrolyte.

**galvanic isolator**   A device installed in series with the green grounding conductor of the AC shore-power cable designed to block galvanic DC current flow but permit the passage of AC if required.

**galvanic potential**   A reference to where a given metal may fall on a galvanic series of metals table. "Anodes" and "zincs," as they are commonly called, have a higher galvanic potential than Monel, stainless steel, and bronze.

**gang plug**   Plug assembly used for connecting multiple conductors.

**gapping**   Adjusting the air gap between two electrodes.

**gel-cell battery**   Type of battery with the active electrolyte contained in a gelatinous medium.

**generator**   Generally, a machine that produces electricity.

**GPS**   Global positioning system.

**ground**   At the potential of the Earth's surface. A surface or mass at the electrical potential of the Earth's surface, established at this potential by an electrically conducting connection, either intentional or accidental, with the Earth, including any metal area that forms part of the wetted surface of the boat's hull.

**ground-fault circuit interrupter (GFCI)** A device intended to protect people that functions to de-energize a circuit or a portion of a circuit when a current to ground exceeds a predetermined value (5 milliamps in the U.S.).

**harness** A group of conductors running together.

**heat-shrink tubing** Insulating sheath that shrinks to size when heated.

**heat sink** A mounting for an electronic component designed to dissipate heat generated by the component to the surrounding air.

**Hertz (Hz)** The unit of frequency of an alternating current. One Hertz is equivalent to one cycle per second.

**horsepower** A measure of power. One horsepower is equivalent to 746 watts.

**hot** Generally considered the power feed conductor in electrical circuitry.

**house battery** Used to supply DC loads other than the engine stater motor.

**hydrometer** A float-type device used to measure the specific gravity of a fluid relative to another. In electrical work, the battery hydrometer is used to measure the specific gravity of the battery electrolyte relative to pure water.

**ignition protected** A critical designation for any electrical device that is to be used in an area where gasoline, battery, or CNG or LPG vapors may accumulate. The ABYC describes ignition protection as: "the design and construction of a device such that under design operating conditions: it will not ignite a flammable hydrocarbon mixture surrounding the device when an ignition source causes an internal explosion, or it is capable of releasing sufficient electrical or thermal energy to ignite a hydrocarbon mixture, or the source of the ignition is hermetically sealed." It is important to note that unlike most of the ABYC standards, ignition-protection requirements are also mandated by USCG regulations, and compliance is not voluntary, but mandatory.

**impedance** A form of resistance, the ratio of voltage to current.

**inductance** See *cross-induction*.

**induction** See *cross-induction*.

**inductive pickup** Used with measuring instruments to sense electrical current flow through wires.

**in-line (fuses, etc.)** A series connection.

**insulator** Material with a high electrical resistance.

**intercircuit short** Anywhere two circuits inadvertently become connected.

**intermittent rating** See *continuous rating*.

**internal short** Short circuit within the case of an electrical appliance.

**inverter** A device that converts DC voltage to AC voltage.

**joule** A measurement of energy. One Joule equals one watt for one second.

**jumpers** Short lengths of conductors, either wire or strapping.

**key** To activate.

**kilo (k)** A common prefix meaning 10 to the third power, or 1,000.

**lead** A length of wire, usually fairly short. As in "meter lead."

**lead-acid battery** Typical battery using lead plates and sulfuric acid electrolyte.

**LED outlet tester** Tester used to verify AC plug outlet wiring connection status that uses light-emitting diodes (LEDs) to signal status of connections at the outlet and its connected wiring.

**life cycles** The estimated number of times a battery can be discharged to a specified level and brought back up to full charge before it fails.

**live** Meaning power is available.

**load** Any device in a circuit that dissipates power.

**lugs** A short, threaded stud used for wire termination.

**magnetic circuit breaker**   Breaker that uses the magnetic field generated by a current-carrying coil to open the circuit.

**magnetic field**   Magnetic lines of flux, invisible but present around all conductors with electrical current flowing through them. The magnetic lines of flux surrounding the Earth are the basis for the function of a magnetic compass.

**magnetic separation**   Insulating or moving away from excessive magnetism.

**mega (M)**   Prefix meaning 10 to the sixth power, or one million.

**micro (μ)**   Prefix meaning 10 to the minus sixth power, or one millionth.

**milli (m)**   Prefix meaning 10 to the minus third power, or one thousandth. As in milliamp or millivolt.

**multimeter**   Electrical meter with multiple functionality.

**ohm (Ω)**   The unit of measurement of electrical resistance.

**ohmmeter**   A device that measures electrical resistance.

**Ohm's law**   The mathematical equation that explains the relationship between volts, amps, and ohms.

**open**   See *open circuit*.

**overcharging**   Forcing excessive current into a battery. Overcharging causes excessive battery gassing and loss of electrolyte, a dangerous situation in either event.

**open circuit**   A break in a circuit that interrupts the flow of current.

**open-circuit voltage**   The voltage reading across the terminals of a battery at rest, with no charge going in and nothing drawing power from it.

**overcurrent-protection device**   A fuse, circuit breaker, or other device installed in a circuit and intended to interrupt the circuit when the current flow exceeds design ratings.

**overrating**   Applying more voltage or amperage to a device or component than it was designed to take.

**panelboard**   Electrical distribution panel. Includes branch circuit breakers or fuses, and both negative and positive bus bars. May also contain system volt and amp meters and in the case of AC panels, a reverse-polarity indicator.

**parallel circuit**   A circuit that allows more than one path for current to flow.

**pie formula**   $P \times I = E$, or $W = V \times A$

**pinging**   Knocking noise from engine that sounds like marbles are bouncing inside.

**polarity**   The distinction between + and – in a circuit or on a load device.

**potential**   See *electrical potential*.

**power**   The rate at which energy is used or converted. The unit of measurement is the watt, which equals amperage times the voltage. One horsepower equals 746 watts. See also *horsepower*.

**pulsar coils**   See *trigger coils*.

**radome**   See *scanner*.

**reference voltage**   The open-circuit voltage of a power source.

**relay**   An electromechanical switch. See also *solenoid*.

**reserve capacity**   The time in minutes that a battery can deliver 25 amps before dying.

**resistance**   Measured in ohms. The opposition to electrical current flow (amps).

**reverse polarity**   Connecting battery cables backwards. Or, in AC, the reversal of the black and white conductors.

**RFI**   Radio frequency interference, emitted by electrical devices. Can produce radio "noise," and can cause navigation equipment to malfunction.

**ripple voltage**   Small amount of AC voltage that typically leaks past rectifiers inside alternators.

**root-mean-square (RMS) multimeter** One using peak AC voltage values to calculate its readings.

**rotor** The moving component inside an alternator that has the field winding wrapped around it.

**rpm** Revolutions per minute.

**scanner** Moving radar antenna (rotating).

**self-discharge** The gradual loss of a battery's capacity as it sits in storage.

**self-limiting** An electrical power source whose maximum output is restricted by its magnetic and electrical characteristics.

**self-scaling (auto-ranging) ammeter** A meter that automatically selects its best range for a measurement.

**series circuit** A circuit having only one path for current to flow through.

**series-parallel circuit** A circuit combining elements of both a series and parallel circuit.

**sheath** A material used as an insulating protective cover for electrical wiring.

**shore power** Power delivered from the dock.

**short circuit** A circuit fault that effectively shortens the designed path of current flow through a circuit. Short circuits usually eliminate the load from the circuit, allowing excessive current to flow.

**shunt** A short electrical bypass, generally associated with an ammeter.

**single loads** An individual electrical load in a circuit, as compared to multiple loads supplied by a circuit.

**sine wave** The waveform made when alternating current is charted over time.

**slave relay** See *solenoid*.

**slow-blow (MDL) fuse** A fuse with a delayed action used in motor circuits and other circuits where start-up load is significantly greater than the continuous current draw on the circuit.

**smart charger** Computerized multistage battery charger.

**socket** The female part of a plug and socket connector.

**solenoid** An extra-heavy-duty relay. Used for switching high-current-draw circuits such as starter-motor circuits.

**specific gravity** The density of a fluid. In electrical terms, the density of battery electrolyte as compared to pure water. Indicates state of charge in a battery cell.

**spike** Sudden surge in voltage.

**starting battery** Cranking battery capable of delivering high amperage for brief periods.

**static charge** Surface charge on a battery. High voltage but no amperage to back it up.

**stator** The stationary armature on an alternator that the rotor spins inside of, where alternator current is produced.

**stray-current corrosion** Corrosive activity induced by electrical leakage. See *corrosion*.

**sulfation** The normal chemical transformation of battery plates when a battery discharges. If left unattended, the sulfate turns to a crystalline substance and attaches itself permanently to the battery plates, ultimately ruining the battery as less and less plate area is exposed to the surrounding electrolyte solution.

**surface charge** See *static charge*.

**surge (spike)** See *spike*.

**switch** A device used to open and close a circuit.

**tachometer** Revolution counter.

**terminal** A point of connection to any electrical device. As in battery clamp, ring eye connector, etc.

**tilt switch** Mercury switch designed to turn off the starting circuit on an outboard engine when it's tilted up out of the water.

**timing** Engine's ignition timing. Point at which the spark plug fires in a cylinder.

**transducer** Two-way sender-receiver used with depth-sounder.

**transformer** An electrical device consisting of two or more coils used to magnetically couple one circuit or section of a circuit to another. Transformers come in three basic configurations: one-to-one, where voltage on both sides of the transformer (primary and secondary) stays the same; step-up, where the voltage is increased from the primary to the secondary side of the unit; and step-down, where the opposite occurs.

**trigger coils** Used to send an electrical charge to a CDI's control box to tell it which cylinder to fire next.

**trim gauge** Used to indicate relative IO drive or outboard engine trim angle.

**trip (breaker)** To open the circuit.

**trip-free circuit breaker** A breaker designed in such a way that the resetting means cannot be manually held in to override the current-interrupting mechanism.

**underrating** Not having adequate ampacity. See also *ampacity*.

**ungrounded conductor** A current-carrying conductor that is insulated from ground. Often thought of as the "hot" wire in a circuit.

**volt** The unit of voltage or potential difference from one side of a circuit to another.

**voltage drop** The loss of voltage as it works its way through a circuit. Excessive voltage drop indicates unwanted resistance in a circuit or circuit component.

**voltage regulation** Maintenance of voltage output despite variation in output current within engineered parameters.

**watt** A unit of power. The English unit of measurement is the horsepower, which equals 550 foot-pounds per second or 746 watts.

**waveform** Voltage as a function of time of a recurring signal. The waveform of AC voltage is the sinusoid, much like that of an ocean wave.

**wet-cell battery** A typical cranking or deep-cycle battery, as compared to a dry-cell flashlight battery. Wet-cell batteries can be recharged; most dry-cells cannot.

# Resources

A number of products and tools are mentioned throughout the *Powerboater's Guide to Electrical Systems*. In most cases your local marine store or chandlery has or can get you the equipment we've discussed. Here are some other useful resources:

## Blue Sea Systems

A great resource for parts as well as technical advice. Call 1-800-222-7617 for customer service, or 360-738-8230 for the technical support line; or go to www.bluesea.com.

## Boat/U.S.

Check them out at www.boatus.com or call 703-461-4666.

## Boater's World

Call 1-877-690-0004 or visit their website at www.boatersworld.com.

## Defender Industries

Call 1-800-628-8225 or go to www.defender.com.

## MAC Tools Corp.

MAC distributes through local franchised mobile vendors. To find a dealer near you, go to www.mactools.com or call 1-800-622-8665.

## NAPA Auto Parts Stores

NAPA has an excellent line of marine parts and mechanic's tools. You can find the stores nearest you at www.napaonline.com.

## Snap-On

In my view, Snap-On produces the finest tools for the mechanic available anywhere in the world. If you are looking for the best, check out www.snapon.com. Like MAC, Snap-On distributes through local mobile vendors, but the distribution network is worldwide.

## West Marine

Call 1-800-685-4838 or go to www.westmarine.com.

# Index

Numbers in **bold** refer to pages with illustrations

## A